THE FRAGMENTATION OF THE CHURCH
AND ITS UNITY IN PEACEMAKING

The Fragmentation of the Church and Its Unity in Peacemaking

Edited by

Jeffrey Gros
and
John D. Rempel

WILLIAM B. EERDMANS PUBLISHING COMPANY
GRAND RAPIDS, MICHIGAN / CAMBRIDGE, U.K.

Wm. B. Eerdmans Publishing Co.

255 Jefferson Ave. S.E., Grand Rapids, Michigan 49503 /

P.O. Box 163, Cambridge CB3 9PU U.K.

www.eerdmans.com

Printed in the United States of America

06 05 04 03 02 01   7 6 5 4 3 2 1

Library of Congress Cataloging-in-Publication Data

The fragmentation of the Church and its unity in peacemaking /
edited by Jeffrey Gros and John D. Rempel.

p.   cm.

Includes bibliographical references.

ISBN 0-8028-4745-5 (pbk.: alk. paper)

1. Christian union.   2. Peace — Religious aspects — Christianity.
I. Gros, Jeffrey, 1938-   II. Rempel, John D.

BX8.2.F66   2001

280′.042 — dc21

00-052145

The essay by Murray Dempster entitled "Pacifism in Pentecostalism: The Case of the Assemblies of God" appeared previously in *Proclaim Peace: Christian Pacifism from Unexpected Quarters,* edited by Theron Schlabach and Richard Hughes (Urbana: University of Illinois Press, 1997) and is reprinted here by permission of the Board of Trustees of the University of Illinois.

Unless otherwise noted, the Scripture quotations in this publication are from the New Revised Standard Version of the Bible, copyright © 1989 by the Division of Christian Education of the National Council of Churches of Christ in the U.S.A., and used by permission.

John Howard Yoder
(1927-1997)
Servant of the churches and their peacemaking calling
and their unity in obedience to the
Kingdom of Christ

Contents

CONTENTS

Foreword

For Christians, the common commitment to love of neighbor and peace-making should not obscure the fact that we are divided from one another by different beliefs about what the gospel demands of us in facing war and violence and about appropriate Christian relations with civil government. The historic peace churches (Quakers, Mennonites, and Brethren) differ significantly among themselves but bear a common heritage of pacifism and a witness to reconciliation in society. Anglican, Protestant, Catholic, and Orthodox churches also are called by the gospel to bring peace to the world, but they interpret the biblical mandate differently from the peace churches and from one another.

For the sake of realizing Christ's prayer — "that they all may be one. As you, Father, are in me and I am in you, may they also be in us, so that the world may believe that you have sent me" (John 17:21) — it is necessary for all Christians to explore their common ground, treat honestly those things that divide them, and seek for means of witnessing to God's will for peace among the peoples of the world.

This volume presents the histories and testimonies of representatives from a variety of churches on the question of peacemaking and the unity to which we are called. We hope that readers will find it a useful contribution to our knowledge of one another and our hope for a common witness in Christ. As the conference that stimulated this volume[1] noted:

1. This volume was engendered by a consultation of the US Faith and Order Commission at Notre Dame in 1995. The goal of the Faith and Order movement is "To call

In a world of violence, be it in the streets or in warfare, churches affirm that peace is the will of God, and that peace has been shown to us most clearly in the life, teachings, death, and resurrection of Jesus Christ. Peacemaking is most deeply rooted in Christ and the unity of the church, and such unity is a gift of the Holy Spirit linked to repentance and forgiveness. Through the power of the Holy Spirit, we are enabled to practice peacemaking as a way of participation in the life and death of Christ. A primary vocation of every believer is love, out of which peacemaking flows. Our peace with God impels us toward peace with neighbor and love of enemies.

Among us as Christians there are painful memories of tensions with and even persecutions against our fellow Christians. We can learn humility, knowing that the forebears of some of our churches have, in the name of the gospel, not only advocated the use of force in war but also persecuted members of the peace churches. As we commemorate Christ's birth in the year 2000, we turn to these churches with openness and repentance for that past persecution. We are all blessed by the martyrs celebrated in the peace churches and can learn from them the tenacity the gospel calls for in modern culture.

It is our hope that this volume will make a significant contribution to the healing of memories among Christians and the enabling of a common witness to the peace Christ desires the Church to bring to the world. These historical and theological reflections contribute to unity among Christians and to the renewal of the human community by stimulating our ability to confess together the apostolic faith and explore what it demands of us in our lives today.

Prayer, formation for peacemaking and ecumenism, and conversion are central to our loyalty to Christ and our relationship to one another. To quote again the conference document: "While areas of disagreement continue, peacemaking is an essential element of the apostolic faith acknowl-

---

the churches to the goal of visible unity in one faith and in one eucharistic fellowship expressed in worship and common life in Christ, and to advance toward that unity that the world may believe." This consultation was the second in a series focusing on The Apostolic Character of the Church's Peace Witness in the context of a worldwide study of what is necessary for a Common Confession of the Apostolic Faith Today. The report of the Consultation begins on p. 218 of this volume.

edged by all. We continue to recognize divergences in the approach to this apostolic mandate in our pilgrimage toward full communion."

We hope that this work of the Faith and Order Commission of the National Council of Churches in the United States will serve all of the churches in the United States, and Christians around the world, in their search for the unity of the Church and their commitment to peace in the modern world.

Dr. Paul Meyendorff
Archbishop Alexander Brunett

Introduction

LAUREE HERSCH MEYER
AND JEFFREY GROS

During the 1980s, many churches were deeply involved in exploration of the demands of the gospel relative to the witness of peace. Despite the end of the cold war and the shift away from clearly identifiable superpower enemies and massive weapons of "deterrence," however, the world has not automatically become more peaceful. Church bodies have not lost the imperative to find a witness that is both consistent with the gospel and effective in service to the human community.

In the West, Augustine's just war theory has formed the basis throughout the centuries for most church traditions' approach to the concept of peace. In more recent years, however, this theory has become the subject of debate, and many churches have begun to move away from it and toward a more confessional, nonviolent witness. The context has been made even more complex by interethnic violence in the Balkans, Africa, and other parts of the world. The use of restraining force in humanitarian crises has placed the discussion of both force and pastoral practice in a new context. In a similar way, postmodern philosophies and the relativism of secular society have put in question the churches' hopes of finding a common confession of the apostolic faith that is both faithful to the Christian heritage and embedded in the rich varieties of postcolonial Christianity around the globe.

As the churches study together in the ecumenical movement, ethical questions are emerging along with creedal ones as central to reconcilia-

1

tion.[1] One cannot discuss unity in the faith delivered to the apostles without finding a common basis for confessing apostolic commitments to discipleship, ethics, and especially peacemaking.

Since the 1960s, churches with different perspectives on pacifism have taken up the cause of nonviolent engagement in situations of conflict. The influence of Gandhi's nonviolent movement, especially as it has been carried on through the ministry of Dr. Martin Luther King Jr., can be seen in the spiritual lives of many Christians and in some churches. For many, the heritage and resources of the peace churches have come into their lives through this openness to a nonviolent Christian discipline and spirituality. As churches move forward in their pilgrimage toward full communion in faith, sacramental life, and witness in the world, unity with those churches who carry a special gift for peacemaking becomes an important challenge and opportunity.

John Howard Yoder, to whom this volume is dedicated, contended for almost half a century that the issues of theology and ethics cannot be separated.[2] The ecclesiological focus of his work was recorded in his *New York Times* obituary: He "stressed that the work of Jesus was not a new set of ideals or principles for reforming or even revolutionizing society, but the establishment of a new community, a people that embodied forgiveness, sharing and self-sacrificing love in its rituals and discipline. In that sense, the visible church for him was not the bearer of Christ's message; it was itself to be the message."[3]

Previous Study

This volume is the second in a series exploring the confessional bases for the Church's peace witness in ecumenical dialogue. The earlier vol-

1. Thomas Best and Martin Robra, eds., *Ecclesiology and Ethics: Costly Commitment* (Geneva: World Council of Churches, 1995); Joint Working Group, World Council of Churches/Catholic Church, "The Ecumenical Dialogue on Moral Issues," in *Deepening Communion*, ed. William Rusch and Jeffrey Gros (Washington: US Catholic Conference, 1998), pp. 597-612.

2. John Howard Yoder, *The Royal Priesthood: Essays Ecclesiological and Ecumenical* (Grand Rapids: Eerdmans, 1994).

3. Peter Steinfels, "John H. Yoder, Theologian at Notre Dame, Is Dead at 70," *The New York Times*, 7 January 1988, p. A14.

ume[4] developed the biblical perspectives from which the churches draw their convictions, and focused primarily on the biblical basis for the churches' decisions about peacemaking. In that volume, the problem of the divisions between the historic peace churches represented in the discussion (Mennonite, Church of the Brethren, and Religious Society of Friends), the ecumenical methodology and its development in the Faith and Order movement, and the hopes of this dialogical process were sketched out in some detail.[5]

It is not necessary to rehash that discussion here. It is only necessary to recall that those essays served and continue to serve both the visible unity of the Church and the common witness of church denominations around the world as they move forward on the pilgrimage toward unity. They also help all churches test together the resources they bring both for their own renewal and for sharing with one another as they learn together what the gospel demands of them in the world. The essays were provided by competent scholars in a variety of disciplines and represent a diverse group of church bodies, from churches within the peace church traditions, churches historically involved in the ecumenical movement, and churches not often represented in the ecumenical dialogue. They moved the biblical conversation in a new direction.

This Study

This set of essays attempts to touch on the relationship of the nature of the Church to its mission of peacemaking from the standpoint of history and the contemporary context. These essays therefore emphasize history, though they are not limited to that perspective. Some of them draw on the confessional positions and formal arguments of the churches or use the testimonies of individuals who have influenced a given church's development. While all of the major Christian traditions are not represented here, Orthodox, Catholic, classical Reformation, and some Pentecostal and evangelical scholars provide a representative range of voices, with the peace churches being given ample space.

4. Marlin Miller and Barbara Nelson Gingerich, eds., *The Church's Peace Witness* (Grand Rapids: Eerdmans, 1994).
5. Jeffrey Gros, "Introduction," in *The Church's Peace Witness*, pp. 1-14.

There are other dialogues on these themes underway, notably between the Mennonites and Lutherans, and the Reformed and Roman Catholics. These essays note what the dialogues have accomplished and what are their hopes. As John Howard Yoder noted, the discussions make a contribution to the ecumenical methodology as well as provide specific conclusions and recommendations for the churches: "In order for Faith and Order to deal with [the peace churches as well as the Churches of Christ and Pentecostals] they have come to us and have to adjust to an alien idiom."[6] Looking at history, the nature of the Church, worship, and the significant personal and pastoral influences on the development of a point of view are all elements of understanding one another. Christians have to learn several "idioms" if they are to experience the richness of Christianity's embodiment in the variety of traditions and cultures represented in this dialogue. Looking at one's own Christian history with new partners, new events, and the impetus of desiring unity in the Church stimulates a new set of interpretive perspectives.

If differences are to be resolved, it is essential for us to understand churches other than our own. The internal complexity of a church is a clue to how it understands itself and the unity that it seeks in the gospel. Conversion entails listening to these analyses of the peacemaking function and resources of each church, and to what each church understands to be the nature of the Church. This call to conversion is a challenge to deepen the common commitment to Christ that draws us together and at the same time keeps us loyal to the convictions that divide us. This call is for the renewal of our own churches. Most important, the call is to seek the unity Christ wills for the Church. For the peace of the world, the churches are challenged to find peace around the table of the Lord. This dialogue is not merely an exercise in understanding; it is more specifically a dialogue of conversion, deepening the spiritual lives of the participants and enriching the churches' relationship in Christ.

The peace churches have gospel resources that have enriched each of the dialogue partners in the conversation. The earlier consultation of Faith and Order raised several issues that are addressed, in part, in this volume:

---

6. Letter to Norman Hjelm, 17 July 1995, evaluating the Notre Dame Conference *The Fragmentation of the Church and Its Unity in Peacemaking*, which was the stimulus for this volume.

4

Should our review of historical traditions in our search for Christian unity involve the reexamination of confessional condemnations by churches teaching the just war doctrine of churches rejecting participation in war and violence?

According to the non-historic peace churches, is a Christian pacifist stance (together with participation in war under certain conditions) also compatible with the apostolic faith? Is this still a church-dividing issue for these Christians?

According to the historic peace churches, are churches that accept both Christian pacifism and Christian participation in war under certain conditions acting in harmony with or contrary to the apostolic faith?[7]

The diverse group of essays in this volume, coming from many different points of view, addresses these issues. In some of the essays, it is clear that the concerns are more complex than these questions make it appear. By explicating the history and present state of the question, however, wisdom can be gained through this conversation. The report of the 1995 consultation *The Fragmentation of the Church and Its Unity in Peacemaking*, which was the stimulus for this volume, makes it clear that, at this stage, there is not a precise, common, church-uniting answer to these questions.[8]

The results of the earlier study also states: "Further questions about a possible change in paradigm of churchly and scholarly understandings of peace and the significance of such a change for traditionally church-dividing positions merit further examination, clarification, and response. Has there been a paradigm shift? If so, what is its character and what are its implications for significant convergence in the churches' peace witness?"[9] Certainly this volume documents more diversity within and among the churches than can yet be comprehended in one unified "paradigm."

The earlier study also documents quite well, however, that dialogue itself entails a paradigm shift, an openness to learn and to extend the frame of one's own church reference. It reinforces the common Christianity shared in our differences. It highlights our real, if yet imperfect communion, which exists even when we approach society and peace in differ-

---

7. Miller and Gingerich, eds., *The Church's Peace Witness*, p. 213.

8. *The Fragmentation of the Church and Its Unity in Peacemaking: A Report*, #14-18, pp. 222-23 in this volume.

9. Miller and Gingerich, eds., *The Church's Peace Witness*, p. 214.

ent ways. It makes it necessary for us to reevaluate our categories for interpreting history and evaluating other ecclesial communities with which we are in dialogue.

The conference suggested

> That unity and peacemaking require special programs of faith formation, in and among the churches, that assist in developing the skills of nonviolent Christian living and understandings of the churches and their quest for visible unity.
>
> That the churches develop programs of prayer for peace, for the unity of the church, and for one another. These prayers nourish communion in Christ and move Christians to the conversion to God's will for the unity of the Church and the peace of the world.
>
> That the churches provide opportunities for a dialogue of conversion, whereby Christians can encounter one another in their common quest for understanding, deepening their commitment to peace and justice in the world, and growing in their zeal for the unity of the Church.
>
> That those churches who have condemned one another's positions on pacifism and engagement in the world reconsider whether these condemnations can be put aside through public acts of reconciliation. That those churches which in the past have persecuted the Peace Churches, or have contributed to the estrangement of other churches, can find occasions for public repentance and petitions of pardon in communal acts of reconciliation, forgiveness, prayer and confession together.[10]

These Essays

These essays explore the nature of the Church's unity in peacemaking that Christians are called to embody in Jesus Christ. Recognizing that our life as Church is fragmented, the authors reflect on how Christians' shared concern for peace and peacemaking can unite us *as* Church, as living members of Christ; our Risen Lord's Body unites us even amid our fragmentation over many matters of faith and order central to our particular

10. *Report*, #20-23, p. 224 in this volume.

legacies. Authors write from the center of their confessional faith, aware that brothers and sisters in Christ who are also committed to peacemaking may embody that commitment in ways others find troubling.

Largely confessional and historical, these essays are not primarily intended to suggest how to overcome our different understandings of peace and living as peacemakers, but are meant to illumine these differences. Christians who seek to live and find unity in peace and as peacemakers differ strongly on the question of what peace and peacemaking mean. Those differences are visible in the various historical traditions and contextual realities, which often seem logically opposed to one another.

John Howard Yoder admonished us, saying that for the Church to achieve unity in matters of faith and order, other churches must adjust to the Historic Peace Churches' "alien idiom" of peacemaking. This is an invitation to conversation. The invitation is a two-way street, however, for the Historic Peace Churches must also adjust to the "alien idiom" of churches which are genuinely concerned for and committed to peace but which have rarely expressed this commitment in terms of non-resistance or understood peacemaking to mean pacifism.

In this volume we begin with a paper that highlights the Reformation issue from a Lutheran perspective. Gritsch explores the classical Lutheran doctrine of the two kingdoms, traces its course in history, and emphasizes the debates that have arisen over the roles taken by church bodies throughout history, particularly during the Nazi era. His historical and confessional perspective focuses the volume as both rooted in our memories, painful as some of them are, and oriented toward our future together in the pilgrimage toward unity for the sake of the peace of the world.

Rempel's paper, from a Mennonite perspective, centers our attention on the nature of the Church, a core issue in all of the contributions in the dialogue. Claims that the Church should be "a gathered church committed to Jesus' teaching with a high view of sanctification [that] will be pacifist" are challenged not only by the number of Christians with differing positions, but also by the realities of Mennonite life. Looking again at the biblical understanding of the Church and its peacemaking demands is a challenge not only for those churches who have been more accommodating to the dominant culture but also for the peace churches. This essay inserts the Mennonite witness squarely in the center of the ecumenical tradition of the churches in dialogue together, and outlines some ways forward.

Erickson's essay is a concise and enlightening look at the issue of peace from an Orthodox perspective. Orthodoxy, unlike most faith traditions, refuses to be labeled either a denomination or a sect. Moreover, it has inherited neither the just war tradition nor the crusading culture of the West. Erickson examines his tradition in order to uncover an accurate understanding of Orthodox attitudes toward peace and war throughout the centuries. He then touches on what this tradition has to say to us today about peace and peacemaking and on what it has to say about the relationship between Christian unity and peacemaking.

The essay from the perspective of the Church of the Brethren, the most ecumenically engaged denomination in the larger Brethren tradition, helps us see the peace churches with a human face. The history recounted includes the martyr witness that is so central to peace-church ecclesiology. Durnbaugh documents the acculturation of members of the peace churches in America, and recounts with care the ambivalent impact of the ecumenical movement on these churches. His essay focuses the ecumenical role and history of all of the peace churches, and as such is central to the whole volume.

Puglisi's paper, from a Catholic perspective, outlines developments in the Catholic Church's teaching on peace, the importance and vision of the search for unity among the churches, and the role of conversion in addressing Christ's call to peacemaking and visible unity. It includes an important discussion of dialogue and its role among the churches and of the process of reception of the results of ecumenical dialogues as Christians move forward together.

The Historic Peace Churches are characterized by a "restorationist" ecclesiology, that is, the claim to move over history and return to the biblical form of the church in the apostolic period. This approach to history is shared with the Churches of Christ, the Baptists, and the Pentecostals. While these churches all claim apostolic restoration, their analyses of the primitive Christian community provide quite different results. The Religious Society of Friends (Quakers) is the most radical of these restorationist movements in its understanding of the human person, the working of the Holy Spirit, and what the Church demands, as Paxson demonstrates in his essay.

The Reformed churches, along with the Lutheran, Anglican, and Anabaptist, are the heirs of the Reformation of the sixteenth century. They have lived beside or in conflict with the peace churches since their foundation. In his paper, Sell documents well the variety of positions within these churches, especially in the English-speaking world, and the resources they provide for peacemaking. His documentation of the diversity of Reformed positions, both among thinkers and in formal church statements, illuminates the paradox of the plurality engendered by biblical seriousness about the churches' obligation in society. He also notes the dialogue between Reformed and Mennonite churches, an important contribution to the goal of this volume.

The Pentecostal churches are among the newest (1906) and fastest growing churches in the world. As Dempster documents in his essay, there was a much stronger pacifist witness in the early days of the movement than exists now, due to the acculturation of many streams of pentecostalism. The pentecostals' restorationist notion of the Church, employing Spirit-led revival intended to unify, contains both ecclesiological elements common to the peace churches and ones in striking contrast.

Barrett presents another Mennonite perspective, giving insight into the spiritual life and discipline of the Mennonite community as well as the biblical basis from which its piety and church life emerge. The essay is particularly important for those not acquainted with the view of history, internal life style, and understanding of the human being characteristic of Mennonites.

Among Baptists there are serious debates about the origins of their tradition: is it an offshoot of British Calvinist separatism or does it have significant continental Anabaptist influences and affinities to the peace churches? Stassen's essay is clearly committed to the latter position and provides historical arguments to substantiate it. He also proposes an approach to peacemaking which has significant ecumenical participation and which he offers as a way forward in the discussions among the churches about their common peace witness.

The Olbricht essay is possibly the most characteristically American of all of the contributions. He delineates the history of the restorationist and ecumenical Campbell-Stone movement, which has given rise to the Christian Churches, the Disciples of Christ, and the Independent Christian Churches. There are significant pacifist strains in the early Campbellite movement and resources for both ecumenism and peacemaking which he outlines in some detail. As in the other restorationist churches — whether they be peace churches, Baptist, Pentecostal, or Churches of

Christ — there is here an attempt to get beyond the "Constantinianism" of the classical Reformed, Orthodox, and Catholic churches to a more pure expression of the gospel.

The Larger Context of This Study

Studies of the apostolic faith and the fourth century, the era of Constantine and the early councils, have shown that the problems of acculturation, church-state relations, and pacifism during this period are more complex than traditionally affirmed by the restorationist movements.[11] While it is necessary for each church to explain its own story, its own view of the Church, and the rationale for its approach to peacemaking, common work on Christian history is as important as common study of the Scripture. In the healing of memories and projection of a common future in response to Christ's call, common reflection on both the sins and gifts of our predecessors is part of the interpretive project of the Faith and Order movement.[12]

The Faith and Order movement has learned that all churches find it difficult to see God's incarnate presence and life in another church's "alien idioms" of belief or behavior. Christians often resist recognizing those with profoundly different beliefs and actions as sisters and brothers or as true, full members of the same Church. It seems particularly challenging for Christians in Europe and North America to embrace as peers those with very different traditions. The tendency to seek unity in sameness fits a philosophical legacy of cultures whose church leaders viewed "their" church's polity and confession as true and non-negotiable in matters of Christian unity.

By addressing their traditions' understandings of peace and the demands of living as peacemakers, these essays illumine ways various ecclesial traditions embody their faith as peacemakers. Each essay presupposes, and many identify, the contextual realities that have shaped them

---

11. S. Mark Heim, ed., *Faith to Creed: Ecumenical Perspectives on the Affirmation of the Apostolic Faith in the Fourth Century* (Grand Rapids: Eerdmans, 1991); Timothy J. Wengert and Charles W. Brockwell Jr., eds., *Telling the Churches' Stories: Ecumenical Perspectives on Writing Christian History* (Grand Rapids: Eerdmans, 1995).

12. Cf. Alan Falconer, ed., *Faith and Order in Moshi* (Geneva: World Council of Churches, 1998).

in their specific life and legacy. It is eminently clear that each church tradition was formed by, and continues to flourish in, its particular situation, age, and place. The legacy of each shaped its commitment to serve God and neighbor in incarnate social, cultural, historical, theological, and ecclesial contexts in which believers widely differ from one another. These historical and practical differences *make* a difference. It is instructive to hear how the particularities of each legacy are integral to the history, identity, story, and specific expressions of what it means for that community to be faithful, to be Church. Deeply integrated into the cultural involvements and historical traditions of their various traditions, Christians know and express life-giving faith in God's righteousness and grace through Christ Jesus "incarnately" — in other words, in their specific realities and experiences.

While Christians in the ecumenical movement can affirm that all communions' efforts to live as peacemakers are expressions of their faith and integrity, we also recognize that national, political, ethnic, and even ecclesial faith and order concerns remain "dividing walls of hostility" that separate us from, rather than unite us in, peace as members of Christ's one, risen, living Body, the Church. Indeed, we hear these diverse voices identify their commitment to make peace and their ways of being peacemakers while painfully aware that the mass violence in the Western world in recent centuries is largely a story of Christians killing other Christians.

Challenges of the Future

New questions present themselves to us today. For us to honor one another as brothers and sisters, as members of Christ who are committed to being peacemakers, all communions must ask questions that are bigger than those of our traditions, confessing that many who love and serve Christ dwell outside the boundaries of our tradition. It seems important, perhaps urgent (though it lies beyond the scope of this volume), to inquire into the theological and doctrinal significance for Christian unity of these "incarnate" differences. For example:

— Is coercion part of all communions' historical and contemporary practice? Consider the dynamic similarities and/or differences between the just war theory (largely affirmed by churches that identify with the larger society of which they are part and feel "responsible" for its safety and well-being) and shunning (an Anabaptist practice in which members within a "set-apart community" are not spoken to or acknowledged when leaders believe their beliefs or actions threaten the integrity of others in the community).

— How do we engage the theological and doctrinal significance for Christian unity of various communions' "incarnate" differences in their understandings of peace and practices of peacemaking? Lisa Cahill and others have provided a sociological basis for this reflection by noting that differences in Christians' identification with "our community" or "all people" in a specific geographical area, city, or nation seem to correlate with the positions taken by that communion in matters of peacemaking. A theological dialogue of peacemaking is particularly complex and important in the global context, when it is begun with Christians from Asia, Africa, Latin America, etc. — places where the worldview and presuppositions of Western theology are often "alien idioms."

— How do Christians think theologically about peacemaking in relation to matters of external, physical, material coercion and internal, spiritual, psychological coercion?

— What does it mean that no tradition can establish universal terms of and norms for peacemaking except by using coercion?

— How do churches committed to peacemaking interpret their own history of killing or of condemning those (internal or external to their communion) whom they named "heretics"?

— Communions clarify their identities by identifying their boundaries — by illumining *their* faith and order, relational dynamics, beliefs, and behavior. A communion's boundaries clarify how it is Church. By what authority then does a communion judge whom God deems righteous or unrighteous, a heretic or peacemaker? How *do* peacemakers assess and relate to those whose faith and order lie outside the boundaries of "their" boundaries and outside their understandings of truth, their confessions of faith, and their affirmations of the actions that "make for peace"?

— Christians ground their identity primarily in Jesus, Scripture, the Church's history, and the work of the Holy Spirit. Simultaneously each ecclesial history is a story that reveals the mark of a specific historical context while also recording significant changes in that com-

12

munion over time. Given the churches' common dynamics of story and change, and our specific and diverse particularities, what ecclesial and theological questions must churches ask in searching for peace, unity, and faithfulness as peacemakers in this world God so loves?

— Spiritually, Christians may live amid or at the margins of a larger society. At home in a society, we often feel at ease, flourish, and identify with it. At its margins, we are apt to feel threatened, suffer, and seek invisibility. A communion's existential legacy-location is often mirrored in its ecclesiology and expectations about peacemaking. For example, Christians whose forebears were killed as heretics are apt to wonder how Christians can seek to control or justify killing others and still view themselves as peacemakers. Christians who identify with the powerful, on the other hand, may readily ponder what the less powerful (in terms of race, gender, ethnicity, etc.) should "be allowed" — betraying that they feel themselves part of, not apart from, those with the power to decide appropriate boundaries for "marginal" individuals. What are the theological reasons grounded in peacemaking and spiritual integrity by which Christians who are mutual members of Christ engage one another in an attitude of cultural advantage and power?

— Christians who are open to and engaged in "alien idioms" learn that some previous ways of expressing faith are no longer life-giving. Open to the new things God is doing, they may seek the life-giving gift God now offers — in a place or way as alien to their legacy and expectation as was God-with-us, arriving as infant Jesus in a stable. How do we peacemakers learn to hear and receive the amazing divine words "Fear not"?

— Communions change in response to new experiences, perspectives, and questions. Their stories document their abilities to thrive in changing contexts and to adapt to external ecclesial, social, cultural, and political conditions they cannot control. Communions do adapt to difficult situations, in part by "controlling" their integration of spiritual, cultural, social, and political life in and as community (even in adverse external situations). What has led and leads the Church and churches to examine their stories, repent of certain aspects of their legacies, be converted, and embody a new way of being the people of faith?

It is an ecclesial contribution to the Church's unity in peacemaking to raise questions at the denominational, ethnic, cultural, national, political, and economic levels of our legacies as Christians. Questions of and concerns for peacemaking are as incarnate, concrete, and practical today as they were for Jesus and his companions. They cannot be faithfully answered once-for-all-time in normative behavioral terms, as if incarnate reality were secondary. Yet basic practical, actual, ecclesial questions will not go away. For example: Who *is* our enemy? How do we believe Christians engage enemies? What guides our Christian self-understanding as peacemakers and what guidelines and boundaries for faith and practice are thereby called for? Of what community are we most basically citizens? At times we dissent from or oppose the expectations or positions of our parish, communion, tradition, ethnic group, or whatever "people" our lives are connected to; at such times, what informs our decision to either do what we were asked or diverge even if such action takes us beyond our community's boundaries?

The 1995 conference brought to the surface other issues in the discussion. The centrality of peace formation for all of the churches emerged as an important common priority, for which the peace churches have important resources to offer. Also, the importance of ecumenical formation — for example, getting to know one's own ecumenical tradition, the churches with which one lives and is in dialogue, and the results of the ecumenical tradition — became evident.[13] The conference also clarified remaining points of contention among church bodies needing further study and made some recommendations. The full report is included at the end of the essays.

The invitational strength of these essays is their affirmation that the Church's "unity in peacemaking" rests in a multiplicity of idioms, incarnate situations, and diverse experiential questions. The human, and ecclesial, tendency to identify one (usually our) way as true and right, is hereby called into question. Each confession of peacemaking and all work

13. Cf. Joint Working Group, World Council/Catholic Church, "Ecumenical Formation," in *Deepening Communion*, 573-82; John Lindner, ed., "Ecumenical Formation: A Methodology for a Pluralistic Age, The Case of the Ecumenical Institute at Bossesy," *Theological Education* 34, Supplement (Autumn 1997); Pontifical Council for Promoting Christian Unity, "The Ecumenical Dimension in the Formation of Pastoral Workers," *Origins* 27, no. 39 (19 March 1998): 653-61.

for peace is part of some specific cultural, spiritual, and religious identity and legacy.

At the same time, each Christian communion and people is basic to the life, meaning, and hope of all, inasmuch as all are members of our source, and Prince, of Peace. However difficult it seems to open our hearts to people whose "alien idioms" of faith and practice (seem to) undermine, challenge, and offend us, one way God in Christ nurtures and converts us through the Holy Spirit is meeting the Holy One again for the first time in situations and places we, based on our own experience and understanding, would overlook or reject. Even so, we remember and receive with open hearts the Divine Word of Epiphany to "fear not," and engage alien idioms each time our faith in God's living presence is stronger than our fear of change, losing face, relinquishing authority and power, or feeling out of control.

As the consultants affirmed together in 1995:

> The divisions in the Body of Christ in the world are a counter witness to the peace sought and proclaimed by the Church as the follower of the Prince of Peace who prayed that his disciples might be one. The movement toward unity among the churches is itself a sign and model of their peacemaking vocation.[14]

14. *Report*, #4, p. 219 in this volume.

Christian Unity and Peacemaking:
A Lutheran Perspective

ERIC W. GRITSCH

A Neuralgic Legacy

Lutheran statements and actions on war and peace have been widely and hotly debated (especially in this century when Germany rose and fell as a superpower in two world wars). They are "neuralgic," as it were, causing acute pain raditating along the nerves of church bodies, detected by "doctors" of theology and history. Martin Luther's "two-kingdoms ethic," as it is called, has been the center of the debate among theologians and historians. Luther tried to described the Christian life as existence in two "realms" (later called "kingdoms"), the realm of God and realm of Satan. these realms must be carefully distinguished even through there is an enduring temptation to unite them — to create the kingdom of God as a result of Satan's conquest by Christ. Luther insisted that as long as the world exists Christians must live in both realms, concretely manifested in church and state. The church is the community of faith in God's salvation through Christ; the state is the guardian of law and order in the face of sin and chaos. Spiritual freedom and political obedience represent the proper distinction of the two realms in Luther's "two kingdoms ethic." But both realms could easily be separated or united, creating a theocracy (the domination of the church over the state) or an idealistic spiritual community (the separation of the church from the "secular" world).

Some Luther scholars in Germany have viewed Luther and Luther-

16

anism either as the source of a cultural community based on sound Christian and constitutional principles (*Kulturstaat)* or as the theological rationale for an idealistic, indeed utopian, idea of political authority *(Obrigkeit).*[1] The Swiss theologian Karl Barth condemned Luther as the source of Adolf Hitler's tyranny, and the American theologian Reinhold Niebuhr saw in Luther's distinction of "office" and "person" a perverse morality that encouraged such tyranny.[2] The best-selling history of Germany under Hitler by the American journalist William L. Shirer called Luther a "ferocious believer in absolute obedience to political authority."[3] The neuralgic history of the "two-kingdoms ethic" has been debated within and outside of Lutheranism.[4]

The questions of war, peace, and resistance to political tyranny have been debated on the basis of Article XVI of *The Augsburg Confession* of 1530, which asserts "that Christians may without sin exercise political authority . . . punish evildoers with the sword, wage just wars; serve as soldiers. . . . But if a command of the political authority cannot be followed without sin, one must obey God rather than human beings (Acts 5:29)."[5] Here Lutheranism stayed within the teaching tradition of the Western medieval church and upheld the just war theory. It was viewed as a significant component of what Lutheranism after Luther called the "first use of the law," that is, the advocacy of justice through "the righteousness of reason."[6]

1. The former view was held by Karl Holl and his disciples, the latter by Ernst Troeltsch and his followers. See Karl Holl, *The Cultural Significance of the Reformation,* trans. Karl and Barbara Hertz and John H. Lichtblau (New York: Meridian, 1959), p. 63; Ernst Troeltsch, *The Social Teaching of the Christian Churches,* trans. Oliver Wyon (New York: Macmillan, 1931), p. 552. For details regarding Luther's "two-kingdom ethic" see Eric W. Gritsch, *Martin — God's Court Jester: Luther in Retrospect,* 2nd ed. (Ramsey, N.J.: Sigler Press, 1990), ch. 6.

2. Karl Barth, *Eine Schweizer Stimme,* 1938-1934 (Zollikon-Zurich: Evangelischer Verlag), 113; Reinhold Niebuhr, *The Nature and Destiny of Man,* 2 vols. (New York: Scribner's Sons, 1953), pp. 194-95.

3. William L. Shirer, *The Rise and Fall of the Third Reich* (New York: Scribner's Sons, 1960), p. 236.

4. See Ulrich Duchrow and Heiner Hoffman, eds., *Two Kingdoms: The Use and Misuse of a Lutheran Theological Concept* (Geneva: Lutheran World Federation, 1977).

5. German text of *The Augsburg Confession* in *The Book of Concord. The Confessions of the Evangelical Lutheran Church* (hereafter cited *AC* and *BC),* trans. Charles Arand et al., ed. Robert Kolb and Timothy J. Wengert (Minneapolis: Fortress Press, 2000), p. 48, section 2 (hereafter 48:2) and 50:7.

6. *BC* 124:22.

This righteousness unites all people, regardless of religion, for the purpose of keeping law and order in the world, and is based on the universal sense of "natural law" reflected in the Decalogue.[7] But keeping law and order does not initiate a better world; evil cannot be overcome in this world — only contained. That is why the chief function of divine law is the disclosure of evil (Rom. 3:20). Its purpose is to accuse, indeed terrify, consciences that cannot do enough good to be freed from sin.[8] Consequently, war at best preserves justice but cannot be a crusade for a world without evil. That is why normative Lutheran teaching rejects both pacifism and crusades as utopian options that either confuse or separate the divine and earthly kingdoms.[9]

These political teachings, however, have a history that has disclosed the perversion of the proverbial wisdom that "abuse does not eliminate proper use" *(abusus non tollit usum)*. The history of the effect of Luther's political advice and its formal confessional adoption reveals more abuse than proper use.[10] Two basic abuses have dominated. The first is the collapse of the two "kingdoms" (or "regiments" or "realms," according to Luther) into one governance consisting of Luther's three divinely ordered "estates" (family, state, church), with the state dominating; its worst political reality was Hitler's establishment of a national (Nazi) church *(Reichskirche)*, a "caesaropapism" with the slogan "one kingdom, one people, one leader" *(ein Reich, ein Volk, ein Führer)*. The second is the separation of the two kingdoms and three estates into an idealistic system of independent spheres of life which are dominated by the political estate. Both abuses represent a dangerous shift from Christian political responsibility to a "diaconal charity" that degrades Luther's holistic care for the neighbor in need and separates religion from politics.

The trajectory of an uncritical alliance or allegiance of Lutheranism and the state began with Philip Melanchthon's contention that Article XVI of the Augsburg Confession meant the subjection of the realm of the

7. *BC* 121:8.

8. *BC* 126:38.

9. *BC* 231:3-4.

10. See Eric W. Gritsch, *Martin — God's Court Jester. Luther in Retrospect,* 2nd ed. (Ramsey, N.J.: Sigler Press, 1990), ch. 6: "Christ and Caesar"; "The Use and Abuse of Luther's Political Advice," *Lutherjahrbuch* 57 (1990): 207-19; Ulrich Duchrow, ed., *Lutheran Churches — Salt or Mirror of Society?* (Geneva: Department of Studies, Lutheran World Federation, 1977).

gospel to the realm of law in the form of political government, "just as we have been necessarily placed under the laws of seasons (changes of winter and summer) as divine ordinances."[11] After Luther's death and a national war over religion, Melanchthon defended the doctrine of "territorial religion," as the Peace of Augsburg decreed it in 1555. The critical interaction between church and state was gone; the territorial prince was acknowledged as the head of both church and state *(summus episcopus)*. Problems continued in later centuries; seventeenth-century "orthodox" Lutherans revived the medieval synthesis of prince and priest, cementing the relationship between the head of a territory and all the baptized in it, and resulting in a *"Landeskirche"* in a given territory. The episcopal rule of territorial prince when bishops become unfaithful to the gospel, what Luther had once called an emergency action, had now become a legitimate tradition.[12] There was, however, radical opposition to these practices, and those who idolized Luther labeled the dominance of princes over the church "a new political Antichrist."[13] The English champion of religious liberty, Roger Williams, joined such critics, espousing the more positive view that Luther advocated freedom of conscience as the critical link between the two kingdoms: conscience must remain free and the state must not be permitted to control spiritual matters.[14]

The abuse continued with a call for the establishment of the kingdom of God on earth through good works of love and justice. Opponents of Lutheran territorial orthodoxy, called "Pietists," called on the Prussian government to fight the kingdom of Satan for the sake of the kingdom of God.[15] At times, Pietists allied themselves with political underdogs, such as the peasants opposed to the monarchy in Scandinavia. Dualistic views of Luther's two-kingdom ethic prevailed. Politicians and intellectuals in

---

11. *BC* 232:6.

12. See Luther's *To the Christian Nobility of the German Nation* (1520). *Luther's Works,* American Edition, 55 vols., ed. Jaroslav Pelikan and Helmut Lehmann (Philadelphia: Fortress Press; St. Louis: Concordia, 1955-1986), 44:129. Hereafter cited *LW.*

13. The slogan of the most ardent Luther disciple, Matthias Flacius. See Joerg Baur, "Flacius — radikale Theologie," *Zeitschrift für Theologie und Kirche* 72 (1975): 368.

14. See "The Bloody Tenant Yet More Bloody" (1644), in *The Complete Writings,* 6 vols. (New York, 1963), 4:19-20.

15. A view advocated by the most influential Pietist, August H. Francke. See Erich Beyreuther, *August Hermann Francke 1663-1727* (Marburg an der Lahn, Verlag der Francke-Buchhandlung, 1956), pp. 181-82.

Germany contended that Luther would have approved of their notion that an inward spiritual life of faith had no bearing on external political decisions. The influential "German Evangelical-Social Congress," led by Friedrich Naumann (1860-1919), declared that Lutheranism teaches the separation of the inner spiritual life from external political power.[16]

This recurring abuse of Luther's two-kingdoms ethic was only rarely interrupted by its proper use as the theological foundation for a view of the church as a pilgrim on the way to the eternal "promised land," our destination after the second coming of Christ. Luther expressed this view with the statement that Christians will always remain "simultaneously righteous and sinners" *(simul justi et peccatores)* as long as they live in this world.[17]

This proper view became the ideological cornerstone for resistance against Nazism in Norway in 1941 when Hitler tried to convert the country into a state of political slavery.[18] The leading bishop of the church, Eivind Berggrav, contended that Lutheranism could not submit to tyranny because tyranny confuses brutal power with just law. In such a situation, he argued, it was a Christian duty to be disobedient by refusing to cooperate with the imposed Nazi government. The office of the word of God must rebuke the office of the sword when the sword is wielded without just law.[19] Bishop Berggrav was put under house arrest, but continued a successful campaign against a Nazi puppet government. The Lutheran Church of Norway went virtually underground, with few in it supporting the Nazi regime. Hitler had the choice of creating massive martyrdom or of tolerating the Norwegian situation until the end of the war; he opted for the latter and lost the ideological war against Norwegian Lutherans.

The question of war and peace has been debated in the shadow of this neuralgic legacy of Lutheran teaching on Christian responsibility in

16. Duchrow, ed., *Lutheran Churches — Salt or Mirror of Society?* p. 15.

17. Just how decisive this view is for Luther's entire thought structure has been shown by Kjell O. Nilsson, *Simul* (Göttingen: Vandenhoeck & Ruprecht, 1966).

18. See Arne Fjellbu, "Luther as a Resource of Arms in the Fight for Democracy," in *World Lutheranism of Today. A Tribute to Anders Nygren* (Stockholm, 1950), pp. 81-97. The history of Norwegian resistance is told by Bjarne Hoeye and Trygve M. Ager, *The Fight of the Norwegian Church Against Nazism* (New York: Macmillan, 1943).

19. Berggrav's views are summarized in *Man and the State* (Fr. George Aus, Philadelphia: Fortress, 1951), pp. 287-99.

the world. The Lutheran World Federation has agreed that the Lutheran confessional teaching of the just war theory, based on Article XVI of the Augsburg Confession, is no longer accepted in its entirety by all of the 58 million Lutherans around the world.[20] Moreover, Lutheran differences on the meaning of war and peace reflect the difficulty of the ecumenical conciliar attempts at increasing unity; the apostolic injunction to have peace on earth is interpreted in many different ways by Christians. Lutherans, therefore, find themselves in the same boat with other Christians — a situation which reflects the historical tradition of Lutheranism, since sixteenth-century Lutherans viewed themselves as a reform movement within the church catholic rather than as a new church.[21] That is why the most recent Lutheran efforts to find consensus on peace call for a complementary consensus on what constitutes Christian unity.[22] But calls for "a culture of peace" and pious expressions of hope for peace do not create much critical interest or sharp debate on the true meaning of peace. A "Working Group on Faith and Order" of the World Council of Churches has been encouraged by most member churches to continue the conciliar attempts to reach a consensus. At issue is the biblical meaning of peace for our time, a chief component of the apostolic character of the church's witness in the world.[23]

20. This has been shown in a series of Lutheran essays in *War, Confession and Conciliarity. What Does "Just War" in the Augsburg Confession Mean Today?* ed. Viggo Mortensen, "Vorlagen" 18 (Hanover: Lutherisches Verlagshaus, 1993).

21. A view still popular among serious students of the Lutheran Confessions in *BC*. See Eric W. Gritsch and Robert W. Jenson, *Lutheranism: The Theological Movement and Its Confessional Writings* (Philadelphia: Fortress, 1976).

22. See, for example, the struggle for a consensus on peace in the Evangelical Lutheran Church in America (ELCA) in its "consultations" responding to the Lutheran World Federation Paper on "War, Confession and Conciliarity" (Chicago, 1994) and the "Social Statement" proposed for consideration by the 1995 Churchwide Assembly of the ELCA, entitled "For Peace in God's World" (Chicago, 1994).

23. This is the mandate given to the "Major Consultation of Faith and Order, USA," where this paper is discussed together with other papers representing various Christian communions. See Marlin E. Miller and Barbara Nelson Gingerich, eds., *The Church's Peace Witness* (Grand Rapids: Eerdmans, 1994), pp. 214-15.

Normative Fundamental Insights

Normative Lutheran teaching was affected by Luther's unsystematic reflections about personal and public Christian life. Luther rejected the Roman Catholic medieval view of two different levels of life and morals, a priestly monastic level, which aimed for spiritual perfection by embodying the "beatitudes" of the Sermon on the Mount (the "evangelical counsels" — *concilia evangelica* — from Matt. 5:1-11) and a lay level, obedient to ecclesiastical authority. Instead, he viewed the Sermon on the Mount not as a divine law to be realized in life, but as a narration of the fruits of faith which follow when one relies completely on Christ as the only source of salvation. The most basic gift of faith is peace with God and with the people of the world — brothers and sisters who become "the neighbor" one loves in Christ's name.[24]

Luther did not follow this view of the Sermon on the Mount when he dealt with public life. According to Luther, for example, a Christian who is a soldier may participate in a defensive, "just" war without committing the sin of killing because such a war is part of the divine way to maintain creation. There must be equity in the face of evil, and there must be soldiers who defend those who till the soil for food. In this sense, Christians are obliged to forgo their personal commitment to peace and nonviolence for the sake of fulfilling the office of soldiering and preserving the peaceful life of the neighbor.[25] They act like physicians who must do painful surgery in order to keep the body alive. That is why war is as godly and useful as eating, drinking, and other enterprises that keep the world going.[26]

Luther's distinction between person and office, as well as his ambiguous use of the Sermon on the Mount as a source of peace, affected the drafting of Article XVI and its approval of just wars. But today, in an age of ABC weapons (atomic, bacteriological, and chemical), Lutheran ethics has virtually rejected the just war theory.[27] Some Lutherans have formed a

24. This has been persuasively shown by Heinz-Horst Schrey, "Frieden V," *Theologische Realenzyklopaedie,* ed. Gerhard Krause and Gerhard Mueller (Berlin and New York: De Gruyter, 1976–), 11:635-37.

25. See Martin Luther, *Whether Soldiers, Too, Can Be Saved* (1526). *LW* 46:102-3, 121-22, 128.

26. Luther, *Whether Soldiers,* 46:97.

27. See the arguments in the study commissioned by The Lutheran Council USA, *Peace and the Just War Tradition. Lutheran Perspectives in a Nuclear Age* (St. Louis: Con-

"peace fellowship" without, however, embracing pacifism. Contemporary Lutheranism has joined Christians around the globe in a call for peace, but this call is neither well argued nor grounded in a consensus on Christian unity and world peace. The time has come to mine the Lutheran tradition for evidence that provides a Lutheran perspective on Christian unity and world peace. What follows is an attempt to provide such evidence.

1. Peace With God

Luther rediscovered Paul's and John's apostolic witness that God's incarnation in Jesus is the only source for inner peace. Such peace comes through faith rather than through merits with God. That is why news of God's incarnation in Christ is a "power" (*dynamis* in Greek) known through faith; it is why "the righteous shall live by faith" (cf. Hab. 2:4; Rom. 1:16-17). Luther also learned from Paul that one must have the mind of Christ who "emptied himself" in total obedience to his mission of saving humankind from sin, avoiding the temptation to be like God and have faith only in the power of the ego (Phil. 2:5-8; cf. Gen. 3:5). John taught him that divine truth is not an idea or dogma, but a person, "the glory as of a father's only son, full of grace and truth" (John 1:14). So true faith is trust in Christ alone. Being right with God ("justified") means to have peace with God (Rom. 5:1). Luther knew this peace as a personal state of mind when he had to deal with his own anxiety and doubt (called *Anfechtung* in German). He expected that peace to come with full power at the end of earthly history. His strong anticipation of the last day may have reduced his desire to work for political peace in the interim between Christ's first and second coming; consequently, he was concerned with law and order mainly as a means of maintaining a balance between good and evil until the day when the peace of another world would come and never end.

---

cordia, 1986). Esp. Gilbert Meilaender, "Whether (in this Nuclear Age) Soldiers, too, Can Be Saved," pp. 88-105. The essay argues for a Lutheran "road less traveled," that is, to view war as a futile attempt to maintain peace with justice. But no clear alternative is offered.

2. Law and Gospel

Luther and normative Lutheran teaching adopted the Pauline view of history as the story of God and his people, first Israel and then all people. Paul described this history as the movement from Jewish law to its fulfillment in Christ and in those who are his disciples (Rom. 8:4; 9:30–10:4). But since Christ has not yet established the life promised in the gospel — the good news of a future of love, peace, and unity — law and gospel must be properly distinguished. Luther labeled both law and gospel "the word of God" that must be distinguished from human words. The word of God is handed on ("traditioned") from generation to generation as God's will for law and order in the face of the chaos resulting from the violation of the First Commandment ("You shall have no other gods"). But the word of God also discloses God's love for the world in Christ, the good news ("gospel") that through the man Jesus the sin of disobedience has been forgiven.[28] Scripture is the God-willed vessel of the word of God. Its center is Christ who is proleptically already present in the Old Testament. The New Testament is the apostolic witness of the final act of God in the history of salvation, the resurrection of Jesus; that resurrection is the foundation of a future without sin and death for all who, like the first disciples, have faith in Jesus alone.

Normative Lutheranism pledges allegiance to the "prophetic and apostolic writings of the Old and New Testaments as the pure, clear fountain of Israel."[29] Here Lutheranism follows the catholic tradition in the West by equating the Old Testament with "law" and the New Testament with "gospel." The Lutheran Confessions speak of three functions of the law: law as justice, or "civil" law, to prevent chaos; law as the instrument of penance leading to the gospel; and law as Christian discipline for an effective ministry of the church in the world.[30]

---

28. It is not as well known as it should be that Luther subordinated his anti-Roman Catholic principle of "Scripture alone" *(sola scriptura)* to his definition of "tradition" as the life of the word of God in time, beginning at creation and ending on the Last Day. He saw more tension between the divine and human word than between Scripture and tradition. See Eric W. Gritsch, "Martin Luther's View of Tradition," *The Quadrilog. Tradition and the Future of Ecumenism. Essays in Honor of George H. Tavard,* ed. Kenneth Hagen (Collegeville, Minn.: The Liturgical Press, 1994), pp. 61-75.

29. *BC* 527:3. Since this is a pledge to the theological, not literal, meaning of the Bible, it rejects any notions of biblical inerrancy or fundamentalism.

30. The third function of the law has been debated in Lutheranism. The first stage

24

The first use or function of the law is to resist evil, the result of the original, inherited sin of idolatry or playing God (Gen. 3:5). Such resistance is based on the diagnostic work of reason, for law is linked to reason as the chief power of human life; in the Book of Concord we read that, in this world, "God requires the righteousness of reason."[31] The use of reason can therefore initiate specific steps toward justice, the best possible balance between good and evil. (It is for this reason that the scale is an appropriate symbol of justice.) Justice is linked to government as a divinely sanctioned instrument to provide law and order (Rom. 13:1). In this sense, the law is laid down for the lawless (1 Tim. 1:9).[32] This was the Lutheran theological foundation for the just war which, as the most reasonable form of violence, must be used to curb unreasonable, unjust violence. Here Christians join non-Christians in the work of justice, ranging from courtroom to battlefield. The battlefield, however, has become, increasingly, an unreasonable way to create justice — making the just war virtually irrelevant.

The second use or function of the law is to create change of mind, or penance (*metanoia* in the Greek New Testament, e.g., Mark 1:15). This use of the law provides an unwelcome reality check, namely, that the most honest attempts to obey the law only reveal our inability to do so. The law reveals sin (Rom. 3:20; 7:18b-19). Such diagnosis shows the limits of the human mind; it cannot save from evil, even though it is always tempted to assume it can. In the light of law as part of the word of God, reason becomes "the old witch," a whore, who tries to trick God into forgiving sins by merit rather than by trust in Christ alone.[33] Reason is idolatrous when it tries to be salvific.

The Lutheran Confessions have the highest regard for this function of the law because it reveals the real state of affairs in the world. The "chief function" of the law is not to create a better world, or to realize the kingdom of God on earth, or whatever human imagination dreams up; the chief function is to show the need for the gospel which is itself the only power to change humankind since it is the power of the future in another, radically different world. The law is at its best when it "terrifies

---

of the debate affirmed it in the *Formula of Concord* of 1577. (See *BC* 587:1–591:25.) It can be viewed as Christian discipline, spiritual formation, or ministry.

31. *BC* 124:22.
32. *BC* 124:22-23.
33. *BC* 623:41.

consciences."[34] That is why *Christian* reasoning is at best diagnostic: used to detect what is truly real before God, to overcome illusions, and to yearn for faith in Christ, who alone liberates from evil. This second function of the law can provide for us today a Lutheran theological foundation for rejecting the just war as a political illusion, in the face of the might and speed of arms that make it impossible to distinguish between justice and injustice. Just as human reason cannot justify ego power as the solution for the world's evil and for a relationship with God, so war can no longer be used to justify nationalism or any other way to dominate others or to be segregated from them. War, then, is always destructive rather than constructive and so must be rejected as a way to create the best way of life.

The third use or function of the law is to shape Christian life for ministry, whether for ordained or non-ordained vocations anchored in baptism. Worship and education are the twin pillars of the church, equipping members for ministry in the world. Both provide spiritual formation and discipline. The Lutheran Confessions speak of "a return to baptism" when they speak of such formation: the task of penance, by drowning the old Adam and Eve every day so that they can rise up "before God in righteousness and purity forever in God's presence."[35] The liturgy of baptism calls this formation "exorcism": expelling evil by invoking the power of the Holy Spirit. Baptism commits to a "new obedience" that produces works of love not for merit before God but for service of the neighbor in the world.[36] This new obedience reflects the gospel promise that already in this life the way of the new world of selfless love is embodied by those who follow Christ, even though they only "see in a mirror, dimly" (1 Cor. 13:12). The Lutheran Confessions stress this new way of life as the consequence of a rebirth through the Holy Spirit: "after they have been reborn . . . they may have a sure guide, according to which they can orient and conduct their entire life."[37] This third function of the law can create a Lutheran theological foundation for an ethic of freedom that rejects war as a demonic exercise of futility. Dietrich Bonhoeffer is so far the only Lutheran who has created such an ethic and applied it to war. "War is a

34. *BC* 126:38.
35. *BC* 360:12.
36. *AC* 6. *BC* 40, 41.
37. *BC* 502, VI:1.

struggle for life using dehumanized means," he said. "The Church that prays to Our Father appeals to God only for peace."[38]

3. Reason and Love

The threefold function of the law is grounded in the double commandment of love: to love God and the neighbor (Matt. 22:37-39). "On these two commandments hang all the law and the prophets" (Matt. 22:40). The Lutheran Confessions view all of Christian life as a way to nurture love for others in the face of the enduring temptation to believe only in oneself and "to wrest heaven from God."[39] Accordingly, human reason must always be bent sideways, as it were. Reason without faith in Christ always tries to storm heaven and make good works meritorious. But the good Samaritan (Luke 10:25-37) uses his mind to help the victim without asking the question, "What's in it for me?" The bad Samaritan just looks at the victim and says, "Whoever did this to you needs a lot of help."

All three uses or functions of the law use reason to do the best possible ministry in the world: first, create just conditions, accepting the help even of non-Christians; second, do a reality check of what is real before God and so move minds toward change and penance; and, third, create a spiritual discipline for the sake of a better witness of the church in the world. Law and reason are at their best when they help helpless victims.

These fundamental insights call for a paradigm shift, based on a contemporary reading of the Bible and on what such a reading yields for the task of creating Christian unity and peace.

Apostolic Mandates

1. Serpenthood

The Matthean Jesus connected discipleship, spiritual discipline, and mission in the world using the paradigm of serpenthood. When the disciples

38. Quoted in Eberhard Bethge, *Dietrich Bonhoeffer: Man of Vision, Man of Courage,* trans. Eric Mosbacher et al. (New York, San Francisco, London: Harper & Row, paperback, 1985), p. 144. There is no solid evidence that Bonhoeffer was an advocate of pacifism in any ideological sense.

39. *BC* 388:22.

were sent to communicate the message of Jesus they were sent out "like sheep into the midst of wolves." But naive, humble servanthood is not the most faithful ministry in a world of life-threatening opposition to the Christian mission, where religious and secular authorities persecute the disciples of Jesus, family members oppose each other over the gospel, children rise against their parents, and disciples of the Lord are maligned even as their master was called "Beelzebul" (Matt. 10:17-25). This is why we must "be wise as serpents and innocent as doves" (Matt. 10:16).

Jesus lifted up the image of the serpent because the serpent is linked in tradition (if not in scientific fact) with the powers of wisdom, healing, and sharp discernment. Doves are "innocent": they coo with naive joy, usually while making love on rooftops, only to be shot down by hunters desiring culinary pleasure. But the serpent is depicted as surviving the longest because of its wisdom. Matthew was aware of the history of the image of the serpent in the Old Testament. First, the serpent was the instrument of temptation in the garden, promising Adam and Eve that they would "be like God" (Gen. 3:5). Then the serpent became a symbol of salvation from death during the exodus of the people of Israel from Egypt; Moses was told by God to make a bronze serpent, and anyone afraid of being bitten by a poisonous snake was saved by looking at the bronze image (Num. 21:9). Finally, the Johannine Jesus told the Jewish leader Nicodemus that "just as Moses lifted up the serpent in the wilderness, so must the Son of Man be lifted up, that whoever believes in him may have eternal life" (John 3:14).

The ancient Greeks also saw the serpent as an image of healing, and such a portrayal has survived even in modern medicine, where the serpent is sometimes shown curling around a staff on a garment or elsewhere. In the Bible, however, the image of the serpent became Christocentric, signaling healing and salvation from evil and death. But healing and salvation do not happen without a precise, cold-blooded diagnosis. To be wise as a serpent means using the mind for proper diagnosis in order to move to a realistic prognosis. Serpenthood is sharp discernment of disease and evil, the toughest form of love. Lutherans call it "the preaching of the law."

Luther modeled for his reform movement both ways of discipleship, being wise as a serpent and innocent as a dove; he was like a cooing dove when he preached about the wonder of the incarnation at his parish in Wittenberg, like a wise serpent when he campaigned against the abuses of his church, ranging from those of financial stewardship to problems with scholastic casuistry.[40] Luther even developed a way of speaking about God in terms that remind one of the images of serpent and dove. The gospel, he contended, must be expressed in contrary terms *(sub contrario)*: God is a baby in the child Jesus at Bethlehem; an itinerant teacher who makes sophisticated Pharisees doubt their own argumentation; a man who dies on a cross, but is raised from the dead. That is why Christians have a greater wisdom than that offered by this world; they are wise by being "fools for the sake of Christ" (1 Cor. 4:10). Luther called himself a court jester, hiding behind a familiar mask in order to communicate a wisdom that transcends traditional politics and religion.[41] It was possible to be free and witty because the future with God had already begun in this life by faith in Christ alone. In this sense, Luther shared with some of his contemporaries a strong notion of the imminent end of the world, marked by an increase of the struggle between good and evil. To him, the meantime had become quite mean for those who had rediscovered the apostolic witness to Jesus Christ as their only Lord; that is why a serpenthood was needed that knew how to interpret the "signs of the times" (Matt. 16:3).

The Lutheran Confessions assert that Christ's presence in word and sacrament is the only norm for the unity and mission of the church.[42] In this sense, "the sign of Jona" (Matt. 12:39-40) is sufficient. All other components are negotiable as instruments of mission; they are not means of salvation. Accordingly, language communication, ritual, polity, doctrine, ethics, and other human instruments are the "word" used by the Holy Spirit to give faith when and where the Spirit deems it right and necessary.[43] Clever serpenthood is needed to distinguish between "word" and "spirit," "law" and "gospel," "essentials for salvation" and "non-essentials" (*adiaphora* — things neither commanded nor prohibited).[44] It is needed

---

40. Luther's homiletical cooing, as it were, has been well reconstructed by Roland H. Bainton, *The Martin Luther Christmas Book* (Philadelphia: Fortress, no date). His serpentine style of debate is well disclosed in the treatise *Against Latomus* (1521), *LW* 32:137-60.

41. *LW* 44:123.

42. *BC* 42, VII:2.

43. *BC* 43, V:2.

44. A significant Lutheran term. How *adiaphora* function is shown in *BC* 635, X-640. See also Gritsch and Jenson, *Lutheranism*, ch. 14: "Adiaphora — Freedom or Bondage?"

to distinguish between the "church militant" or "in conflict" and the "church triumphant" or "at rest." These distinctions cannot be made properly without serpenthood — the work of sharp discernment, of clear reasoning, and of frequent debate.

2. Pilgrim Peace

Like many Christians, Lutherans have been sheep among wolves rather than innocent doves and wise serpents. The German Lutheran church leadership failed to maintain a faithful witness to Christ during the Nazi regime (1933-1945) but revised their position during the struggle against Communism by creating substantial support for a nonviolent, successful revolt against the Communist regime in East Germany (1989). When confessionally alert, Lutheranism is thus a vigilant guardian of the sheep who have heard and know the voice of their shepherd (John 10:4). At their best, Lutherans can be confessionally grounded serpents who would be not only pioneers of Christian unity (as they were in this century through leaders like Nathan Soederblom),[45] but also serpentine agents for peace in a world filled with violence and war.

Normative Lutheran teaching is not exclusively guided by the Lutheran Confessions of the sixteenth century. All subsequent "confessions of faith" in Lutheran church constitutions show that the sixteenth-century norms appear in a hierarchy of truths, as it were, beginning with the confession of Christ as the living "word" written in the Scriptures, confessed in the trinitarian creeds, and communicated in the world in the context of a tradition that is faithful to its origins. From this perspective it becomes quite obvious that sixteenth-century normative teachings about "created order," "government," and "obedience" need to be redefined in the light of contemporary life after Hitler, Stalin, and the holocaust of millions. The Lutheran Confessions, designed to reform the Western medieval church, could not imagine non-Christian political leaders and thus called for obedience to leaders, maintaining at the same time that they should be "preserving and propagating on earth 'divine matters,' that is,

---

45. See the sketch on the Lutheran link to the ecumenical movement in Eric W. Gritsch, *Fortress Introduction to Lutheranism* (Minneapolis: Fortress, 1994), pp. 81-85.

Christ's Gospel, and as vicars of God defend[ing] the life and welfare of the innocent."[46]

Half-a-millennium of wrestling with Scripture and tradition have produced insights that are still anchored in the Lutheran theology of law and gospel but come to new conclusions regarding Christian unity and world peace. Lutheran dialogue with the "left wing of the Reformation" (for example, Anabaptists, now known as Mennonites and Hutterites) as well as with "the right wing" (Roman Catholics) has transcended polemics and removed decrees of condemnation. Christian unity can still be understood as unity in word and sacrament,[47] but this unity is now intimately linked to the peace that comes through word and sacrament. It is a pilgrim peace, instilled in a global Christian movement aware of its interim existence between the first and second coming of Christ. The Old Testament talks about a "covenant" between God and the people of God, and about the peace *(shalom)* connected with it, which has implications for family life, friendship, and humankind in general (Ps. 133). This peace must be nurtured and guarded against the sin of jealousy, illustrated by the quick change from friendship to enmity between Saul and David (1 Sam. 18). But the covenantal force of peace prevails in the face of suffering, evil, and death. The divine plan of peace is executed and totally realized at the end of time with the arrival of the "Prince of Peace" (Isa. 9:6). Discipleship of Christ means peace with God and with all of humankind (Rom. 5:1; cf. 4:3). It means pressing on to the promised land (2 Pet. 3:13). Biblical peace is part of being well with God and world, even in the face of evil. The "church militant" must hold on to a vision of peace when swords will be beaten into plowshares and the wolf will live with the lamb (Isa. 2:4; 11:6). Pilgrim peace is part of a faith and love that can move mountains (1 Cor. 13:2); when teamed with apostolic serpenthood, it can even wind its way into the hearts and minds of wolves and end up dancing with them.

---

46. *BC* 244:44. This is an appeal to Emperor Charles V to exercise his "special responsibility before God to maintain and propagate sound doctrine and defend those who teach it [Lutherans who want to be better Catholics]."

47. *AC* 7. *BC* 42, VII:2.

3. Conciliar Penance

In their best and brightest moments Lutherans have faced challenges with a Christian realism shaped by a weighty dialectic of sin and grace. The "two-kingdoms ethic" is the center of this dialectic. It insists that Christian life must be lived in a daily struggle against private and public sin. The Lutheran eschatological vision, anchored in the biblical promise of eternal peace, is dialectically connected with a sharp discernment of what is evil in the world. To use once more the paradigm of the Matthean Jesus' call for mission, the vision is innocent dovehood, the discernment wise serpenthood. Lutherans have to learn a lesson from the historical abuses of their social-political ethic and put this ethic to proper use today. When this is done, Lutheranism will be committed to peace — not at any price as the pacifists are, but in close, critical encounter with all enemies of peace. Such encounter will deal with the whole range of strategies for global peace that have been developed and strengthened since World War II.

The Lutheran confessional commitment to Christian unity and world peace is possible only through a revival of conciliar fellowship with other Christians. Conciliar fellowship means that issues in the church are settled by mutuality, best embodied in an ecumenical council. Its earliest form was the consultation between Paul and the Jerusalem leadership on the divisive question of whether Christians should be circumcised before they were baptized. Sharp debate and reasonable compromise avoided the creation of a Jewish Christian sect (Acts 15). Ecumenical peace prevailed against the sin of ethnic pride. Luther solemnly appealed for an ecumenical council on November 28, 1518, in the Holy Spirit Chapel of the Wittenberg Town Church,[48] but Rome did not call for an ecumenical council until 1545 (at Trent), confirming a schism rather than overcoming it.

Lutherans and other Christians need to make peace with each other before they can become trusted peacemakers in a world still inhabited by people who glorify war. Unfortunately, conciliar fellowship as a means to create Christian unity seems to flourish only when churches suffer through persecution or other enmity, and ecumenical efforts often dimin-

---

48. *Appeal of Friar Martin Luther to a Council,* 1518, as quoted in Gritsch, *Martin — God's Court Jester,* pp. 26-27.

ish as human comfort increases. Christian unity has been more manifest when people have suffered rather than when they have prospered. Cruciformity and unity are intimately related. In the wake of World War II, marked by nationalist and ethnic violence, refugees, and starvation, there was a greater effort towards Christian unity. But major churches are still divided over issues of faith and life. It seems that institutional prosperity still has a greater priority than unity for those who suffer for Christ's sake.

Christian unity and the peaceful unity of humankind belong together. There must be peace among Christians before there can be peace in the world. Why is it not possible in our day to witness to the freedom of the gospel in the eucharistic celebrations of all churches? Why is there no move from mutual consultations to a conciliar framework that would allow a fair measure of collegiality among those in positions of church leadership? Why could there not be an ecumenical council, representing all Christians, delegated to do penance for the sins of separation, schism, and institutional pride? Normative Lutheran teachings press for answers to these questions within and outside of Lutheranism.

The biblical vision of peace is holistic and inclusive. Accordingly, peace is neither simply the absence of war nor a mystical state of mind lacking implications for the total rhythm of human life in the world. Massive conciliar penance is needed among Christians if Christianity is to become a trustworthy agent of peace.

The Unity of the Church and the Christian Peace Witness: A Mennonite Perspective

JOHN D. REMPEL

I. The Issue

In her recent book, *Love Your Enemies,* Lisa Cahill claims that pacifism and the just war theory emerge from different understandings of the church. Personal conversion and a gathered church give birth to the former; a people's church gives birth to the latter. Just war thinking is an ethical theory; pacifist thinking is the embodiment of a conversion experience.[1] Both the magisterial churches and the peace churches agree with this delineation of the issue, but its ecclesiological grounding is seldom as clearly highlighted as it is in Cahill's writing.

My plan in this essay is to pursue the relationship between ecclesiology and peace ethics. Because this is a vast topic, I limit the scope of my writing in two ways: I confine myself to engagements with peace theology made by churches in Europe and North America (though it would be profitable to examine the topic's relation to liberation theology in Latin America and elsewhere), and, within that realm, I focus on the Protestant world, the world I know best.

My goal is to shed more light on the relationship between ecclesiology and peace ethics. I approach my task as a Mennonite theologian but do so in the awareness that in many countries, and particularly the United

1. Lisa Sowle Cahill, *Love Your Enemies: Discipleship, Pacifism and Just War Theory* (Minneapolis: Fortress, 1994), pp. 1-3 et passim.

34

States, the social location from which both types of churches return to the Bible has changed measurably. Knowing that the typology I use is itself in flux, my initial questions are these: What is the nature and extent of the correlation between pacifism and a gathered church? What is the nature and extent of the correlation between the just war theory and a people's church? I use the term "gathered church" because it is broader than "believers' church"; it implies a community which is not coterminous with society yet has a confessional and not an ethnic or national identity. Ethical imperatives arise out of this confessional identity which set its members apart. I use the term "people's church" in the sense of "Volkskirche," in which church and society are coterminous. Ethical imperatives are derived from universal notions of citizenship and justice, applicable to all members of society.

Jesus' moral teaching was binding on the early church, whose membership rested on a profession of faith in him and obedience to him. This understanding prevailed, more or less, until the Constantinian settlement. Monasticism arose to carry on the gathered church ecclesiology grounded in Jesus as the moral norm,[2] but the church as a whole became an imperial institution. The reformations of the sixteenth century coincided with the rise of nation states. By an extension of the Constantinian settlement, church and nation were fused in Magisterial Protestantism.

The first modern challenge to this Protestant arrangement arose in Europe after the carnage of World War I. The body of Christ had been rent asunder by Christians in one country murdering Christians in another because they belonged to enemy nations. This contradictory situation was one of the chief stimuli of the ecumenical movement. In 1925, a Life and Work Conference was convened in Stockholm, and a liberal internationalism (in some cases of a pacifist variety) was invoked there against the scandal of churches subservient to the politics of nation states. At the Conference for Practical Christianity in Fano in 1934, Dietrich Bonhoeffer made a pacifist appeal for a universal Protestant peace council.[3] The next significant change in the relationship between ecclesiology

2. Roberta Bondi summarizes the unity of doctrine, ethics, and ecclesiology in early monasticism in *Faith to Creed,* ed. S. Mark Heim (Grand Rapids: Eerdmans, 1991), pp. 60-82.

3. Heino Falcke spells out Bonhoeffer's proposal in *Vom Gebot Christi, dass die Kirche uns die Waffen aus der Hand nimmt und den Krieg verbietet* (Stuttgart: Radius, 1986), pp. 26-35. Konrad Raiser, the current general secretary of the World Council of

and the ethics of war came in 1937 at the Oxford Faith and Order Conference. There it was said that the Christian rejection of both war and extreme nationalism follows from the very nature of the church, which has one Lord whose following cannot be confined by political boundaries. For the majority of those in attendance this declaration was not pacifist, but it did entail a relativizing of the relationship between people's church and nation state. The *corpus christianum* was under investigation. With its motto, "let the church be the church," the Oxford Conference began an auspicious shift, that of placing Christian deliberation on war and peace back into its original context of the church as "a new humanity" (Eph. 2) and God's primary agent of reconciliation (2 Cor. 5). It set in motion the present trend of insisting that ecclesiology and ethics cannot be separated.[4] (The church is ontologically prior to ethics but its mission in history cannot be thought of apart from its moral engagement.) This trend also received liturgical expression in the half-century-long ecumenical study that led to the conference document entitled *Baptism, Eucharist, and Ministry,* and it is most evident in the section of the document on the Lord's Supper, whose celebration always has to do with the whole church. The text makes clear that injustice and racism are challenged when we share in the body and blood of Christ.[5]

Both pacifists and non-pacifists have tended to debate the ethics of violence as if it were an isolated ethical problem. The cardinal question is usually, "Can killing be an act of love?" At most, the discussion has included the larger moral teaching of Jesus as presented in the New Testament. But little attention has been given to the character of the moral actor, either the individual member or the whole body of Christ. Is she someone acting out of existential faith, grounded in a discerning commu-

---

Churches, traces the reception which Bonhoeffer's proposal of a peace council has received in the intervening years in *Wir Stehen noch am Anfang* (Gütersloh: Christian Kaiser-Gütersloher Verlagshaus, 1994), pp. 50-61.

4. Thomas Best and Martin Robra, eds., *Ecclesiology and Ethics* (Geneva: WCC Publications, 1997), gathers together the work of three major WCC Faith & Order conferences (Ronde, Jerusalem, and Johannesburg) with Orthodox, Catholic, and Protestant voices setting some of the dilemmas and consequences of making ecclesiology and ethics inseparable. An earlier volume by the same editors, *Costly Commitment* (Geneva: WCC Publications, 1995), illustrates how the conference in Jerusalem related this thrust to violence and killing, pp. 10, 26, 52, et passim.

5. *Baptism, Eucharist, and Ministry,* Faith and Order Paper #111 (Geneva: World Council of Churches, 1982), esp. p. 24.

nity? Is this community without ethnic or national borders? Is its ultimate loyalty in matters religious and political given only to Jesus Christ? Does it "obey God rather than men" in matters of life and death? Speaking out of the violent setting of Northern Ireland, Enda McDonagh makes the startling proposal that the churches there should stop baptizing until they have answered these questions.[6]

Scholars on both sides of the historic peace divide see the shift of power and status in the churches (those of both persuasions) as a latent source of convergence on ecclesiology and the ethics of war.[7] What are the criteria for such developments in doctrine? On what basis can we claim that new views were implicit in old ones (to borrow from John Henry Newman)? Or are the churches admitting they were in error?

II. Coherence Between Claim and Reality: Mennonites as a Case Study

In carrying forward with integrity the debate on peace, each partner needs to account not only for the theological and ecclesiological claims of his confession but, also, for its social and ethical reality. We know that every human striving falls short of its intention, but, according to the prophetic voice in biblical revelation, true religion needs to manifest coherence between claim and reality.

Let me illustrate this challenge using the concluding discussion of the Notre Dame conference, out of which this set of essays emerged. The assembly was trying to formulate an agreement on the "peacemaking nature of the gospel." Could an "engaged pacifism" and a "chastened just war position" both be seen as legitimate interpretations of New Testament ethics? If so, the remaining confessional differences regarding peace ethics would not be a church-dividing issue. The HPC (Historic Peace Churches — Quaker, Brethren, and Mennonite) participants pressed

6. Enda McDonagh, *Between Chaos and New Creation* (Dublin: Gill & Macmillan, 1986), pp. 84-85.

7. Harry Hiller in *Baptism, Peace, and the State*, ed. Ross Bender and Alan Sell (Waterloo: Wilfred Laurier University Press, 1991), pp. 191-97. In *The Limits of Perfection* (Scottdale: Herald, 1992) J. Lawrence Burkholder calls on Mennonites to begin their moral reflection from their social position rather than that of their sixteenth-century forebears.

their pacifist claims on the assembly. At one point a delegate from one of the other churches asked how consistently the peace churches had practiced this position in the United States during World War II. To the consternation of most of those present, the Mennonites confessed that just over half of their members had been conscientious objectors, while the Brethren had only 20 percent and the Quakers 10.

As a Mennonite,[8] I acknowledge that the shock among the participants was appropriate because we claim to be a "believers' church," one in which people baptized on profession of faith pledge to live what they profess in accordance with their church's teaching. Most of the Mennonites who went to war gladly confessed God as Trinity, Christ as both divine and human, and the Bible as the binding authority over the church. But they rejected their own denomination's conviction that one cannot faithfully make this confession and go to war.

During the war, many Mennonite congregations excommunicated members who enlisted, and after the war various conferences made conscientious efforts to teach the next generation the peace position, urging young men to undertake alternate service and women to volunteer for peace service. But the contradiction between teaching and practice did not go away. As Mennonites in North America moved further from being a "sect" and closer to being a "church," their stake in society grew. People concluded that social responsibility (and economic opportunity) called for identification with the nation they were privileged to live in — including, in some cases, with its military ambitions.

As Mennonites came to be at home among their neighbors, evangelistic outreach became more and more important to them. Many Mennonites discovered that the peace teaching conflicted with their neighbors' core values and interfered with their own missionary undertakings. Many

8. The Mennonite Central Committee (MCC) is the relief, development, and peace agency of almost all conferences. But its "engaged pacifism" is accepted only by the mainstream, made up of a moderate evangelical majority and a moderate liberal minority. The old order groups are nonresistant but reject active peacemaking in society. The right wing evangelicals view the peace teaching as marginal to their mission. J. R. Burkholder discusses Mennonite views in relation to evangelical and conciliar trends in *Mennonites in Ecumenical Dialogue on Peace and Justice*, MCC Occasional Paper No. 7 (Akron: MCC, 1988). For a synopsis of recent Mennonite developments in peace ethics see Howard Loewen in *Baptism, Peace, and the State in the Reformed and Mennonite Traditions*, ed. Ross Bender and Alan Sell, pp. 87-122.

theologians and ministers worked hard at making peace and evangelism a seamless garment, but, for others, evangelism (narrowly defined) was such a priority that any proclamation which made reconciliation with God more important than private evangelism was spurned. As a consequence, Mennonite congregations have grown up in which the peacemaking nature of the gospel, to say nothing of pacifism, is strictly a matter of individual conscience. There are now active Mennonites for whom even the "chastened just war theory" of current ecumenical thinking would overly restrict the loyalty the Christian citizen owes his nation.

To what extent, then, are the Mennonites a "historic peace church"? According to historic Mennonite criteria, chief of which is the inseparability of belief and practice, Mennonites are probably not a peace church. According to the criteria of the magisterial Christian traditions, the Mennonites might well make that claim, because in the mainline churches the peace question, in and of itself, does not have confessional status. But to accept that generous judgment would go against the Mennonite understanding of the church!

III. Inevitable Ecclesiology?

Three related aspects of the "problem" of ecclesiology need to be named to provide a frame of reference for the search to make peace no longer a church-dividing question. The first aspect is internal to the ecclesiology of "believers' churches." Mennonite theology holds that a gathered church committed to Jesus' teaching and holding a high view of sanctification will be pacifist. This is theologically an arguable position, as the peace churches have insisted and as Lisa Cahill, the Catholic ethicist, has recently argued in a highly nuanced way.[9] But it is not uniformly true historically. For example, Baptists hold to all the tenets of a gathered church ecclesiology but, with notable exceptions, are not pacifist.[10] This has been

9. Cahill, *Love Your Enemies*, esp. pp. 228-46.

10. In his outline of early Baptist understandings of the state and warfare, B. R. White notes that during the Civil War General Baptists (Arminians) were wary of the state and of involvement in warfare whereas Particular Baptists (Calvinists) favored full participation in both. Those Baptists who moved to an explicitly pacifist position in the mid-seventeenth century tended to become Quakers. It is noteworthy, however, that the early Russian Baptists (1850s) were officially pacifist until 1924 when a concordat with the So-

a source of anguish for Mennonites across the centuries, an anguish peculiar to siblings. The historical evidence thus makes it clear that the relationship between ecclesiology and ethics is not as direct and inevitable as Mennonites have thought.

Let us briefly return to Christian origins to examine this correlation more fully. In the early church, personal conversion and a church of believers made for a general (but, after A.D. 200, not universal) pacifist commitment. What accounts for the difference between the majority view in the pre-Constantinian church and the majority view in the church after Constantine? The answer lies chiefly in the fact that the former sustained an eschatological tension and would not be reconciled to the exigencies of history. The latter believed that the church's concordat with the state expressed the providence of God. Augustine's theology of history and of the created order most profoundly expresses this altered relationship between church and kingdom.[11] It was not only a matter of doctrine but of radically altered practice. It is on the basis of a Christian state that Augustine cemented the theology of infant baptism and, if necessary, its implementation by coercion. Gregory Dix documents such a change as it expressed itself in public worship. "As the church came to feel at home in world, so she became reconciled to time. The eschatological emphasis in the eucharist inevitably faded."[12] Though Dix is a champion of worship as it developed in the patristic era, he is not loath to point out that the alliance of church and military might have had the effect of taking "liturgy," the work of the people, away from the people. In the West, these developments marked the end of a gathered and nonviolent church, except in monasticism.

Let it be said, however, that neither the social setting in which pacifism emerged nor the one in which just war theory arose exist today. Pacifists interpreted Jesus' teaching from within a powerless and marginalized subculture, just war theorists from within a Christianized society. Pacifists cannot retreat into a restorationism which tries to go back in time before the Christianization of European civilization. At the same time, their primitivism has kept pacifism alive in the church across the

viet state, on which their survival depended, dropped the peace teaching from their confession of faith. In the U.S., black Baptists have been leaders in the movement for nonviolent change but have not been pacifist as denominations. See *The English Baptists of the 17th Century* (Didcot: The Baptist Historical Society, 1996), pp. 53-58.

11. Cahill, *Love Your Enemies*, pp. 55-80, esp. pp. 75-80.

12. G. Dix, *The Shape of the Liturgy* (London: Dacre Press, 1975), p. 305.

centuries,[13] and it reflects the eschatology and ecclesiology of many non-Western denominations.

As was mentioned above, however, the comparison between Mennonites and Baptists shows that a common ecclesiology and eschatology do not, by themselves, determine a community's convictions regarding violence and warfare. This striking example leaves us with unanswered questions. Which theological and social factors account for the differences between Baptists and Anabaptists? How do these factors shape the hermeneutical community's reading of the New Testament, in particular their reading of Jesus' teachings about the reign of God and love of enemies, or of Paul's notion of the body of Christ? How significant were the differences in context? Because of unrelenting persecution, the Anabaptists were confined to a more marginal social location than the Baptists. They were the subjects of many small states with conflicting religious and military loyalties, while the Baptists lived in a single, sovereign nation-state in which there were political alternatives — a monarchy versus a republic. Do these data relativize all theological vantage points or do they suggest that the more powerless a church, the closer it stands to the kingdom? By itself, however, even this latter claim — if it is granted — does not offer the church in the West today, where all the communities engaged in the debate on peacemaking are power-holders, an ethic.[14] Finally, is there an ecclesiology anywhere along the spectrum of Christian orthodoxy which is necessarily pacifist?

IV. Independent Churches

The second preliminary ecclesiological problem concerns the recent emergence in North America of independent churches which disclaim accountability to the larger Christian tradition (theologically, ethically, or liturgi-

13. This is illuminatingly documented in the growth of American-born denominations in the eighteenth and nineteenth centuries, a process seen in *Proclaim Peace: Christian Pacifism from Unexpected Quarters,* ed. T. Schlabach and R. Hughes (Urbana: University of Illinois Press, 1997).

14. On a practical level, the WCC's Programme to Overcome Violence moves beyond former antagonisms to make nonviolent peace building integral to the mission of the church. See Salpy Eskidjian, *Overcome Violence* (Geneva: World Council of Churches, 1997), esp. pp. 22, 27-29.

cally) as it has been mediated through Orthodoxy, Roman Catholicism, and even most forms of Protestantism.[15] These churches, in fact, see most tradition as a barrier to direct dependence on the Bible and the work of the Holy Spirit. In contrast to the earlier leading American revivals such as the Stone-Campbell movement and Pentecostalism, which saw pacifism as integral to life in the Spirit, this new wave of revivalism seems to lack that eschatology. In its alliance with the nation-state, it exhibits more of a post- than a pre-Constantinian ethic and ecclesiology. Because their focus is almost entirely on church growth, these independent churches leave many matters of great importance throughout historic Christianity, such as the celebration of sacraments and the ethics of war and peace, to the conscience of ministers or congregants. Few of them venture critical judgments concerning the widespread legitimation of violence and militant nationalism in the United States; both pacifism and a chastened just war theory seem to be beyond the scope of discourse in these communities.

This situation is relevant to our discussion of Christian peacemaking in America because many of the powerful independent churches and para-church agencies with a similar approach to mission seem to aspire to be the national conscience — if not the new national religion — of the United States. But they do so without the ethical constraints which earlier national churches, from the time of Augustine onward, imposed upon themselves.[16] From a Mennonite point of view, ethical reflection on war and peace in independent evangelicalism seems to show less accountabil-

---

15. I restrict my observations to independent churches in the United States, but the movement is international. It has parallels with earlier generations of restorationism, but many of those churches, among them the Pentecostal and African Independent Churches, now have their own tradition and are cautiously in conversation with the ecumenical movement. The HPC were all restorationist in character, but the Anabaptists sought to prove their orthodoxy and considered themselves the true continuation of the church, not only of the apostolic era, but of the early centuries as well. The Church of the Brethren was less concerned than were the Mennonites with doctrinal orthodoxy and continuity but considered itself a part of historic Christianity. The Quakers were perhaps the closest to today's independent churches in that they saw tradition as a barrier to rather than a medium of the Spirit's work. But, for the most part, they have sought alliances with orthodox Christians.

16. It is instructive that on the eve of the Gulf War, Billy Graham (who, though a Baptist, seems not to see himself accountable to traditional just war theory) was inside the White House and made no public statement, while Edmond Browning (presiding bishop of the Episcopal Church) was outside the White House arguing that the attack on Iraq could not be considered a just war.

ity to the New Testament and its interpretation across the centuries than does the just war theory as it is practiced today in light of the conditions of modern warfare.

This state of affairs is troubling for a host of reasons, only two of which I will name. One of them is that, although in ecclesiological matters Mennonites have much in common with these churches (baptism upon confession of faith, the giftedness of each member, sanctification as the power to live what Jesus taught), in social ethics their positions are in conflict. A second, and different, reason for bringing independent evangelicalism into a discussion on peacemaking is that it has brought aspects of the gospel within reach of many people who did not know Christ in a way that the historic churches have not. These churches speak the language of the people in the way monasticism did in the fourth century and countless renewal movements have done since. For the sake of church unity and mission, this movement cannot remain, by its own initiative or that of others, aloof from the search for peace. How can the historic confessions (just war and pacifist) in the United States engage and be engaged by these churches and their political constituencies on all questions of faithfulness and, specifically, on questions relating to peace?

V. A Conciliar Process

Now, to the final preliminary question concerning ecclesiology. In the West, monasticism and the reformations of the sixteenth century arose as correctives to the failures of the medieval church. The striving from below for a "pure" church carried over from monasticism into the Radical Reformation. The striving from above for a people's church whose clergy and sacraments were Spirit-filled carried over from medieval Catholic reform movements into the Magisterial and Counter-Reformations. Each movement provided a corrective to the tradition, often becoming more defined by its corrective measures than by the larger tradition it sought to reform.

The ecumenical movement arose among Protestants at the onset of the twentieth century after they acknowledged that the correctives of the sixteenth and subsequent centuries had not restored wholeness to the body of Christ in any one of the existing denominations or among all of them together. The logic of the early conciliar movement was as follows: when all the confessions grounded in trinitarian faith have adopted each other's correctives to the failings of the church,[17] then they will have found the fullness of Christ, the unity of his body. In this approach, the true church is simply the sum of all its parts.

By itself, this model is inadequate to the task set before the Faith and Order Commission of the National Council of Churches (NCC, F&O), which was to address "the fragmentation of the church and its unity in peacemaking." In making the apostolic church its norm through the prism of the sixteenth century, the earlier ecumenical movement is too narrow and too Protestant. But could it serve as a starting point for healing a wound in the body of Christ that has so far been incapable of healing, not only in Protestantism but also in Orthodoxy and Catholicism? The ecumenical movement is experimenting with a broader version of this notion, with a larger sense of tradition and of the church (i.e., beyond European Christianity).[18] In most parts of the world the *corpus christianum* does not exist. In North America it has a residual existence; in Western Europe a Christian shell exists within a dechristianized world. This altered social situation gives the denominations *de facto* if not always *de jure* common ground ecclesiologically and missiologically. From this vantage point they are returning to the New Testament together.[19] In the

---

17. I think this was the meaning of being "catholic, evangelical, and reformed," a description of the ecumenical movement which was widespread in the mid-century thought of the conciliar movement.

18. Mennonites have found their way into this process, especially as it bears on questions of ecclesiology and ethics. John Howard Yoder is the pioneer; see, for example, his discussion of tradition in *The Priestly Kingdom* (Notre Dame: Notre Dame University Press, 1984), pp. 63ff. and 92ff. A. James Reimer delves into the relationship between dogma and ethics in the fourth-century church in *Faith to Creed*, ed. Heim, pp. 129-61, and Howard Loewen reappraises Mennonite pacifism in conversation with other traditions in *Baptism, Peace, and the State*, ed. Bender and Sell, pp. 87-122.

19. In *Shalom: Biblical Perspectives on Creation, Justice, and Peace* (Geneva: WCC Publications, 1989), Ulrich Duchrow and Gerhard Liedke do an admirable job of relating biblical imperatives to questions of ecology, injustice, and violence in Europe. They draw models of the church for this time in history from the inseparability of ecclesiology and ethics. Their chapter, "Different Ways of Being the Church," is an exercise in convergence thinking grounded in the peacemaking nature of the gospel (pp. 154-85). It has direct applicability to the NCC Faith & Order process in which we are presently engaged. In this regard, Glen Stassen's *Just Peacemaking: Transforming Initiatives for Justice and Peace* (Louisville: Westminster/John Knox Press, 1992) and Duane Friesen's *Christian Peacemaking and International Conflict: A Realist Pacifist Perspective* (Scottdale: Herald Press, 1986) need to be mentioned.

realm of peace and justice certain aspects of Bonhoeffer's dream of a universal peace council are already under deliberation. The fact that this process includes the Catholic and Orthodox churches exceeds what he believed to be possible.

Theologians, lay people, and entire denominations within the just-war churches have accepted the pacifist claim that the heart of the biblical proclamation of reconciliation and forgiveness is its power to overcome alienation, violence, vengeance, and idolatry of the nation. The Roman Catholic and United Methodist pastoral letters on peace and, to an even greater degree, the United Church of Christ's declaration that it is "a just peace church" are remarkable manifestations of this trend. As a consequence, they are reinvigorating the notion of ethical as well as doctrinal heresy — in other words, the notion that orthodoxy consists not only in believing rightly but also in obeying rightly. In turn, the mainstream of the HPC have accepted two major correctives: first, their need for a theology of creation in order to live responsibly in society and, second, the realization that their model of the church is not purely deduced from the apostolic age, but, like others', was shaped by the conditions under which it arose.

The conciliar movement in the United States, particularly among all the denominations working within the National Council of Churches' Faith & Order Commission (Roman Catholics and evangelicals, in addition to NCC member churches), is in a process of discernment and forward movement on a matter that has remained an intractable point of division since the fourth century. Churches involved in this movement believe that peace should no longer be a church-dividing issue.[20] Both a classical pacifism and the classical just war theory are incomplete expressions of gospel reconciliation, and some other common ground needs to be found.

If representatives of certain denominations in the United States believe that they have gained common ground on matters of ecclesiology and ethics, by whose authority would this conclusion be reached? I pro-

---

20. It is tempting not to qualify the word "church," but the historical process being described is that of the Western church. Orthodoxy has never developed a formal theory of just war and has identified itself with national cultures in a different way from that in the West, especially after 1945. But, of course, the ecumenical movement can be universal only when the Orthodox are part of it. How can the conversation be expanded in a way that respects the distinctive developments of Eastern Christianity?

pose two moves by which the new common ground might be built on. One of them is for Faith and Order to formally communicate the present level of agreement to the participating churches for additional action. Such action might happen on a pastoral as well as a scholarly level. The recent grassroots ecumenical initiative "Every Church a Peace Church," for example, might be formally recognized by participating denominations as an expression of a reclaimed dimension of unity. Second, the mutual accountability built into the "Fragmentation of the Church and Its Unity in Peacemaking" process by the Faith and Order Commission should be expanded. We now know that there are just war Catholic and Protestant voices as well as Orthodox, and Peace Church voices who are in the middle of a conversation that has changed them all. They need a structure to help them continue their work and to draw previously unengaged participants — like the independent churches — into it. But the question remains: who would receive the consensus of the representatives — their own denominations, bilateral dialogues, the NCC? How would this reception become part of each denomination's doctrine and practice? How would it shape its catechesis and worship?

VI. Conclusions

I began my inquiry with two questions: What is the nature and extent of the correlation between pacifism and a gathered church? What is the nature and extent of the correlation between the just war theory and a people's church? Two claims emerged from these questions. One of them is that in the ancient church, from the first to the fourth century, the correlation is very high. This link continued in monasticism, the Radical Reformation, and eighteenth and nineteenth century American-born denominations. I noted that a high correlation is not inevitable, however, as is illustrated by the comparison of early Baptists and Anabaptists and of peace churches and independent churches in the late twentieth century.

The matter of coherence between claim and reality is acutely problematical. The Historic Peace Churches themselves, especially if measured by the particulars of their own ecclesiologies, do not always live up to their claims. The movement in the World Council of Churches and various denominations to reassert the inseparability of ecclesiology and ethics and to take ethical heresy as seriously as doctrinal heresy provides common resources for peacemaking not just as an ideal but as a way of life. In my judgment, this process is far enough along that it needs to be received and owned by the churches as a reality that is essential to the unity of the church.

The question of war and violence is not an isolated moral issue. The only fruitful and faithful way forward is to acknowledge that it is an issue integral to the relationship between ecclesiology and ethics and to the mission of the church. Would Enda McDonagh's proposal for the churches in Northern Ireland bring the issues at stake into focus? Now that we have been given even a little more of the truth, can we any longer baptize people into communities that live off of violence? What if all the churches stopped baptizing, for even one day, as a sign of remorse for the contradiction they perpetuate? Such a revolutionary act would confront us with the frightening, and potentially liberating, truth: that as followers of the Lover of Enemies, we do not realize what we are doing when we initiate people into his company.

An Orthodox Peace Witness?

JOHN H. ERICKSON

In the mid-960s, a dispute arose between the patriarch of Constantinople, Polyeuktos, and the emperor of the day, Nikephoros II Phokas. The emperor, possibly influenced by the Islamic concept of the holy war, the *jihad,* wished to have soldiers killed in battle honored as holy martyrs. The patriarch successfully opposed him by citing an ancient church canon from the "canonical epistles" of St. Basil the Great:

> Our fathers did not reckon killings in war as murders, but granted pardon, it seems to me, to those fighting in defense of virtue and piety. Perhaps, however, it is advisable that, since their hands are not clean, they should abstain from communion alone for a period of three years. (Canon 13)

This episode is of some interest not only because of what it says about attitudes toward war — more of this at a later point — but also because of the patriarch's way of dealing with this imperial request. He cited an ancient canon. This was not done out of legalism. The canon had not been applied for centuries, if ever, as the medieval Byzantine canonists pointed out. The penitential system which it presupposes had long since fallen into desuetude; its very wording suggests that it was more a counsel than a prescription, and, in any case, the Byzantine canonical tradition had always allowed for some *oikonomia* (flexibility, accommodation) in the application of the canons. What is striking in this episode is the patriarch's creative reappropriation of an element from the church's tradition that by this point had been practically forgotten, at least by the emperor.

To reread one's tradition in the light of present realities — is that not what all of our churches are doing, or at least what they should be doing? From within the Lutheran tradition, Eric Gritsch urges such an approach when, after tracing the long history of abuses of Luther's "two-kingdoms ethic," he states: "The time has come to mine the Lutheran tradition for evidence that provides a Lutheran perspective on Christian unity and world peace."[1] We also see this approach at work in the National Conference of Catholic Bishops' 1983 Pastoral Letter *The Challenge of Peace,* which attempts to reread the rich and variegated tradition of the Catholic Church, fully aware that "its development cannot be sketched in a straight line and [that] it seldom gives a simple answer to complex questions" yet at the same time confident that this tradition does have something important to say at this "moment of supreme crisis" in human history.[2] At this "moment of supreme crisis" many other churches also have been rediscovering what their tradition has to contribute to the discussion and the pursuit of peace. The Mennonites, for example, are finding again their sixteenth-century Anabaptist heritage, especially its pacifist strain. Paolo Siepierski certainly is correct when he notes that "an event does not exhaust itself in its occurrence or in the documents that record its occurrence. . . . A past event has the ability to cause other events, in the present and the future." The task of the interpreter therefore is not only to explain what happened or what was said in the past but also to "direct the effective power" of the past toward present issues.[3] This, in effect, is what Patriarch Polyeuktos was doing in his dispute with Emperor Nikephoros Phokas.

In this essay I would like to pursue Patriarch Polyeuktos' rereading of the Orthodox tradition. What does this tradition have to say about

---

1. Eric Gritsch, "Christian Unity and Peacemaking: A Lutheran Perspective," pp. 16-32 in this volume.

2. *The Challenge of Peace: God's Promise and Our Response* (Washington, D.C.: United States Catholic Conference Office of Publishing Services, 1983), Publication No. 863, p. 3.

3. Paolo Siepierski, "Reflections on a *Kainotic* History: Basil of Caesarea as a Paradigm for Ecumenical Dialogue," in *Faith to Creed: Ecumenical Perspectives on the Affirmation of the Apostolic Faith in the Fourth Century,* ed. S. Mark Heim (Grand Rapids: Eerdmans, 1991), pp. 104-5.

peace and peacemaking for us today? And, more broadly, what does it say about the church's relationship to society and to civil authorities? Then, following a brief survey of historical and ethical issues, I will touch upon "the overarching ecclesial concern" that prompted the Faith and Order Commission of the National Council of Churches to organize a special consultation on "The Fragmentation of the Church and Its Unity in Peacemaking," namely, what is the relationship between peacemaking and Christian unity?

We must note, first of all, that Orthodoxy has had a long history of concern for the public order. It has refused to identify itself either as a *sect* set apart from the wider society or as a *denomination* happy to exist side by side with other denominations within the wider society. (In the United States we Orthodox sometimes have shown tendencies in both directions, but historically, at least, this is true). In most places, Orthodoxy, like Catholicism, has had a strong sense of being *church,* of being open to all, expected by all, in a sense expected of all, with a high sense of responsibility toward all. To use James Joyce's expression, "Here comes everybody." On the one hand, this has meant considerable involvement of Orthodox Christians and church leaders in public affairs. Patriarch Polyeuktos and Emperor Nikephoros Phokas disagreed about the canonizing of fallen soldiers as martyrs for the faith, but that the issue should arise at all suggests the high level of interpenetration of ecclesiastical and civil that existed in medieval Byzantium, where the ideal of *symphonia* (of a single Christian commonwealth whose well-being depended on the close cooperation of the imperial and priestly authorities rather than on their separation) was strong.

Even after the fall of Constantinople to the Turks in 1453, Orthodoxy has been the dominant faith. In the Ottoman Empire, for example, the Patriarch was the *milet bashi,* the head of *Rum milet,* the "Roman" (*i.e.,* the Orthodox Christian) nation, and ultimately responsible before the Sultan for most aspects of its daily life. This has been true, *a fortiori,* where Orthodoxy continued to take some measure of establishment for granted. This has been true where Orthodoxy has been the dominant faith.

As a result, the Orthodox Church has sometimes reacted with bewilderment when faced with situations of radical disestablishment like ours in North America. For example, in the last century it appeared desirable to move the see of the Russian North American diocese from Alaska, the former Russian America, to the lower states, in order to minister more effectively to the Orthodox immigrants who were then arriving by the boatload, but for a long time the Holy Governing Synod and the Foreign Office in St. Petersburg hesitated. After all, the establishment or suppression of episcopal sees was a matter for the civil authority; in Russia it required an imperial *ukase*. Wouldn't a change in the diocesan see be regarded by the United States as an infringement on its sovereignty?

Orthodoxy has also been closely identified with the nation, the people. It has shared the nation's sufferings — and these have been many, for in fact every segment of Orthodoxy has experienced long periods of domination and sporadic persecution at the hands of hostile powers. It also has shared the nation's triumphs. One result of this has been an ambivalent attitude toward peace and peacemaking. Innocent victims of suffering and martyrdom, both ancient and modern, have been accorded special veneration, but so have kingly warrior saints. For example, seven out of the nine Serbian saints of the Middle Ages were princes or kings whose various activities included both patricidal and fratricidal civil wars as well as defensive and offensive foreign wars. And at times the martyr and the kingly warrior, redemptive suffering and national glory, are seen in one and the same figure: The greatest of Serbian national holidays commemorates not a victory but the great defeat at Kossovo in 1389. St. Lazar, the king who had fought "for the cross and freedom," was cruelly tortured and slain by the Turkish victors; his *vita* draws out every possible parallel between his passion and that of Christ.[4]

From what has been said so far, one might be tempted to conclude that Emperor Nikephoros Phokas won a posthumous victory over Patriarch Polyeuktos; that in matters relating to war and peace Orthodoxy has had "a neuralgic legacy" analogous to Gritsch's description of Lutheranism; that the current suffering in Bosnia and so much of the ethnic strife throughout Eastern Europe is ascribable to the pathological state of Orthodoxy; that the Orthodox should be classed among the historic war churches, as it were, with little to contribute to a dialogue with the historic peace churches. This at least is the picture conveyed in many news accounts. Yet there are other elements in the Orthodox tradition

4. See Alexander F. C. Webster, "Varieties of Christian Military Saints: From Martyrs Under Caesar to Warrior Princes," *St. Vladimir's Theological Quarterly* 24 (1980): 3-35.

which suggest the need for a more nuanced assessment and which may in fact contribute to a discussion of peacemaking.

Let me begin by recounting a recent exchange of views within Orthodoxy in the United States. The inaugural issue of a stimulating but short-lived magazine entitled *American Orthodoxy* carried an article reviewing some criticisms of the Gulf War from the National Council of Churches and juxtaposing them against some official statements by Orthodox jurisdictions here in the United States.[5] The thrust of the article was twofold: that Orthodoxy accepted a just war theory, albeit imprecisely, and that much of the official U.S. Orthodox response to the Gulf War rejected this just-war approach by succumbing to the NCC's anti-American, anti–just-war rhetoric.

A subsequent issue carried a response by Fr. Stanley Harakas, then distinguished professor of ethics at Holy Cross Greek Orthodox School of Theology.[6] In it he recounted the evolution of his own thought on the subject of the "just war." Initially in his teaching and public speaking he had followed the position set forth in the lectures and handbooks of professors in the Athens theological faculty where he had studied, which basically supported a just-war approach and rejected the principle of conscientious objection (and especially of selective conscientious objection) as showing an unbecoming lack of responsibility toward society and disobedience toward duly constituted civil authority. Fr. Harakas began to question this position, however, when he discovered what he called the "stratification of pacifism" in the ancient canons, which prohibit any form of military activity to the clergy while allowing it for the laity.[7] Then, when asked to comment on the U.S. Catholic bishops' Pastoral Letter, he reviewed the Eastern patristic and canonical sources yet again and found, to

5. Lawrence Uzzell, "Rumors of War in the NCC," *American Orthodoxy* 1 (Fall 1991): 7-9.

6. Fr. Stanley Harakas, "No 'Rumors of War' in the Greek Fathers," *American Orthodoxy* 2 (Winter 1992): 8-9. The author would like to express his deep gratitude to Fr. Harakas, who originally had been scheduled to speak at the NCC Faith and Order consultation on "The Fragmentation of the Church and Its Unity in Peacemaking," for generously sharing with him his thoughts as well as copies of his many articles on the subject of peace.

7. Cf. his reflections in "The Morality of War," in *Orthodox Synthesis: The Unity of Theological Thought*, ed. Joseph J. Allen (Crestwood, N.Y.: St. Vladimir's Seminary Press, 1981), pp. 67-94.

his surprise, that he could not find any of the traditional components of the Western just war theory, whether *jus ad bellum* or *jus in bello*. Rather, he found

> an amazing consistency in the almost totally negative moral assessment of war coupled with an admission that war may be necessary under certain circumstances to protect the innocent and to limit even greater evils! In this framework war may be an unavoidable alternative, but it nevertheless remains an evil. Virtually absent in the tradition is any mention of a "just war" much less a "good" war. The tradition also precludes the possibility of a crusade. For the Eastern Orthodox tradition . . . war can be seen only as a "necessary evil" with all the difficulty and imprecision such a designation carries.[8]

The end point of the evolution of his thought and the key to discussion of whole subject, Fr. Harakas recounts, came with a conference devoted to "The Orthodox Concern with Peace." His own paper, and indeed those of the other participants, documented what he calls the "pro-peace" stance of the fathers of the Eastern Church as well as the biblical sources of their thought. He concluded:

> The East did not seek to answer questions concerning the correct conditions for entering war and the correct conduct of war on the basis of the possibility of a "just war" precisely because it did not hold to such a view. Its view of war, unlike that of the West, was that it is a necessary evil. The peace ideal continued to remain normative, and no theoretical efforts were made to make conduct of war into a positive norm.[9]

It is unnecessary to reexamine here all the evidence that Fr. Harakas adduces in his various articles on the subject. Some aspects of this — above all the biblical understanding of *shalom/eirene* — will be familiar to theologians of every Christian tradition. Rooted in the Bible, the Greek

---

8. Harakas, "No 'Rumors of War'"; cf. Fr. Harakas' essay "The NCCB Pastoral Letter: 'The Challenge of Peace' — An Eastern Orthodox Response," in *Peace in a Nuclear Age: The Bishops' Pastoral Letter in Perspective,* ed. Charles J. Reid Jr. (Washington, D.C.: The Catholic University of America Press, 1986), chap. 16.

9. "The Teaching on Peace in the Fathers," in *Un Regard Orthodoxe sur la Paix* (Chambésy-Geneva: Editions du Centre Orthodoxe du Patriarcat Oecumenique, 1986), pp. 32-47, quote on p. 43.

fathers and the Byzantine tradition as a whole saw peace not simply as the absence of war but, rather, as a gift of God closely related to well-being and salvation, making it practically synonymous with the work of Christ. Several points should be emphasized, however.

First, the crusade mentality which from time to time has gripped the West, whether in the Middle Ages or since, is strikingly absent in the Christian East. In the West, possibly as one aspect of Christianity's adaption to Germanic heroic ideals, even churchmen looked for signs of God's judgment on the battlefield. (Inculturation brings mixed blessings!) As one contemporary source observes, "one rode in blood up to the knees and even to the horses' bridles, by the just and marvelous Judgment of God."[10] Here the evils of war are almost completely ignored. Instead, war is presented as a good and noble means of achieving a good and noble purpose — even, as with the Prussian General Karl von Clausewitz in the nineteenth century, as a boon to culture, science, and progress. At the very least, as with World War II and other secular "crusades" (whether actual or metaphorical), it is a righteous struggle against Evil, in which the enemy is inevitably demonized, dehumanized, and denied any share in the image of God. In the East, by contrast, as the secular historian George Ostrogorsky observes, "the crusading movement as the West conceived it was something entirely foreign. . . . There was nothing new in a war against the infidel, but to the Byzantines, this was the outcome of hard political necessity."[11] Eastern contemporaries were simply horrified at the sight of churchmen wielding swords in battle. Killing in war should not be reckoned as murder, as the canon of St. Basil invoked by Patriarch Polyeuktos observed, yet it remains a sin, albeit an involuntary one, and therefore subject to ecclesiastical penance.

While the letter of this canon was seldom enforced, a "pro-peace" stance is evident in Byzantium in secular as well as ecclesiastical sources. Interesting in this regard are handbooks of military strategy; one of the first begins by observing that "war is a great evil, even the greatest of evils," and, like others of the genre, it goes on to argue for avoidance of open battle, inasmuch as the object of warfare is the defeat of the enemy

10. Raimundus de Agiles, quoted in H. J. Muller, *Freedom in the Western World* (New York, Evanston, and London: Harper and Row, 1963), p. 48.

11. George Ostrogorsky, *History of the Byzantine State* (New Brunswick, N.J.: Rutgers University Press, 1957), p. 90.

through disruption, not slaughter.[12] No hint here of the glory of battle or of the heroism that war stimulates!

At the same time, most forms of pacifism were also rejected. The Byzantine Church probably would have regarded as evidence of Manichean heresy the Anabaptist Schleitheim Confession's rejection of the sword of the magistrate along with the sword of war as well as its call for "separation from the abomination." Does such a view represent a radical shift from the attitude of the pre-Constantinian church, as a number of church historians have argued?[13] I think not, though the scope of this paper does not allow for full discussion of this question. The sources suggest that pre-Constantinian objection to military service on the part of Christians arose above all because of the compulsory pagan religious observances that formed part of a soldier's life. Otherwise, the maintenance of public order, the enforcement of justice, and the protection of the body politic from external attack were accepted values in the pre-Constantinian church.[14]

Here, of course, we must keep in mind how pervasive and persuasive was the notion of a *pax romana*. Centuries of official peace had blunted ancient militarism, with its adulation of the triumphant general and its culture of death. Both pagans and Christians in the Late Empire, like their Byzantine heirs, had come to look on the far-flung Roman legions, if not as peacemakers, then at least as peacekeepers, rather like today's U.N. forces in the world's various trouble-spots.

A final point must be mentioned. While the Christian East never developed a just war theory, a concern for justice has never been absent from its understanding of peace and peacemaking. It is not easy, however, to balance the demands of peace and justice. The Catholic bishops' Pasto-

12. Cited by Harakas, "The Teaching on Peace," p. 44.

13. Cf., for example, John Howard Yoder, "The Authority of Tradition," in *The Priestly Kingdom: Social Ethics as Gospel* (Notre Dame: University of Notre Dame Press, 1984), pp. 63-79; cf. also A. James Reimer, "Trinitarian Orthodoxy, Constantinianism, and Theology from a Radical Protestant Perspective," in *Faith to Creed*, pp. 129-61 and the literature analyzed there.

14. On this point see especially John Helgeland, Robert J. Daly, and J. Patout Burns, *Christians and the Military: The Early Experience* (Philadelphia: Fortress, 1985); but see also the critical observations of David G. Hunter, "The Christian Church and the Roman Army in the First Three Centuries," in *The Church's Peace Witness*, ed. Marlin E. Miller and Barbara Nelson Gingerich (Grand Rapids: Eerdmans, 1994), pp. 161-81.

ral Letter *The Challenge of Peace* (1983) identifies the problem with great precision:

> In the kingdom of God, peace and justice will be fully realized. Justice is always the foundation of peace. In history, efforts to pursue both peace and justice are at times in tension, and the struggle for justice may threaten certain forms of peace.[15]

On the whole, I would say that we Orthodox have tended to insist more on justice than peace. This is what the late Fr. John Meyendorff had to say in a 1982 editorial on "Peace and Disarmament":

> The major task of Christians . . . should not be empty, general talk about "peace," but also — and primarily — efforts in favor of human rights and the restoration of conditions which would make mutual confidence possible and war unthinkable. This is not empty moralism, but the only realistic approach to the problem of peace and disarmament. There will always be danger of war as long as justice will be forgotten and human freedom curtailed. Peace is inseparable from openness and confidence.[16]

Or, in the words of the modern Greek Orthodox thinker Alexander Tsirindanes, "Desires for international peace which do not comprehend a state of international justice . . . are nothing else but a participation in international crime."[17]

It might be added that what holds true for international relations also holds true in domestic matters. In Byzantium the emperor, of course, was an absolute monarch, but this did not absolve him from respect for justice and just laws. An emperor identified as a *tyrannos* might well have lost his throne and his life. This in fact was the fate of Nikephoros Phokas. Characteristically, his slayer, General John Tzimisces, succeeded

---

15. *The Challenge of Peace*, p. 19.

16. Fr. John Meyendorff, originally in *The Orthodox Church* (the newspaper of the Orthodox Church in America), reprinted in his *Witness to the World* (Crestwood, N.Y.: St. Vladimir's Seminary Press, 1987), p. 92. On the intimate connections between justice and peace and their significance for ecumenism see the inter-Orthodox statement "Orthodox Perspectives on Justice and Peace," in *Justice, Peace and the Integrity of Creation: Insights from Orthodoxy*, ed. Gennadios Limouris (Geneva: WCC Publications, 1990), pp. 16-27.

17. Alexander Tsirindanes, cited in Harakas, "The Morality of War," p. 93.

him; but equally characteristically, Patriarch Polyeuktos refused to proceed with the imperial coronation until Tzimisces had fulfilled a suitable penance.

A few words about the relationship between peacemaking and Christian unity are also necessary. These days many Orthodox become suspicious or cynical whenever either ecumenism or peace is mentioned. (This phenomenon is, it should be noted, not limited to the United States, where some seem bent on portraying Orthodoxy as the Eastern version of the Christian Coalition.) Since the fall of Communism, many in Eastern Europe appear intent on rejecting anything and everything that they were once forced to praise. A personal story may illustrate this point. A few years ago I was expressing my enthusiasm for ecumenism to a young Orthodox student from what is now the Czech Republic. He was frankly shocked and scandalized. As he explained, under the Communists they had been obliged to be ecumenical, but now that they were free, they could be true Orthodox.

The word "peace" likewise has fallen into disrepute because of its abuse by calculating liars who would "make a desert and call it peace."[18] Earlier I referred to Fr. Harakas' participation in a conference devoted to "The Orthodox Concern for Peace" and how decisive it was for the development of his own thought. This conference was one of a series devoted to preparation of the tenth agenda item for the long-awaited Great and Holy Council of the Orthodox Church and was called "The Contribution of the Local Orthodox Churches to the Adoption of the Christian Ideals of Peace, Freedom, Brotherhood, and Love Among the Peoples of the World and the Elimination of Racial Prejudice." The topic, needless to add, had been included on the agenda at the insistence of the churches from what was then the Communist bloc. Even at the time it provoked sarcastic comments; today practically every word seems blasphemous.

How can our debased vocabulary be purified? Can anyone speaking of peace, brotherhood, freedom, love — or Christian unity — ever be believed again? Certainly this will not happen if, in their social analysis and rhetoric, our theologians simply parrot evanescent secular solutions. Peace (like freedom and justice and love) must be approached from the perspective of the gospel, as a serious matter of "faith and order." Its ultimate referent is God, whose gift of peace is our reconciliation with him

18. Tacitus, *Agricola* 30.

and with each other through the death of his Son. We must not allow the issue of peace to be dismissed or marginalized, as though it were somehow irrelevant to genuine theological concerns. That would distort the gospel itself. But neither should we allow a counterfeit peace, a caricature of God's peace, to become a substitute for the gospel.

The Brethren Peace Witness
in Ecumenical Perspective

DONALD F. DURNBAUGH

On June 16, 1705, a Swiss Reformed pastor and the mayor of the village of Frenkendorf, near Basel, complained to the Basel city council that a certain Andreas Bohni (1673-1741) was causing trouble. A native of Frenkendorf and a weaver by trade, Bohni had as a journeyman lived in Heidelberg where he came into contact with Radical Pietist views.[1] After his wife's death, Bohni returned to his home where he communicated his new convictions first to his family and then to others. The local officials expressed fear that a dissenting movement would spread rapidly unless it were immediately checked.[2]

1. The best discussion of Radical Pietism is found in Hans Schneider, "Der radikale Pietismus im 17. Jahrhundert," in *Geschichte des Pietismus, Band 1,* ed. Martin Brecht (Göttingen: Vandenhoeck & Ruprecht, 1993), pp. 391-437, and "Der radikale Pietismus im 18. Jahrhundert," in *Geschichte des Pietismus, Band 2,* ed. Martin Brecht and Klaus Deppermann (Göttingen: Vandenhoeck & Ruprecht, 1995), pp. 107-97. For a recent treatment in English, see W. R. Ward, *The Protestant Evangelical Awakening* (Cambridge: Cambridge University Press, 1992), pp. 160ff.

2. The incidents are discussed in Donald F. Durnbaugh, *Brethren Beginnings: The Origins of the Church of the Brethren in Early Eighteenth-Century Europe* (Philadelphia:

This essay is adapted from a paper originally presented at a conference held at the University of Toronto in May 1991, published in *The Pacifist Impulse in Historical Perspective,* ed. Harvey L. Dyck (Toronto: University of Toronto Press, 1996), pp. 125-44.

According to the pastor and mayor, Bohni was guilty of three "Anabaptist" errors: (1) he refused to bear arms or drill with the militia; (2) he categorically rejected the taking of oaths; and (3) he renounced the sacrament of Holy Communion. More than a year later, during which time Bohni sojourned again in the Palatinate, the pastor issued a further complaint. He reported that Bohni had shown up at a service of infant baptism and publicly challenged the pastor to show from the New Testament ("which he always carries with him") where pedobaptism and godparents were commanded. At the time he was not wearing the customary sidearm bayonet, and Bohni and his brother were haled before the Basel magistrates. Their interrogation revealed that Bohni had often visited local Mennonites.

An assessment by the Basel clergy reported that an early examination had revealed that Bohni rejected the use of the sword. Now, after another sojourn in Heidelberg, "he has absorbed all the other errors of the Anabaptists, enthusiasts, and fanatics," they claimed. Moreover, "[h]e holds so obstinately and stubbornly to these doctrines that, although he is defeated and done in with God's Word, he still remains firm in his opinion. . . . He is completely assured of it through Scriptures as well as through the inner instruction of the Spirit."[3]

Although these incidents took place several years before the inception of the Brethren in 1708, they reveal the basic orientation of its founders, of whom Andreas Bohni was one. The Brethren were separatists of Radical Pietist persuasion who adopted an Anabaptist view of the church. Coming primarily from the Reformed faith, the separatists were profoundly influenced by Anabaptism and Pietism.[4]

Brethren Encyclopedia, Inc., 1992), pp. 15-18; many of the documents are given in translation in Donald F. Durnbaugh, ed., *European Origins of the Brethren* (Elgin, Ill.: Brethren Press, 1958), pp. 87-105.

A current Swiss research project places Bohni in a larger context: "Religiöser Non-Konformismus im frühen 18. Jahrhundert: Der Fall des Pietisten Andreas Bohni von Frenkendorf," conducted by a Mennonite scholar, Hanspeter Jecker under the sponsorship of Prof. Ulrich Gäbler, University of Basel.

3. Durnbaugh, *Brethren Beginnings,* pp. 16-18; Durnbaugh, *European Origins,* pp. 94-105.

4. Good surveys of Anabaptist history and belief are found in Cornelius J. Dyck, *An Introduction to Mennonite History,* 3rd ed. (Scottdale, Pa.: Herald Press, 1993), and William R. Estep, *The Anabaptist Story,* 3rd ed. (Grand Rapids: Eerdmans, 1996).

Anabaptist Nonresistance

Much attention has been given, and rightly so, to the topic of Anabaptist nonresistance. An older generation of largely Mennonite scholarship found the tenet of nonresistance to be close to the core of the early Anabaptist essence, with Harold S. Bender's "Anabaptist Vision" a useful reference; the third element in Bender's delineation of the Anabaptist Vision was "the ethic of love and nonresistance as applied to all human relationships."

More recent scholarship has questioned that interpretation. Scholars such as James M. Stayer in North America and Hans-Jürgen Goertz in Europe, to take leading examples, have demonstrated a variety of Anabaptist reactions to the problem of violence, ranging from absolutist rejection to apocalyptic crusade. Intriguing and important as the discussion is, it can be bypassed for the present. There is consensus that by the end of the sixteenth century the Anabaptist/Mennonite position was almost entirely nonresistant. Thus Stayer can conclude his narrative analysis: "By the late sixteenth century virtually all Anabaptists had adopted the idea . . . that 'the Sword is ordained by God outside the perfection of Christ.'" The position of the Brotherly Union of Schleitheim (or Schleitheim Confession) of 1527 had become normative for the movement.[5]

By the early eighteenth century, therefore, the form of Anabaptism the Brethren encountered was thoroughly nonresistant. This was graphically recognized by Alexander Mack Sr. (1679-1735) in some early writ-

---

5. Harold S. Bender, "The Anabaptist Vision," in *The Recovery of the Anabaptist Vision,* ed. Guy F. Hershberger (Scottdale, Pa.: Herald Press, 1957), p. 51; the essay was originally published in *Church History* 13 (March 1944): 3-24 and was republished (with slight revisions) in *The Mennonite Quarterly Review* 18 (April 1944): 67-88. See the literature cited in John S. Oyer, "The Anabaptist Vision" in *The Mennonite Encyclopedia,* vol. 5 (Scottdale, Pa./Waterloo, Ont.: Herald Press, 1990), p. 26; Albert N. Keim, "History of the Anabaptist Vision," *Mennonite Historical Bulletin* 54 (October 1993): 1-7; and especially the discussion in Albert N. Keim, *Harold S. Bender, 1897-1962* (Scottdale, Pa.: Herald Press, 1998), 306-31. See also James M. Stayer, *Anabaptists and the Sword* (Lawrence, Kans.: Coronado Press, 1972), p. 328; a revised version was published by the same press (1975); his recent book, *The German Peasants' War and Anabaptist Community of Goods* (Montreal/Kingston: McGill-Queens University Press, 1991), is also relevant. See as well Hans-Jürgen Goertz, *Die Täufer: Geschichte und Deutung,* 2nd, rev. ed. (Munich: C. H. Beck, 1988).

ing. Responding to an interlocutor who had asked if he felt his movement would turn out better than had the former Anabaptists', Mack replied:

We cannot testify for our descendants — as their faith is, so shall be their outcome. Nevertheless, we can say this, that the outcome of the former Anabaptists has turned out far better than that of all other religions. The Anabaptist seed is far better than the seed of L[uther], C[alvin], and also that of the C[atholics]. These have had a completely wild, yes, bestial outcome, which is self-evident. The Jews and the Turks are scandalized by the horrible wickedness of these three religions. Not even with gallows and torture can they keep them, who are of one faith, from murdering one another in their homes. . . . What is still more horrible, they go publicly to war, and slaughter one another by the thousands.

Mack conceded that the Mennonites he knew had lost much of their original fervor, had indeed been sadly diminished. Yet, he maintained: "No Anabaptist will be found in war. . . . The majority of them are inclined to peacefulness. . . . It would indeed be desirable that the whole world were full of these 'deteriorated' Anabaptists."[6] Peter Brock's studies have described the attenuation of this nonresistant position among the rapidly acculturating Dutch and North German Mennonites in modern times, but the Palatine Anabaptists with whom the early Brethren had contact in the first decades of the eighteenth century were from Switzerland and South Germany and still faithfully maintained the peace testimony.[7]

A bridge from the Anabaptist stance on peace to the Brethren's was offered by the *Dompelaars* (also *Dompelaers*), a little-studied immersionist movement among seventeenth-century Mennonites, with congregations

6. Durnbaugh, *European Origins,* pp. 342-43; the original title was "Eberhard Ludwig Grubers Grundforschende Fragen, welche denen Neuen Täuffern, im Witgensteinischen, insonderheit zu beantworten, vorgelegt waren," a manuscript circulated in 1713; it was later published in North America. Although historians had long considered this to have been the first Brethren publication, it has recently been discovered that Mack's responses were based on a booklet by Gruber, entitled *Grundforschende Fragen von der Wassertaufe* (Idstein: 1713). See the paper by Hans Schneider, " 'Basic Questions on Water Baptism': An Early Anti-Brethren Pamphlet," *Brethren Life and Thought* 43 (Summer/Fall 1998): 31-63.

7. Peter Brock, *Pacifism in Europe to 1914* (Princeton, N.J.: Princeton University Press, 1972), pp. 174-254, and *Freedom from Violence: Sectarian Nonresistance from the Middle Ages to the Great War* (Toronto: University of Toronto Press, 1991), pp. 97-130.

in Hamburg/Altona and Krefeld. The mystic Christian Hohburg (1606-75), a Lutheran pastor who became Reformed, often preached at the Dompelaar congregation in Altona. He called for Christians to follow the path of suffering because their weapons are "not muskets, but Bible and prayer to God." When the Brethren movement became active in the early eighteenth century, members established links with these congregations and were themselves called *Dompelaars*.[8]

Pietist Nonresistance

One man played a predominant role in winning to Radical Pietism those who became Brethren. This was the itinerant Radical Pietist evangelist Ernst Christoph Hochmann von Hochenau (1670-1721). Hochmann was a committed nonresistant. This became clear during several interrogations he underwent in the course of his wandering ministry, which revealed that he had read the works of Quaker theologian Robert Barclay (1648-90). Hochmann was also directly influenced by Gottfried Arnold (1666-1714), noted Radical Pietist historian. Arnold's books on the early Christians and on heretical movements included sections on nonresistance, and he is sometimes credited with being the first historian to treat the Anabaptists sympathetically.[9]

8. Brock, *Pacifism in Europe*, pp. 247-48; Durnbaugh, *Brethren Beginnings*, pp. 34, 42, 52, 54, 57; Friedrich Nieper, *Die ersten deutschen Auswanderer von Krefeld nach Pennsylvanien* (Neukirchen/Moers: Buchhandlung des Erziehungsverein, 1940), passim (simply equating the Dompelaars in Krefeld with the Dunkers); Albrecht Ritschl, *Geschichte des Pietismus . . . : Zweiter Band* (Bonn: Adolph Marcus, 1884), pp. 61-63; F. Ernest Stoeffler, *The Rise of Evangelical Pietism* (Leiden: E. J. Brill, 1965), pp. 230-31. See especially the recent study, Dennis L. Slabaugh, "Dunkers and Dompelaars," *Brethren Life and Thought* 43 (Summer/Fall 1998): 68-116.

9. Heinz Renkewitz, *Hochmann von Hochenau (1670-1721): Quellenstudien zur Geschichte des Pietismus*, 2nd, rev. ed. (Witten: Luther-Verlag, 1969), passim; this was issued in English translation (without the scholarly apparatus), trans. William G. Willoughby (Philadelphia: Brethren Encyclopedia, Inc., 1993). A recent study of Gottfried Arnold is Peter C. Erb, *Pietists, Protestants, and Mysticism: The Use of Late Medieval Spiritual Texts in the Work of Gottfried Arnold (1666-1714)* (Metuchen, N.J.: Scarecrow Press, 1989). See also Dale R. Stoffer, *Background and Development of Brethren Doctrines, 1650-1987* (Philadelphia: Brethren Encyclopedia, Inc., 1989): 23-36.

Comments on Arnold's treatment of the Anabaptists are found in Guy F. Hersh-

Hochmann preached directly against Christian participation in war; although wars would continue, he argued that sincere Christians should reject military service because of its incompatibility with Christ's commandment of love. If all who claimed to be Christians were Christians in reality, actually following Christ's message of brotherly love, wars would cease. In any case, it was totally offensive to him that Christians would fight against fellow Christians. A symbol of Hochmann's nonresistance was his name for a retreat in the village of Schwarzenau; he called it *Friedenstadt,* city of peace.[10]

Separatists influenced by Hochmann shared this attitude. Under interrogation, members of a conventicle of Radical Pietists meeting at the home of button maker Martin Lucas (1700s) in Heidelberg testified that love of enemy was central for them. Christian practice, they believed, required not only that they meet for worship and Bible study in small groups, but also that "they love foremost God and their neighbor as themselves, even their enemies." Many of this group later joined the Brethren.[11]

Restitutionism

Although Pietism and Anabaptism differed in some respects, with Pietists tending to emphasize individuality and Anabaptists community, both movements shared one important trait — the concept of restitutionism or primitivism. That is, both movements held the early Christian church to be normative for belief and practice. While willing to draft and affirm confessions of faith, both rejected the creedal emphasis that marked Protestant orthodoxy from the era of the early Reformation through the

---

berger, "Introduction," in Hershberger, ed., *The Recovery of the Anabaptist Vision,* 2, and Franklin H. Littell, *The Anabaptist View of the Church,* 2nd, rev. ed. (Boston: Starr King Press, 1958), p. 152, which was republished as *The Origins of Sectarian Protestantism* (New York: Macmillan, 1964).

10. Renkewitz, *Hochmann,* pp. 335-36; a critical theologian in Wesel also pointed out Hochmann's dependence on Barclay, p. 308. See also Ruth Rouse and Stephen C. Neill, eds., *A History of the Ecumenical Movement, 1517-1948* (Philadelphia: Westminster Press, 1954), pp. 83, 103-4, 228-29.

11. Renkewitz, *Hochmann,* p. 235; Durnbaugh, *European Origins,* p. 76.

bitter confessional strife and bloody religious wars of the later sixteenth and seventeenth centuries.[12]

Anabaptism itself was solemnly and repeatedly anathematized in Lutheran and Reformed creeds. This has recently proved awkward; for example, European Mennonites (who directly carry on Anabaptism) were invited as ecumenical colleagues to celebrate anniversaries of the Formula of Concord in 1977 and the Augsburg Confession (Augustana) in 1980, but in both of these documents they were formally condemned. This led to a series of theological discussions which have proved fruitful. Similar consultations have taken place between Reformed and Mennonite delegations.[13]

Another way to state the issue is to say that both Anabaptism and Pietism understood themselves as restoring and preserving the faith once delivered to the Apostles. In this sense, they thought that they were making contributions "towards the common expression of the apostolic faith" in their day, to adopt the language of the recent studies of the Faith and Order Commission of the national and world conciliar agencies. Contemporary representatives of these traditions have sought to make a similar case in recent Faith and Order discussions.[14]

It is clear from both earlier and later Brethren expressions that they fully accepted and adopted the restitutionist posture. The first historical sketch of the Brethren was penned by Alexander (Sander) Mack Jr.

---

12. In the writings of Franklin H. Littell, the theme of restitution is made central to the understanding of Anabaptism; see especially chapters two and three of his prize-winning book, *The Anabaptist View of the Church* (1952).

13. See, for example, *Texte aus der VELKD 53: Bericht vom Dialog VELKD/Mennoniten, 1989 bis 1992* (Hannover: Lutherisches Kirchenamt, 1953) and *Texte aus der VELKD 54: Material über die Täuferbewegung zum Dialog VELKD/Mennoniten, 1989 bis 1992* (Hannover: Lutherisches Kirchenamt, 1954); Hans Georg van Bergen and others, eds., *Mennonites and Reformed in Dialogue: Studies from the World Alliance of Reformed Churches,* 7 (Geveva: WARC, 1986), which includes Ernst Saxer et al., "The Attitude of the Reformed Churches Today to the Condemnations of the Anabaptists in Reformed Confessional Documents," pp. 42-56, and Heinold Fast, "A Mennonite View of the Reformed Condemnations," pp. 57-60.

14. On this stance, see especially discussions and bibliographical references found in Marlin E. Miller and Barbara Nelson Gingerich, eds., *The Church's Peace Witness* (Grand Rapids: Eerdmans, 1994), especially "Introduction," pp. 1-14, by Jeffrey Gros, FSC, and "Toward Acknowledging Together the Apostolic Character of the Church's Peace Witness," pp. 196-207, by Marlin E. Miller.

(1712-1803), the like-named son of the first minister, in an introduction to his father's doctrinal treatises. After describing the events, including expulsion from their homes, which led a number of religious dissenters to gather in the county of Wittgenstein, he wrote: "Under these circumstances some felt themselves powerfully drawn to seek the footsteps of the primitive Christians, and desired earnestly to receive in faith the ordained testimonies of Jesus Christ according to their true value." Thereupon, he continued, "these eight persons covenanted and united together as brethren and sisters into the covenant of the cross of Christ to form a church of Christian believers." As they studied the New Testament and "authentic histories" they found that "the primitive Christians in the first and second centuries, uniformly, according to the command of Christ, were planted into the death of Jesus Christ by a threefold immersion . . . of holy baptism . . . , they were anxiously desirous . . . to go forward to the fulfillment of all righteousness." Subsequently, they demanded of Alexander Mack Sr., who "led in the preaching of the word, to immerse them according to the example of *the primitive and best Christians,* upon their faith."[15]

This was the background for the first baptism of Brethren in the summer of 1708. Those baptized clearly believed that they were following the precept and example of the early Christian church. The narrative of the best-documented case of suppression of newly-baptized convert, that of six young Brethren men and their landlord from Solingen, began: "As we seven men, who had learned to recognize the suppressed truth according to the understanding of the first Christians, also endeavored to live in harmony with this as far as faith and mercy had appeared to us, we were arrested." A Swiss separatist wrote from Krefeld in 1719 about them also: "Their foundation, as is well known, rests on the mere letter of the Scripture, and is an imitation of the early Christians."[16]

It therefore comes as no surprise that a consolidation of nineteenth-century Brethren periodicals in the United States was entitled *The Primitive Christian* (1876) or that the first systematic exposition of Brethren

---

15. Alexander Mack Jr., "Preface or Introduction," in *A Short and Plain View of the Outward, Yet Sacred Rights and Ordinances of the House of God. . . . Also Ground Searching Questions answered by the Author Alexander Mack . . . ,* ed. Henry Kurtz and James Quinter (Columbiana, Ohio: Gospel Visitor, 1860), pp. 22-24 (emphasis added).

16. See the discussion and bibliographical citations in Donald F. Durnbaugh, "The Genius of the Early Brethren," *Brethren Life and Thought* 4 (Spring 1959): 4-18, esp. 5-6.

theology, by the former Lutheran Peter Nead (1796-1877), was *Primitive Christianity, Or a Vindication of the Word of God* (1834). These attributes were combined in the subtitle of Nead's collected theological writings, *A Vindication of Primitive Christianity* (1850, 1866). Nead was instrumental in initiating an organ of the conservative Brethren, still in publication; its title is *The Vindicator of the Ancient Order* (1870-) Similarly, Henry Kurtz (1796-1874) asserted that his goal in his pioneer Brethren periodical, *The Gospel Visitor* (1851-), was to defend Christ's "unadulterated Gospel . . . in the simplicity with which it was taught and practiced by the apostles and the primitive church."[17]

Brethren were fond of stating that their sole aim was "earnestly contending for the faith once delivered to the saints." They claimed that they had no creed except the New Testament, which they took as a guide to Christian life and doctrine. It was clear to them that the early Christian church was nonresistant and, as restitutionists, they had no choice but to accept and maintain this position.[18]

Thus, the two formative movements that influenced the Brethren, Anabaptism and Pietism, as well as their influential restitutionist and primitivist beliefs, all shaped the tenor and texture of the Brethren peace stance.

Early Brethren Nonresistance

To the surprise and disappointment of modern Brethren, little discussion on peace issues was recorded among the early Brethren. Why would something so central to their faith pilgrimage be scarcely mentioned in the early records? Besides the fact that only scraps of documentation can

17. See the discussion in Donald F. Durnbaugh, *Fruit of the Vine: A History of the Brethren, 1708-1995* (Elgin, Ill.: Brethren Press, 1997), pp. 226, 237-38.

18. The latest study of Brethren development since 1850 agrees that the restoration of the primitive apostolic church was the "primary impulse of the early Brethren" — see Carl F. Bowman, *Brethren Society: The Cultural Transformation of a "Peculiar People"* (Baltimore: Johns Hopkins University Press, 1995), esp. pp. 23-50. See also the following articles: Kenneth I. Morse, "Primitive Christian"; Fred W. Benedict, "Nead, Peter"; Marcus Miller, "Vindicator"; and Dale H. Aukerman, "Nonresistance"; all found in *The Brethren Encyclopedia* (Oak Brook, Ill./Philadelphia: Brethren Encyclopedia, Inc., 1983-1984), pp. 918-20, 944, 1058, 1306-7.

be gleaned from the early records, there are two other reasons for the silence. Early Brethren arose in conscious rejection of the Reformed and Lutheran state churches and what Brethren considered their hyper-creedalism. They designedly refrained from compiling a creed, or even a confession of faith, that would give systematic expression to their views; instead, they tried to stay open to new light that could come to the community. As Alexander Mack Jr. expressed this hermeneutic in the late eighteenth century, referring to differences in church practice:

> I want to say this, that if a brother or some other person can in love and humility demonstrate by the word of the Lord something other than what is now done, we are willing to accept it. . . . Indeed, we do not intend to rest upon old practice but the word of the Lord alone is to be our rule and guideline. . . . Therefore, dear brethren, let us watch and be careful, and above all preserve love, for thus one preserves light.[19]

Because Brethren were not writing complete statements of faith, the few writings they did publish dealt with controversial points. Against the Radical Pietists they debated the necessity of church discipline; against the Mennonites, the method of baptism. Because both of these movements held to a staunch nonresistant position, the Brethren had no occasion to dispute this shared tenet in published form. This explains the relative absence of expression on peace issues.

Similarly, they engaged in some published controversy with a contemporary group, the charismatic New Prophets or Community of True Inspiration, who have become well-known in North America as the Amana Society. These Inspirationists also held a consistent peace stance, so the issue did not become a point of debate with them either.[20]

19. Donald F. Durnbaugh, ed., *The Brethren in Colonial America* (Elgin, Ill.: Brethren Press, 1967), pp. 464, 468. See also Carl F. Bowman, *Brethren Society*, p. 29, et passim, and Durnbaugh, *Fruit of the Vine*, pp. 389-92.

20. There is a voluminous literature on the Inspired or Inspirationists; a recent study in English is Diane L. Barthel, *Amana: From Pietist Sect to American Community* (Lincoln: University of Nebraska Press, 1984). The best monograph on Inspired origins is Ulf-Michael Schneider, *Propheten der Goethezeit: Sprache, Literatur und Wirkung der Inspirierten* (Göttingen: Vandenhoeck & Ruprecht, 1995). On their peace position, see also Peter Brock, *Pacifism in the United States* (Princeton, N.J.: Princeton University Press, 1968), pp. 438-39, 825-27; Brock, *Pacifism in Europe*, pp. 249-50.

The Colonial Period

Space does not permit an extended historical review of the peace witness of the Brethren in the centuries since their foundation in the early eighteenth century, even though their story, unlike that of the Mennonites and the Quakers, is principally an American one. Suffice it to say that by the late 1740s the Brethren had been transplanted in North America, primarily in Pennsylvania; those remaining in Europe either reverted to an individualist Radical Pietism or merged with the Mennonites.[21] The story of Brethren nonresistance has been told well in the magisterial studies by Peter Brock, *Pacifism in the United States* (1968) and *Freedom from Violence* (1991), as well as in the earlier monograph by Rufus D. Bowman, *The Church of the Brethren and War* (1944). A few highlights will illustrate the initial Brethren grounding in nonresistance and recent changes in position.[22]

In the familiar irony of history, most documentation on peace churches has arisen when governments have made military demands on their citizenry, including those of pacifist persuasion, with the result that we know most about the Brethren attitude toward peace during wartimes.[23] The rise of American independence efforts as they came to focus in the Revolutionary War brought sharp demands upon the Brethren and other peace groups. During this era Brethren held staunchly to the nonresistant principle; this is attested by all contemporary accounts. Proud's *History of Pennsylvania,* for example, records of them: "Those people in Pennsylvania, called Dunkards, . . . hold it not becom-

---

21. See Durnbaugh, *Fruit of the Vine,* pp. 61-70.

22. See Brock, *Pacifism in the United States* and *Freedom from Violence;* Rufus D. Bowman, *The Church of the Brethren and War, 1708-1941* (Elgin, Ill.: Brethren Press, 1944), republished with a biographical sketch of the author (New York: Garland Publishing Company, 1971); Rufus D. Bowman, *Seventy Times Seven* (Elgin, Ill.: Brethren Press, 1945), a study guide with additional material on World War II; Dale W. Brown, *Brethren and Pacifism* (Elgin, Ill.: Brethren Press, 1970), a revised and expanded version of which was issued as *Biblical Pacifism: A Peace Church Perspective* (Elgin, Ill.: Brethren Press, 1986). The Brethren peace witness is treated extensively in Durnbaugh, *Fruit of the Vine.*

23. Note especially the discussions in Louise Hawkley and James C. Juhnke, eds., *Nonviolent America: History through the Eyes of Peace* (North Newton, Kans.: Bethel College, 1993).

ing a follower of Jesus Christ to bear arms or fight; because, say they, their true Master has forbid His disciples to resist evil."[24]

Basically, the Germanic peace sects — Mennonites, Brethren, Moravians, and others — wished to stay neutral in the struggle. Their tragedy was that it was not in the rebels' interest to permit this. By a variety of means, such as test or loyalty acts, the Revolutionary camp forced all colonists to take sides. Quite often, members of the German peace groups came down on the Loyalist (Tory) side, and the same is true of the Quakers. This is not surprising. They were truly grateful that the British crown had allowed them religious freedom in the New World. They accepted Romans 13 and God's support for the powers that were; it was not at all clear to them that the rebel cause had supplanted the British in that status. Those Americans taking the most belligerent revolutionary positions came from the Presbyterian and Anglican parties, which had been the most active political opponents of their interests.[25]

A classic statement of the Brethren position is contained in a joint petition of Mennonite and Brethren elders to the Pennsylvania Assembly in 1775; an excerpt, using the masculine language of the time, reads as follows:

> The Advice to those who do not find Freedom of Conscience to take up arms, that they ought to be helpfull to those who are in Need and distressed Circumstances, we receive with Chearfulness towards all men of what Station they may be — it being our Principle to feed the

24. Robert Proud, *History of Pennsylvania; Vols. I and II* (Philadelphia: Zachariah Poulson Jr., 1798), pp. 345-47, as quoted in Rufus D. Bowman, *Brethren and War,* pp. 71-72. The manuscript of Proud's original source, Samuel Smith, remained unpublished until the twentieth century: William M. Mervine, ed., *History of the Province of Pennsylvania by Samuel Smith* (Philadelphia: Colonial Society of Pennsylvania, 1913), pp. 181-83, 188-90, discussed and quoted in Durnbaugh, *Colonial America,* pp. 14-21. See also Roger E. Sappington, "Eighteenth-Century Non-Brethren Sources of Brethren History, IV," *Brethren Life and Thought* 2 (Autumn 1957): 65-75.

These statements are well corroborated by recent studies. See, for example, Richard K. MacMaster et al., eds., *Conscience in Crisis. Mennonites and Other Peace Churches in America, 1739-1789: Interpretation and Documents* (Scottdale, Pa./Kitchener, Ont.: Herald Press, 1979); Richard K. MacMaster, *Land, Piety, Peoplehood: The Establishment of Mennonite Communities in America, 1683-1790,* The Mennonite Experience in America, Vol. I (Scottdale, Pa.: Herald Press, 1985).

25. For more detail, consult Donald F. Durnbaugh, "Religion and Revolution: Options in 1776," *Pennsylvania Mennonite Heritage* 1 (July 1978): 2-9.

Hungry and give the Thirsty Drink; — we have dedicated ourselves to serve all Men in every Thing that can be helpful to the Preservation of Men's Lives, but we find no Freedom in giving, or doing, or assisting in any Thing by which Men's Lives are destroyed or hurt.[26]

A few of the Brethren and Mennonites were so opposed to the Revolutionary cause that they became active Tories. Some were caught up in Loyalist plots in Pennsylvania and Maryland; they did insist, however, that their support be limited to noncombatant activities such as driving wagons. In neither Pennsylvania nor Maryland did these loyalist plots come to fruition, but some participants, including the German sectarians, were executed anyway.[27]

This pro-British support is one reason for the migration to Ontario after the war's end by many members of the peace groups. Among those who left the newly established American state were Mennonites, Amish, Brethren, and the newly-founded River Brethren. Because the latter two groups were both called Tunkers in Canada, there is much confusion in the literature.[28]

The Nineteenth Century

Brethren practice during the Civil War followed that of the late eighteenth century. Membership in the church was still conditioned on a bap-

---

26. The original petition was published in English and German. The document has often been republished. For recent publications, see MacMaster, *Conscience in Crisis*, pp. 266-67; Durnbaugh, *Colonial America*, pp. 362-65. The petition is discussed in the article by Leo Schelbert on a Mennonite dissident, "Christian Funk's *Spiegel für alle Menschen*: An Interpretative Introduction," *Yearbook of German-American Studies* 32 (1997): 153-90.

27. See Durnbaugh, "Religion and Revolution" and *Fruit of the Vine*, 156-59; J. Russell Harper, "Christopher Sower [III], King's Printer and Loyalist," *New Brunswick Historical Society Collections* 14 (1955): 67-109; Carl Van Doren, *Secret History of the American Revolution* (New York: Macmillan, 1941); Emmert Bittinger, *Allegheny Passage: Churches and Families, West Marva District, Church of the Brethren, 1752-1990* (Camden, Maine: Penobscot Press, 1990), pp. 220-26.

28. See Dennis D. Martin and R. Truman Northup, "Ontario," in *The Brethren Encyclopedia*, p. 975; E. Morris Sider, *The Brethren in Christ in Canada: Two Hundred Years of Tradition and Change* (Nappanee, Ind.: Evangel Press, 1988).

tismal pledge by new members that they would be faithful to the nonresistant position, and Brethren held true to this pledge during the war. They were following the direction of the Annual Meeting which pointedly answered this question that came to it in 1865: "Can a brother be held as a member of the church who will, when put in the army, take up arms and aim to shed the blood of his fellowman?" The answer was: "He cannot."[29]

This abstention caused considerable sacrifice, particularly in the Confederacy, since the South had greater need of all of its men of fighting age. Moreover, as it was understood that Brethren hated slavery, their nonresistant principles could easily be interpreted as pro-Union sentiments. Several murders of Brethren, clearly caused by their nonresistance, are known; the most noted was the assassination in 1864 by Confederate irregulars of Elder John Kline (1797-1864) of Broadway, Virginia. He had repeatedly crossed the battle lines (with official permission) to preside over church meetings held in the North. This travel, compounded by his clearly-stated and well-known anti-secession and anti-slavery views, led to his slaying.[30]

Kline, it should be noted, had carefully articulated the Brethren view that nonresistance included acceptance of proper authority. In a letter to the governor of Virginia in 1861, he wrote:

> We teach and are taught obedience to the "powers that be," believing as we do that "the powers that be are ordained of God," and under his divine sanction so far as such powers keep within God's bounds. By God's bounds we understand such laws and their administrations . . . as do not conflict with, oppose, or violate any precept or command contained in the Divine Word which he has given for the moral and spiritual government of his people. By government . . . we understand rightful human authority. And by this, again, we understand, as the

29. This and other relevant minutes are found in L. W. Shultz, comp., *Minutes of the Annual Conference of the Church of the Brethren on War and Peace* (Elgin, Ill.: Board of Christian Education, Church of the Brethren, 1935), p. 7. For this period, see Brock, *Pacifism in the United States,* pp. 797-821, and Rufus D. Bowman, *Brethren and War,* pp. 114-68.

30. See Roger E. Sappington, *Courageous Prophet: Chapters from the Life of John Kline* (Elgin, Ill.: Brethren Press, 1964). A highly-detailed account of his death (based on private papers not accessible to other writers) is found in Ray A. Neff, *Valley of the Shadow* (Terre Haute, Ind.: Rana Publications, 1987).

Apostle Paul puts it, "the power that protects and blesses the good, and punishes the evildoer."[31]

Brethren had not developed much literature on peace, but they presented a small book from this time as their statement to the Confederate government. It was *Non-Resistance, or the Spirit of Christianity Restored* (1862), and its author was William C. Thurman (ca. 1830-1906), a Virginia Baptist who had become convinced through his own biblical study of the importance of nonresistance. He joined the Brethren during the war and soon was given leadership positions, although he remained in them for only a short duration because he began promulgating millenarian views and questioning certain traditional practices, such as the form of footwashing.[32]

The Twentieth Century

By 1917, when the United States entered the Great War, the Brethren attitude toward war had changed. This was because the Brethren had changed. No longer German-speaking farmers living in isolated enclaves, Brethren had moved with the times. Beginning in 1876 they established "Normals," that is, teacher-training schools, which eventually became well-respected and accredited colleges. Many Brethren had moved from the farms to take up managerial and professional positions, particularly as teachers, in towns and cities. A well-endowed General Mission Board was sending scores of missionaries to several continents. In 1911, after painful years of controversy, the Annual Conference ruled that the plain dress or garb could be waived by congregational action. This act was a symbol of the widespread acculturation of the church membership.[33]

31. Found in Benjamin Funk, *Life and Labors of Elder John Kline, the Martyr Missionary* (Elgin, Ill.: Brethren Publishing House, 1900), p. 439; also quoted in Rufus D. Bowman, *Brethren and War*, p. 121.

32. William C. Thurman, *Non-Resistance, or the Spirit of Christianity Restored* (Charlottesville, Va.: author, 1862); Donald F. Durnbaugh, "Thurman, William C.," *The Brethren Encyclopedia*, p. 1264. See also Brock, *Pacifism in the United States*, pp. 814-15; Rufus D. Bowman, *Brethren and War*, p. 141; Roger E. Sappington, *The Brethren in Virginia* (Harrisonburg, Va.: Committee for Brethren History in Virginia, 1973), pp. 190-91.

33. See Carl F. Bowman, *Brethren Society*, passim.

If one event were to be singled out to illustrate this transformation, it would be the election in 1914 of Martin Grove Brumbaugh (1862-1930) as governor of the Commonwealth of Pennsylvania. Brumbaugh, a minister and the first member of the Brethren church to earn a doctorate (Ph.D.), had been a president of the oldest Brethren college (Juniata College founded in 1876), professor of pedagogy at the University of Pennsylvania, and commissioner of education in Puerto Rico after the American victory in the Spanish American War. His achievements as a reforming superintendent of the Philadelphia public school system gave him the credentials for the gubernatorial race, which he won handily.[34]

At Brumbaugh's inauguration in January 1915, he did not take an oath of office; rather, he affirmed his dedication to perform his duties. When the United States entered the war, one of these duties was to command the Pennsylvania militia, which was soon incorporated into the regular U.S. military. Although this involvement, in the eyes of traditional Dunkers, cast doubt on his *bona fides* as a minister of the church, many in the denomination were gratified by his prominence.[35]

The Annual Conference for 1918 was asked to define the church's position "as regards the propriety of our members holding any office under our Civil Government which would necessitate their using, or causing to be used, physical force, carrying carnal weapons, or administering oaths." The answer was equivocal:

1) Annual Meeting reaffirms her position on nonresistance and does not permit the holding of office by her members when such office compels them to violate these nonresistant principles and the taking or administering of oaths. 2) However, we recognize that, in a democracy, it is not wrong for Brethren to serve their communities and municipalities to promote efficiency and honesty in social and civic life when the nonresistant principles and the New Testament doctrines are not violated. 3) Anyone who violates this decision subjects himself to the discipline of the church.[36]

---

34. The definitive biography is Earl C. Kaylor Jr., *Martin Grove Brumbaugh: A Pennsylvanian's Odyssey from Sainted Schoolman to Bedeviled World War I Governor, 1862-1930* (Madison, N.J.: Fairleigh Dickinson University Press for Juniata College, 1996).

35. Durnbaugh, *Fruit of the Vine,* pp. 419-21.

36. Shultz, *Minutes,* p. 26; Rufus D. Bowman, *Brethren and War,* pp. 193-94 (slightly varied); see also Dennis L. Slabaugh, "Brumbaugh, Martin Grove," in *The*

Brumbaugh was never called to task for his war involvement and continued to be respected. He was, however, never called to the highest positions in the church and seldom asked to address it.

The change in tone of the resolutions of the Brethren's Annual Conferences also documents the shift from consistent nonresistance to a more activist pacifism. Through the nineteenth century, conferences dealt with issues involving the church and its members in regard to war. There was no hint that the church felt itself responsible for social or governmental problems. The Annual Meetings of 1875 and 1885 turned down requests for Brethren to cooperate officially with peace associations and conferences.[37] Resolutions in the twentieth century, however, urged such cooperation. More strikingly, by 1915 the church thought it appropriate to praise the course of U.S. President Woodrow Wilson in "his efforts to discourage war and maintain peaceable relations with all the world," commending his "spirit of conservatism, his words encouraging restraint and self-control, his calm temper and manly character." The resolution also applauded Wilson's "humanitarian course in securing advocacy of Christian ideals in all walks of public and private life."

The same conference resolved that the church renew "its allegiance to its time-honored stand for peace and the brotherhood of man, and urged the judicial arbitration of all international differences." It pledged greater zeal in spreading the "peace gospel," more relevant discussions among members, and frequent sermons by ministers "to the end that it may be an increasingly effective power in the hands of the master for the maintenance of peace and goodwill among men and among the nations of the world."[38]

The shift from apolitical nonresistance to a Social Gospel sort of pacifism had been initiated by the conference action of 1910 to appoint a Peace Committee. The language of the second part of the committee's assignment is noteworthy because of the sweeping quality of its parameters:

Brethren Encyclopedia (1983-1984), pp. 222-23, and Salvatore M. Messina, "Martin Grove Brumbaugh: Educator," Ph.D. thesis, University of Pennsylvania, 1965. The recent appraisal by Carl F. Bowman, *Brethren Society,* underscores the pivotal nature of Brumbaugh's political activities; see esp. pp. 245-51.

37. Shultz, *Minutes,* pp. 9, 10.
38. Shultz, *Minutes,* p. 13.

First: to propagate and aid in the distribution of such literature as
may be helpful to the better understanding as to the sinfulness
and folly of resorting to arms in the settlement of differences;
Second: to use every lawful gospel means in bringing about peaceful
settlements of difficulties when such may arise between governments or societies;
Third: to keep the Brotherhood informed, from time to time,
through our publications, as to the true status of the peace movement.[39]

The fact that the Conference did not provide any funds to aid the
Peace Committee in this undertaking does not minimize the significance of
the sea change in orientation. No longer were the Brethren thinking in
terms of two separate realms or kingdoms, that of the church and that of the
world. They began to think of the church as co-responsible with the government for the solution to the world's problems. Bowman quite rightly, if
understatedly, regarded the action as marking a change in the church's
thought when he wrote: "The Brethren were beginning to sense the need of
a peace educational program within the church and the necessity for the
church to become an active force for peace among the nations."[40]

The change in attitude was tested when the entry of the United
States into World War I in April 1917 brought after it draft legislation in
May. Conscientious objectors (COs) such as the Brethren were excused
from combatant duty but required to perform non-combatant service;
the exact nature of such service was to be defined later by executive order.
Such clarification did not come for almost a year, complicating greatly the
plight of the COs. At this time the leadership of the Church of the
Brethren was divided in its advice to young members who began to be
drafted. Many, such as the important church leader Henry C. Early
(1855-1941), believed that as loyal citizens young Brethren men should
accept noncombatant service. Others, arguing that doing that would
make them part of the military machine, urged them to avoid such activity and, indeed, to refuse to wear uniforms or cooperate in any way.[41]

---

39. Quoted in Rufus D. Bowman, *Brethren and War,* p. 161.
40. Rufus D. Bowman, *Brethren and War,* p. 161.
41. The most complete discussion of this shift is found in Rufus D. Bowman,
Brethren and War, pp. 169-233, based in part on interviews with church leaders. See also

The confusion led to the calling in January 1918 of a special Annual Conference, one of the very few times this has happened, in Goshen, Indiana. The most significant conference action was an incisive restatement of the Brethren position on war:

> Therefore this Conference of the Church of the Brethren hereby declares her continued adherence to the principles of nonresistance, held by the Church since its organization in 1708.
>
> I. We believe that war or any participation in war is wrong and entirely incompatible with the spirit, example, and teachings of Jesus Christ.
> II. That we can not conscientiously engage in any activity or perform any function, contributing to the destruction of human life.[42]

These conclusions were buttressed by extensive biblical citations, a statement on church/state relations, and the creation of a Central Service Committee to liaise with the government.

Highly placed U.S. government officials were informed of the conference action by a delegation of church leaders. President Wilson sent a courteous letter to Elder H. C. Early acknowledging its receipt; in it he suggested that the forthcoming list of noncombatant services would probably be broadened enough to satisfy the conscience of the Brethren. The Goshen Statement, as it came to be called, was printed in pamphlet form for distribution to the denomination, and was intended particularly for the use of those male members of the church subject to the draft.

Among the recommendations of the Goshen Statement was one directing Brethren men, when drafted, to refrain from wearing military uniforms and from participating in drilling exercises. This proved to be fateful. When the statement, with these recommendations, came to the attention of the War Department in the summer of 1918, the office of Advocates General threatened prosecution of the officers of the Special

---

Kenneth G. Long, "Attitudes of the Brethren in Training Camps during the World War," B.D. thesis, Bethany Biblical Seminary, 1939, published in part in *Schwarzenau* 1 (July 1939): 57-77. Carl F. Bowman, *Brethren Society*, pp. 349-53, contains an excellent brief description of the shift away from traditional nonresistance. For a biography of Early, see John S. Flory, *H. C. Early: Christian Statesman* (Elgin, Ill.: Brethren Publishing House, 1943).

42. Shultz, *Minutes*, pp. 17-25.

Conference. It grounded its threat on the provisions of the Espionage Law, which called for severe penalties for those discouraging military service. Religious leaders (particularly Jehovah's Witnesses), political radicals, and union leaders were in fact given harsh sentences on this basis.

Brethren leaders managed to avoid prosecution by pledging to cease distribution of the Goshen Statement. J. Maurice Henry (1880-1966), a Brethren participant in the negotiation with the government, wrote: "The Central Service Peace Committee — guided by wisdom from a gracious heavenly Father — had saved the church from a tragic situation: the church which the peaceful saint, Alexander Mack, had founded, for which Christopher Sower had been persecuted, and for which John J. Bowman and John Kline had suffered martyrdom in times of war." Later commentators found this statement fraught with irony; their judgment was that the retraction seriously weakened the church's nonresistant position.[43]

Young Brethren caught in the draft machinery of World War I disliked the mixed signals they received from the church's leadership. Several among them decided to avoid this kind of problem in the future by devoting their lives to strengthening the Brethren peace witness. These included such figures as Michael Robert (M. R.) Zigler (1891-1985), Dan West (1893-1971), and Rufus D. Bowman (1899-1952), who became nationally known as peace advocates.

These men were largely influenced by the liberal pacifism of the time. While always referring to the nonresistant tradition as their foundation, in practice their orientation was liberal and activist rather than conservative and withdrawn. They sought to combine what the church called "creative citizenship" with active peacemaking strategies, hoping to eliminate the causes of war by social stratagems, political intervention, and church activity.[44]

43. J. Maurice Henry, a member of the Central Service Committee appointed to negotiate with the U.S. government, left a full description in a district history: *History of the Church of the Brethren in Maryland* (Elgin, Ill.: Brethren Publishing House, 1936), pp. 525-32. See also Roger E. Sappington, *Brethren Social Policy, 1908-1958* (Elgin, Ill.: Brethren Press, 1961), pp. 38-45; Rufus D. Bowman, *Brethren and War,* pp. 180-89; and Carl F. Bowman, *Brethren Society,* pp. 329-34. The latest extensive assessment is Robert G. Clouse, "The Church of the Brethren and World War I: The Goshen Statement," *Mennonite Life* 45 (December 1990): 29-34.

44. Brief biographical sketches of these men are found in *The Brethren Encyclope-*

The Historic Peace Churches

In addition, these Brethren leaders were keenly ecumenical in attitude. They hoped to extend the Brethren peace witness to the broader Christian world. Quite naturally, they first reached out to sister churches with peace traditions, principally the several varieties of Mennonites and Friends, as well as the Schwenkfelders and others. A little-known series of ten conferences held between 1922 and 1931, in which Brethren played active roles, sought to deepen the sense of unity initiated among these churches by their shared experience as conscientious objectors during World War I.

The first conference was held at Bluffton College, Ohio, in 1922; its title — Conference of Religious Bodies Who Hold that Peace between Nations Can Be Maintained by Following the Teachings of Jesus — explains its viewpoint. Such interaction doubtless influenced one of the most cited Annual Conference papers of the Brethren in 1935, which included these words:

> We believe that all war is sin; that it is wrong for Christians to support or to engage in it; and that war is incompatible with the spirit, example, and teachings of Jesus. . . . Those beliefs are not based upon a popular peace doctrine of our own; they arise from our application of Christian standards to all human relations, whether individual, group, class, or national. To settle conflicts in any of these relationships by war is not efficient, nor constructive, not permanent, and certainly not Christian.[45]

The same year, 1935, saw a landmark conference at North Newton, Kansas, which coined the quickly-popularized term *Historic Peace Church Activity*. Because the storm clouds of the next war were already forming on the horizon, the unresolved theological differences in peace positions of

---

dia. There are full biographies of West and Zigler: Glee Yoder, *Passing on the Gift: The Story of Dan West* (Elgin, Ill.: Brethren Press, 1978); Donald F. Durnbaugh, *Pragmatic Prophet: The Life of Michael Robert Zigler* (Elgin, Ill.: Brethren Press, 1989). All are discussed in Sappington, *Social Policy*. See also Donald F. Durnbaugh, "Bowman, Rufus David," in *Biographical Dictionary of Modern Peace Leaders*, ed. Harold Josephson (Westport, Conn.: Greenwood Press, 1985), pp. 104-5.

45. Quoted in Rufus D. Bowman, *Brethren and War*, p. 241. The series of conferences is described in Durnbaugh, *Fruit of the Vine*, pp. 431-36.

those attending (which were many) were not allowed to deter the cooperative peace effort which ensued. Along with active peace education, seminars, publications, and pronouncements, the Historic Peace Churches sent weighty delegations to the U.S. government.

These delegations, which met twice with President Franklin D. Roosevelt and often with other high officials, tried to accomplish at least two things: first, to place their peace position on record, with particular attention to the vigorous programs they were carrying on through their service agencies in several countries; and, second, to lay the groundwork for a plan for dealing with conscientious objectors in wartime. They did not want a repetition of the unhappy experiences of World War I.[46]

World War II

As it happened, their foresight was rewarded in September 1940 when the Burke/Wadsworth Bill became law as the Selective Training and Service Act, mandating the first peacetime conscription in American history. The Historic Peace Churches had lobbied for improvements in the bill with partial success. While not achieving all they had asked for, they did secure more generous provisions for conscientious objectors than had been originally planned by legislators. The upshot was the creation in 1940-41 of the Civilian Public Service (CPS) program, administered by a cooperative body, chaired by M. R. Zigler, called the National Service Board for Religious Objectors.[47]

The Church of the Brethren, as well as several other smaller Brethren bodies, supported this program of alternative service in a sacrifi-

46. The best recent study of these developments is Albert N. Keim and Grant M. Stoltzfus, *The Politics of Conscience: The Historic Peace Churches and America at War, 1917-1955* (Scottdale, Pa.: Herald Press, 1988).

47. See Keim and Stoltzfus, *Politics*, pp. 78-102, and Albert N. Keim, *The CPS Story: An Illustrated History of Civilian Public Service* (Intercourse, Pa.: Good Books, 1990). A non-peace-church assessment is Lawrence S. Wittner, *Rebels Against War: The American Peace Movement, 1941-1960* (New York/London: Columbia University Press, 1969), pp. 70-84. The NSBRO was later renamed the National Interreligious Service Board for Conscientious Objectors.

A recent book discussing the reaction of American churches to World War II pays little attention to this effort: Gerald L. Sittser, *A Cautious Patriotism: The American Churches and the Second World War* (Lincoln: University of Nebraska Press, 1997).

cial way, contributing $1,300,000 as well as much material aid. A church survey in 1945 estimated that 10 percent of draft-age Brethren men entered CPS, and that another 10 percent accepted noncombatant military service. A majority engaged in full military participation, without falling under the censure of their home congregations.[48]

Of the twelve thousand men in the entire CPS program, Mennonites had by far the largest contingent and Brethren the second largest with over 1,500. Many Brethren COs accepted the CPS alternative as being the best option; it satisfied the military obligation in a sacrificial way and held true to Brethren tradition. Some men, however, opposed the arrangement, concluding that the Brethren were cooperating too closely with the military. These absolutists, who refused CPS or walked away from the CPS assignments, were tried and received prison sentences.[49]

CPS men had volunteered for overseas duty in relief work during World War II, but were blocked by the United States Congress. At war's end, many secured places with the expanded operations of the Historic Peace Church service organizations — the American Friends Service Committee, the Mennonite Central Committee, and the Brethren Service Committee. They assisted these volunteer agencies in worldwide programs providing material aid, resettlement, and general assistance to refugees, displaced persons, and other war victims. This activity received much favorable attention, symbolized by the awarding of the Nobel peace prize to the Friends Service Council (U.K.) and the AFSC in late 1947.[50]

Another rewarding field of service to society was the assignment of

48. The Brethren CPS program was studied in Leslie Eisan, *Pathways of Peace* (Elgin, Ill.: Brethren Publishing House, 1948); a recent interpretation of CPS is Cynthia Eller, *Conscientious Objectors and the Second World War: Moral and Religious Arguments in Support of Pacifism* (New York: Praeger, 1991), based on interviews. See also articles in a special issue of the denominational journal, *Messenger* (October 1990): 10-21.

49. Mulford Q. Sibley and Philip E. Jacob, *Conscription of Conscience: The American State and the Conscientious Objector, 1940-1947* (Ithaca, N.Y.: Cornell University Press, 1952); Richard E. Anderson, *Peace Was in Their Hearts: Conscientious Objectors in World War II* (Watsonville, Calif.: Correlan Publications, 1994); and Heather T. Frazer and John O'Sullivan, *"We Have Just Begun to Not Fight": An Oral History of Conscientious Objectors in Civilian Public Service during World War II* (New York: Twayne Publishers, 1996).

50. Brethren efforts are described in Donald F. Durnbaugh, ed., *To Serve the Present Age: The Brethren Service Story* (Elgin, Ill.: Brethren Press, 1975). See also Durnbaugh, *Pragmatic Prophet*, and Sappington, *Social Policy.*

scores of CPS men to public mental hospitals. Their devoted service, along with exposés they documented of the scandalous conditions then existing, led to remarkable improvements. National mental health reform is widely attributed to their uncomplaining and effective service.[51]

The Later Twentieth Century

The end of the twentieth century finds the Church of the Brethren in a divided position in relation to its peace tradition. Repeated Annual Conference statements have rearticulated the Brethren position on peace but at the same time have attempted to deal with diversity. On one end of the continuum are those who still stand foursquare for traditional nonresistance. Two-kingdom people, they pray for the government, criticize those Brethren who attempt to be politically relevant, and are totally opposed to military service. On the other end are acculturated Brethren who are unhappy with the traditional peace emphasis of the Brethren, write critical letters to the denominational journal questioning the lack of patriotism of the church's leaders, and still consider themselves loyal members of their church.

In between is a small, articulate, and rather influential group of individuals who could be called Neo-Anabaptists. They follow a line that seeks to speak to political issues while at the same time maintaining a clear distinction between an *agape* ethic of love within the church and the ethic of justice and fairness seen as appropriate for the state. During the Vietnam war, they created several *Brethren Peace Fellowships,* which sought a greater intensity of peace action than that sponsored by denominational agencies.[52]

Also present are classical liberal pacifists who seek to extend the way of love through all sectors of society by education, social action, and government programs. A small number follow a just war ethic, especially as it is currently expressed in liberation theology. Most members are content

51. A well-documented survey of these developments is found in Alex Sareyan, *The Turning Point: How Men of Conscience Brought About Major Change in the Care of America's Mentally Ill* (Washington, D.C.: American Psychiatric Press, 1994).

52. See C. Wayne Zunkel, "Brethren Peace Fellowship," in *The Brethren Encyclopedia,* p. 193; Durnbaugh, *Fruit of the Vine,* pp. 536-39.

to support and maintain the denominational peace tradition, without necessarily feeling personally obliged to follow it in their own lives.[53]

Several Annual Conference study papers have sought to clarify matters by identifying these positions but have not succeeded in bringing about complete unity among the differing groups. In part stimulated by this problem, the *On Earth Peace Assembly* was created in 1974 by long-time peace activist and church leader M. R. Zigler; it is centered at New Windsor, Maryland, and works to develop peace-mindedness among Brethren, with a particular focus on young people and vocational groups.[54]

Ecumenical Relations

Brethren have been leaders since 1948 in bringing the Historic Peace Church witness to the National Council of Churches and the World Council of Churches. A number of publications, of which *Peace Is the Will of God* (1953) is the most important, have been presented to World

---

53. Reviews of Brethren and peace in the past three decades are: Robert W. McFadden, "Perspective in Pacifism," *Brethren Life and Thought* 6 (Spring 1961): 36-52, and Richard B. Gardner, "Brethren and Pacifism: An Analysis of Contemporary Brethren Approaches to Peace and War," *Brethren Life and Thought* 8 (Autumn 1963): 17-37. See also Harry K. Zeller Jr., *Peace Is Our Business* (Elgin, Ill.: House of the Church of the Brethren, 1947); Arthur G. Gish, *The New Left and Christian Radicalism* (Grand Rapids: Eerdmans, 1970); Vernard Eller, *King Jesus' Manual of Arms for the 'Armless* (Nashville/ New York: Abingdon Press, 1973), republished as *War and Peace from Genesis to Revelation* (Scottdale, Pa.: Herald Press, 1981); Dale Aukerman, *Darkening Valley: A Biblical Perspective on Nuclear War* (New York: Seabury Press, 1981) and *Reckoning with Apocalypse* (New York: Crossroad, 1993); Brown, *Biblical Pacifism* (1986); Vernard Eller, *Christian Anarchy: Jesus' Primacy Over the Powers* (Grand Rapids: Eerdmans, 1987); Carl F. Bowman, *Brethren Society*, esp. pp. 349-56.

54. Among the relevant recent Annual Conference pronouncements are the following: "Statement of the Church of the Brethren on War" (1968), adapted from an earlier statement of 1948, revised in 1957 to recognize selective objection to war; "Obedience to God and Civil Disobedience" (1969); "Statement on Church/State Relationships" (1988); "Peacemaking: The Calling of God's People in History" (1991).

For the "On Earth Peace Assembly" movement, see Durnbaugh, *Pragmatic Prophet*, pp. 274-88, and Charles L. Boyer, "On Earth Peace," *The Brethren Encyclopedia*, p. 974; Ida S. Howell, "A History of the 'On Earth Peace Conference,'" *Brethren Life and Thought* 23 (Winter 1978): 13-15.

Council assemblies. A significant series of formal theological discussions took place after 1955 at the so-called Puidoux conferences, named after the Swiss retreat house where the first meeting was held. The formal title was: "Conference on Lordship of Christ over Church and State." Its impact on the *Volkskirchen* of West Germany was particularly strong.

Later initiatives have kept the peace issue before the World Council of Churches. One of the latest efforts, *A Declaration on Peace* (1991), was prepared by a team of Brethren, Mennonite, Quaker, and Fellowship of Reconciliation theologians; it seeks to speak to the entire Christian community. The current emphasis of the World Council initiative called the "Programme to Overcome Violence" was launched in 1994, largely as the result of an intervention by Donald E. Miller, executive secretary of the Church of the Brethren.[55]

Sparked by a renewal movement among Friends in the United States after 1970, a concerted attempt to revitalize the peace witness among the Historic Peace Churches became active locally, regionally, and nationally in 1976. It was called *New Call to Peacemaking* and developed around a series of intensive conferences and supporting literature in 1978, 1980, and 1982. Its chief effect was to bring together from across denominational lines those concerned with peace, and after 1982 it sought broader contacts with peace groups in other religious bodies. With minimal organizational overhead, it continues its activities to this day.[56]

A related effort focused on direct peace action at national and international trouble-spots is called *Christian Peacemaker Teams*. It was stimulated by an appeal by Ronald Sider at a world conference of Mennonites, held in Strasbourg in 1984. Sider called for a "peace army" trained and ready to take risky actions for reconciliation and peace wherever needed.

55. The cooperative work of the Historic Peace Churches is traced, with documents, including those named above, in Donald F. Durnbaugh, ed., *On Earth Peace: Discussions on War/Peace Issues Between Friends, Mennonites, Brethren, and European Churches, 1935-1975* (Elgin, Ill.: Brethren Press, 1978). The recent publication is Douglas Gwyn, George Hunsinger, Eugene F. Roop, and John Howard Yoder, *A Declaration on Peace: In God's People the World's Renewal Has Begun* (Scottdale, Pa./Waterloo, Ont.: Herald Press, 1991); see especially the chronology, compiled by John Howard Yoder, "40 Years of Theological Dialogue Efforts on Justice and Peace Issues by the Fellowship of Reconciliation and the Historic Peace Churches," pp. 93-105.

56. See Robert J. Rumsey, "New Call to Peacemaking," *The Brethren Encyclopedia*, pp. 925-26, and the movement's newsletter, *Call to Peacemaking*, initiated in February 1979, and still published.

With primary support coming from Mennonites and Brethren after 1986, teams thus far have concentrated their work among Haitians, Palestinians on the West Bank, and ghetto-dwellers in Washington, D.C. They have sponsored, along with the *New Call to Peacemaking,* a number of national peace conferences.[57]

An interesting initiative has brought representatives of the Historic Peace Churches (Church of the Brethren, Mennonites, and Friends) into dialogue in Europe with leaders of the Evangelical Church of Czech Brethren, Hussite Church, Hutterian Brethren, Moravian Church, and Waldensian Church leaders. This series of meetings, often called the Prague Conferences because the Czech city was the site of the first three conferences, was held there in 1986, 1987, and 1989. A fourth and fifth in the series, sponsored by the World Alliance of Reformed Churches, continued the dialogue in conferences held in 1994 and 1998 in Geneva, Switzerland. They also marked an extension of the discussion by enlarging the circle of participants to include theologians from the Lutheran and Reformed churches. Issues of church and state relations, including pacifism, were prominent in these deliberations, which are intended to continue.[58]

Conclusion

Thus, the theme of Brethren nonresistance and pacifism has become a topic with considerable variety in understandings and responses. Nonresistance in the historic sense is certainly alive among the Brethren, but it would be too much to say that it is still the predominant position. Pacifism in a broader sense, including such meanings as active peacemaking

57. J. R. Burkholder, "Peace," *The Mennonite Encyclopedia* (Scottdale, Pa.: Herald Press, 1990), 5:684. CPC circulates a newsletter called *Signs of the Times.*

58. Papers from the first and second consultation were published in a special issue of *Brethren Life and Thought* 35 (Winter 1990): 4-113. See also the special issue of *Reformed World* 43 (September 1993): 76-124, and Milan Opocenský, ed., *Towards a Renewed Dialogue: Consultation on the First and Second Reformations, Geneva, 28 November to 1 December 1994* (Geneva: WARC, 1996). Sketches of many of these bodies are found in Donald F. Durnbaugh and Charles W. Brockwell Jr., "The Historic Peace Churches: From Sectarian Origins to Ecumenical Witness," in Miller and Gingerich, *The Church's Peace Witness,* pp. 182-95.

and nonviolent resistance, is definitely present among many Brethren. Some Brethren members distance themselves from the historic peace position, yet a substantial number want to keep the peace testimony alive and well, refusing to leave it only a part of a neglected heritage.

Building upon an early history that looked to the early church as its model of life and virtue, articulate Brethren understand the peace witness as part of the apostolic faith they seek, although imperfectly, to incarnate in this new century.

Catholic Commitments to
Peace, Unity, and Dialogue

JAMES F. PUGLISI

Introduction

As a student of sociology and theology at the Catholic University of America in the sixties and seventies, I had the unique opportunity to be active in the Catholic Church's struggle to help the American government and people become aware of its stance toward war, arms, and peace. Many a day was spent demonstrating nonviolently on the Washington Mall, teaching, as a Franciscan and Christian, that war was not the solution to the resolution of conflict and that the ways of peace and justice were the only means of securing a lasting solution to the conflicts of South East Asia and other hot spots in the world.

I remember a professor of sociology who would talk about the conflict of cultural mind-sets that existed between the Far East and the industrialized West regarding the value of life, human dignity, and harmony. He himself was Chinese as well as being a social scientist and a Catholic Christian, and therefore could speak from both perspectives. On the level of sociological theory, I began to understand that the conflict of ideologies could not be resolved by force — there could be no winners at this level. During those years I also occasionally helped meet the planes returning with our wounded soldiers from Vietnam — men as young as eighteen years of age — and then visited them in the "Old Soldiers' Home" in Washington, D.C. These were very depressing experiences, especially when one realized that many of these young men were not only maimed for life physically but were scarred emotionally and psychologically as well.

Commitment to Peace

These recollections serve the purpose of situating the issues of peace in our modern-day world in a concrete fashion — one that touches human lives and this universe in which we live. The Catholic Church's commitment to peace is, after all, a concrete one, based on the Incarnational principle of Christ's peace *(pax Christi)* becoming real in the world when Christians called to follow the spirit of the Beatitudes do so by embodying it in their relationships with people and with the world.

Service to the gospel is rooted in the complexity of the vocation of the Church in the world. The elements of this vocation might be identified as announcing the Good News, bearing witness to the ongoing trial between the Spirit of Jesus and the spirit of the world, and being agents of reconciliation by continually reconstructing that which Babel continually destroys and by living in the communion received from God by grace. In this way, Christians witness to the kingdom of God, a reign of *shalom* or peace, and serve the gospel in a concrete fashion.

This brings us to my first subject: *the anthropology of peace.* From a Catholic perspective, we are bound to the revelation that God makes to his people throughout history and especially in the phase of their formation as a people. In the context of spiritual anthropology it is necessary for us to consider the reality that peace is a condition established by God at the very beginning of creation. In God's creation, a state of *shalom,* peace, harmony and integrity reigned between the creator and the creation. This state existed between all of God's creatures and especially among humans as the apex of God's creative activity; they were made in his image and likeness and hence were an icon of peace. After the fall, however, they lost the natural capacity to live in peace and harmony as they were created to do.

Spiritual traditions of both the East and the West have elaborated on this situation of unification or pacification through the development of concepts in their theological systems of thought.[1] The understanding

1. Concepts such as *quies* in Western theology gave rise to movements like

of the *eschaton* is a traditional way of understanding how the reign of God breaks into our world, hence anticipating that new world where the peaceful kingdom of God will be the only reality. At this point, the Church and its unity enter into the discussion. Catholics believe that the Church of Christ has received the mission of being present in history as a reconciling community. The communion that is in the body of Christ is a foretaste of the eschatological kingdom of peace. The force of the Church's task is striking: she exists as the only community that believes it possible to live in a way faithful to the spirit of the Beatitudes in the world. Therefore, the Church must desire to incarnate concretely that which she announces, that which she celebrates liturgically, and that which she confers sacramentally.

Moreover, Catholics are also members of the *saeculum* where they live a day-to-day existence. It is in this sphere that they become artisans of peace outside the boundaries of the Church. They live as citizens of the world, with diverse responsibilities and influences, and have the task of giving an evangelical face to the other communities of which they are a part. In this way the mission of the Church is expanded to ecclesiastical and political responsibilities. It is this reality which the Second Vatican Council made clear in its Pastoral Constitution on the Church in the Modern World, *Gaudium et spes*. Regarding the purpose of the Church and its role in the world we read that "the Church has but one sole purpose — that the kingdom of God may come and the salvation of the human race may be accomplished" and this because the Church is "the universal sacrament of salvation at once manifesting and actualizing the mystery of God's love for humanity."[2]

Gaudium et spes must be seen within the long line of social teachings that the Catholic Church has made, especially in these past two centuries, and in the context of the interventions which have made concrete

---

"quietism," which refers to "any contemplative spirituality that proscribes human effort, particularly active ascetical practice, in favor of complete passivity and abandonment to God." (See K. R. Barron, "Quietism," in M. Downey, ed., *The Dictionary of Catholic Spirituality* [Collegeville: Liturgical Press, 1993], p. 803). *Hesukhia* in Eastern theology gave rise to "hesychasm." This term can refer to a "hermit as opposed to a cenobitic monk but is normally used to designate one who uses the Jesus Prayer and the physical technique connected with it." (See R. R. Zawilla, "Hesychasm," in M. Downey, ed., *The Dictionary*, pp. 471-73.)

2. *Gaudium et spes* 45.

her teachings. The entire first section of this document seeks to situate the Church's social mission in the person and the gospel of Jesus Christ. It is important to see how the evolution that took place during the Council finds its maturity in this pastoral constitution, one of the Council's last documents. Such themes as human dignity and religious freedom find a rightful place in the articulation of the Church's understanding of its role in society. Even if today there is a tendency to return to a methodology of "natural law," the methodology of *Gaudium et spes* marks a shift away from this tradition[3] by using historical models which include the employment of the tools of the human and social sciences. Its thoroughly biblical and Christological orientation is another striking dimension of its teaching. Finally, these changes in the way the Church conceived of her engagement in the world opened new horizons for the involvement of the laity as members of the Church in its mission to the world. In addition to recognizing that pastors are not always so "expert as to have a ready answer to every problem . . . that arises,"[4] *Gaudium et spes* encourages the laity to acquire a knowledge of the sacred sciences as well as "incorporat[e] the findings of new sciences and teachings and the understanding of the most recent discoveries with Christian morality and thought. . . ."[5] In this way the Council requalified the laity as producers of intellectual and faith capital. All of this is important for understanding how the Catholic Church renders more immediate its intervention in the modern world, regarding not only peace issues but all issues which touch upon the Church's role in society.

The Council document set the tenor for what would eventually develop into a groundswell of Catholic pacifism in the 70s and lead to the American bishops' pastoral letter *The Challenge of Peace*. Chapter five of the pastoral constitution is entitled "Fostering of peace and establishment of a community of nations." It builds on the earlier concepts of human dignity, the value of human labor, economic principles, and free political involvement in the life of one's community. It is possible to see how the bishops intended to indicate what steps Catholic Christians need to take to avoid war, to establish a community of cooperation among nations,

---

3. Natural law was the hallmark of papal teaching especially in the thought of the modern popes (Leo XIII, Pius XI, Pius XII, John XXIII, and John Paul II).

4. *Gaudium et spes* 43.

5. *Gaudium et spes* 62.

and to contribute positively to the development of peoples. In the background of the Council was the encyclical of John XXIII, *Pacem in terris*. For our purposes the positive teaching of the Council is important. Peace is not understood as the "absence of war" but the "effect of righteousness."[6] The righteousness referred to in the document is basically the right relationship and ordering between humans, the basis of which is to be found in the divine command of love. This love is divine because it is the love found between the members of the Trinity and hence that which is to be mirrored in the life of the Church.

The document calls for the condemnation of savage wars and conflict and for the Church to play a key role in finding solutions to these conflicts.[7] The bishops recognize that the principal victims in war-torn circumstances are the poor.[8] From the gospel mandate found in the Beatitudes it is clear that the Church has a responsibility to the poor above all. For this reason the Council decree ends with a plea for the establishment of norms of collaboration among nations to help alleviate situations which lead to armed conflict; these norms include aid to developing nations, the establishment of greater equality among peoples of the same nation, and protection of the rights and dignity of all peoples.[9] The role that Catholics and the Church play is fundamental and is to be based on evangelical principles, above all charity. This teaching will provide the basis for the involvement of all Catholics and local churches in movements of peace and justice and development.

Concrete commitment to peace can be seen by such Catholic movements as "Pax Christi International," the non-governmental organization of Franciscans International at the United Nations, and the international community of St. Egidio, which was founded in Italy by Professor Andrea Ricciardi and now exists in various countries.

Three bishops from the United States have been extremely active in the peace movement of the 70s, 80s, and 90s: Carroll Dozier, Thomas Gumbleton, and Walter Sullivan. All three of these individuals have had pain and suffering inflicted upon them because of their unwavering affirmation of the gospel values of the Beatitudes. The personal

6. *Gaudium et spes* 78.
7. *Gaudium et spes* 79-82.
8. *Gaudium et spes* 81.
9. *Gaudium et spes* 86-90.

experiences I recounted at the beginning of this essay illustrate how much Catholic conscientiousness has grown in the years since the end of the Second World War and the Second Vatican Council. For example, the movement of Pax Christi invites Catholics to join in the call to take an active role in securing "peace based on justice and love." This active role includes prayer for peace, peace education, the seeking of nonviolent alternatives to war, development of justice in the world order, and especially respect of the primacy of conscience and the dignity of the human person.[10]

It might be said that movements like Pax Christi and the Community of St. Egidio are precisely that, only movements within the Catholic Church, and one must therefore ask what the Catholic Church's position on the issue of peace is. In addition to the stance taken by the Second Vatican Council and contemporary popes, a number of episcopal conferences have expressed their views on the issue of peace by means of pastoral letters. While growing out of the position taken by the Council and papal and curial statements, these pastoral letters are a manifestation of how local and regional churches have sought to ground concretely the Catholic Church's teaching on such issues as arms, disarmament, war, deterrence, pacifism, and the struggle for liberation and justice. While it is not possible to analyze these statements here, it is worth citing some examples of how different episcopal conferences have made clear the position and commitment of the Catholic Church on these issues.[11]

Letters or statements have been issued by the French, German, and American episcopal conferences.[12] In all three of these documents, peace is seen as first and foremost a gift from God and the result of the search for justice. All three ground their teachings squarely in the Scriptures and

10. For more details on the programs and rationale of Pax Christi, see M. Jegen, *Pax Christi International. What it is, What it does.* (Antwerp: Pax Christi International, 1989).

11. Further information about the positions of these Episcopal conferences' pastoral letters can be found in R. G. Musto, *The Catholic Peace Tradition* (Maryknoll: Orbis, 1986).

12. Full texts of these letters have been published in the following: French Episcopal conference, J. V. Schall, ed., *Winning the Peace. Joint Pastoral Letter of the French Bishops* (San Francisco: Ignatius Press, 1984); Schall, ed., *Out of Justice, Peace. Joint Pastoral Letter of the West German Bishops* (San Francisco: Ignatius Press, 1984); and National Conference of Catholic Bishops, *The Challenge of Peace: God's Promise and Our Response* (Washington, D.C.: United States Catholic Conference, 1983).

the Catholic peace tradition. One is also struck by the attention given to nonviolence and to the growing Catholic attitude of pacifism; these tendencies were already evident in John XXIII's *Pacem in terris* and taken up in *Gaudium et spes*.[13]

The American bishops urge the Church in their letter to be actively involved in finding nonviolent solutions to situations of tension and conflict.[14] One cannot but think of the delicate position that the Catholic Church in the United States found itself in during the long conflict in Vietnam. It was that experience, of course, which brought to maturity this peace-oriented position among American Catholics and their leaders. In light of recent conflict situations in the Balkans and other parts of the world (East Timor, Sudan, and Ethiopia, for example), the positions taken not only by European and North American episcopal conferences but also by other national and regional conferences of bishops illustrate the Catholic commitment to the search for peace — peace that is built on the gospel principles of justice, integrity, conscience, and human dignity.

Words and theory, however, need to be translated into practice. Maybe we can more clearly understand the Catholic Church's commitment to peace at this level if we note its incarnation in the establishment of "Justice and Peace Commissions," which grew out of the call for the Church to address the international components of development, justice, and peace.[15] Because of this call, Paul VI created in 1976, on the level of the Vatican, the "Pontifical Commission Iustitia et Pax." Similarly, bishops' conferences and local diocesan churches began to establish commissions that dealt with issues surrounding the question of peace and justice. Eventually, a similar concept penetrated the parochial structure, so that by the mid-1990s it was not uncommon to find parishes having justice and peace commissions that took active roles not only within the parish but also in the local and state communities. The wonderful dimension of this is that so many of the laity are now engaged in these commissions and are in this way fulfilling the desire of the Council for active involvement of the laity in the life of the Church. In addition, these commissions demonstrate that all members of the Church have a responsibility to carry forward the evangelical mission of the Church; there should be collabora-

13. *Gaudium et spes* 78.
14. *The Challenge of Peace*, pp. 221-30.
15. See *Gaudium et spes* 90.

tion between the various vocations (priests, religious, and lay) within the life of the Church.[16]

John Paul II has consistently and constantly urged all people of good will to be artisans of peace, justice, and the respect for human rights and the dignity of the human person. It is not possible to explore the richness of his myriad interventions on behalf of world, local, and regional peace; one could note the World Peace Day messages pronounced each January first, the Assisi meeting in favor of peace, the world day of prayer for peace in Sarajevo, and the list could go on. In his encyclical *Ut unum sint,* he places the search for peace squarely in the search for unity among Christians:

> In this context, how can I fail to mention the ecumenical interest in peace, expressed in prayer and action by ever greater numbers of Christians and with a steadily growing theological inspiration? It could not be otherwise. Do we not believe in Jesus Christ, the Prince of Peace? Christians are becoming ever more united in their rejection of violence, every kind of violence, from wars to social injustice.
>
> We are called to make ever greater efforts, so that it may be ever more apparent that religious considerations are not the real cause of current conflicts, even though, unfortunately, there is still a risk of religion being exploited for political and polemical purpose.
>
> In 1986, at Assisi, during the *World Day of Prayer for Peace,* Christians of the various Churches and Ecclesial Communities prayed with one voice to the Lord of history for peace in the world. That same day, in a different but parallel way, Jews and representatives of non-Christian religions also prayed for peace in a harmonious expression of feelings which struck a resonant chord deep in the human spirit.
>
> Nor do I wish to overlook the *Day of Prayer for Peace in Europe, especially in the Balkans,* which took me back to the town of Saint Francis as a pilgrim on 9-10 January 1993, and the *Mass for Peace in the Balkans and especially in Bosnia-Hercegovina,* which I celebrated on 23 January 1994 in Saint Peter's Basilica during the *Week of Prayer for Christian Unity.*

16. Various models of these commissions exist with varying degrees of structure, activity, and independence from authority; see the description given in G. Powers, "Peace and Justice Commissions," in *The New Dictionary of Catholic Social Thought,* ed. J. A. Dwyer (Collegeville: The Liturgical Press, 1994), p. 723.

When we survey the world joy fills our hearts. For we note that Christians feel ever more challenged by the issue of peace. They see it as intimately connected with the proclamation of the Gospel and with the coming of God's Kingdom.[17]

Commitment to Unity

This long "peace paragraph" of John Paul II is an appropriate way to end a section on the Catholic Church's "commitment to peace" because it situates the search for peace in the context of the search for unity and the need for dialogue. Elsewhere, I have written that the search for Christian unity must be punctuated by concrete facts demonstrating that it is indeed the unity of the Church of Christ we are seeking.[18] We likewise receive unity as a gift just as peace is essentially a gift coming from God. Both have their origin in God and both will lead back to God as the source of all gifts.

The Catholic Church's commitment to ecumenism is laid out clearly in the encyclical letter of John Paul II, *Ut unum sint*, cited above. It is perhaps the most personal of John Paul II's many encyclical letters illustrating the passion and desire for the unity of the Church that the Bishop of Rome holds dear to his heart. Others have commented on this letter at length[19] and space does not allow me to do so here. There are some salient points that need to be emphasized, however, in regard to the commitment to unity.

17. John Paul II, *That They May Be One — Ut unum sint. On Commitment to Ecumenism* (Washington, D.C.: United States Catholic Conference, 1995) no. 76.

18. J. F. Puglisi, "On the Path to Christian Unity: Will Words Alone Suffice?" *Bulletin — Centro Pro Unione* 50 (1997): 18-23.

19. For example, see R. Hütter, "Ökumene und Einheit der Christen-abstrakte Wiedervereinigung oder gelebte Einmütigkeit?" *Kerygma und Dogma* 44, no. 3 (1998): 193-206; E. F. Fortino, "L'ecumenismo dal decreto Unitatis redintegratio all'enciclica Ut unum sint," in *Il Concilio Vaticano II carisma e profezia*, ed. T. Stenico (Vatican City: Libreria Editrice Vaticana, 1997), pp. 143-66; H. Chadwick, "Papstamt und Einheit der Christen aus anglikanischer Perspektive," *Kerygma und Dogma* 43, no. 4 (1997): 272-78; Church of England, House of Bishops, *May They All Be One: A Response of the House of Bishops of the Church of England to Ut unum sint*, GS Misc, 495 (London: Church House, 1997); E. J. Yarnold, "Mutual Enrichment: John Paul II's Ecumenical Philosophy," *One in Christ* 32, no. 3 (1996): 212-21.

Since the end of the Second Vatican Council, the Catholic Church has embarked on an extensive program of dialogue with a variety of churches and ecclesial communities. This has been carried out both on the international level by the then Secretariat, now Pontifical Council for Promoting Christian Unity, and on the local or regional level by local churches or national bishops' conferences. The results are staggering when one looks at the quantity and quality of the printed and agreed-upon statements.[20] To this growing number of dialogues was added a new one in 1998 with the "peace church tradition"; this Mennonite-Catholic Dialogue is called "Towards a Healing of Memories."[21] After the first session several themes arose that will need further study. These include the questions of tradition, continuity/discontinuity, mediation of the Church, the Trinity, structures of authority, sacramentality and sacraments, the meaning of baptism, sanctification, faith and works, and the concern for peace.

While many of the dialogues continue to go forward, there is a growing concern among some that the process is showing itself to be an exercise in futility. Where will this path lead and how much longer will the dialogue process need to continue? Jan Cardinal Willebrands has given his reasons for remaining a man of hope in spite of the voices of skepticism being raised. The Cardinal noted how he had lived through

20. To date there are over 25 official dialogues alone on the international level. The most complete collection of the agreed statements is found in the four-volume Italian edition of the *Enchiridion Oecumenicum* published by Dehoniane in Bologna (1986 and following). Volumes 1 and 3 contain the international dialogues while volumes 2 and 4 print the texts of the agreed statements of the local/regional/national official dialogues. See S. J. Voicu and G. Cereti, eds., *Enchiridion Oecumenicum. Documenti del dialogo teologico interconfessionale. 1: Dialoghi internazionali 1931-1984* (Bologna: EDB, 1986), and G. Cereti and J. F. Puglisi, eds., *Enchiridion Oecumenicum. Documenti del dialogo teologico interconfessionale. 3: Dialoghi internazionali 1985-1994* (Bologna: EDB, 1995). Another volume is foreseen for the year 2000. There are partial editions published in German (2 volumes), Spanish (2 volumes), and French (1 volume). Currently the English edition is found in H. Meyer and L. Vischer, eds., *Growth in Agreement: Reports and Agreed Statements of Ecumenical Conversations on a World Level,* Faith and Order Paper 108/Ecumenical Documents 2 (New York/Geneva: Paulist/WCC, 1984).

21. The first session of this five-year dialogue took place at the Mennonite World Conference in Strasbourg, France, from 14-18 October 1998. The author is a member of the Catholic delegation and made the presentation on Catholic Identity. The second session of the dialogue (October 1999) took up the theme "Toward a Common Understanding of the Church."

most of the "modern ecumenical movement" in which the Catholic Church moved from a position which condemned all things ecumenical to one of full and active participation in the ecumenical movement. In such a short time, therefore, so much has been accomplished. His message of hope to young people encouraged patience but also advocated continual prayer and study. Prayer is necessary because in it our heart is transformed by the power of the Spirit of God, allowing us to see reality with eyes of faith and in the context of a deep spirituality that is open to the Spirit. Study, in turn, allows us to understand with our minds that which the Spirit has opened to our hearts in prayer. The two are necessary for us to continually remember that unity is *not* something that will come as the result of human invention; it is a gift of God to be received.[22]

This stance proposed by the Cardinal should not be seen as an attempt to avoid dealing with the real and difficult obstacles and problems that we will encounter on the path toward Christian unity but, rather, as a challenge for us to courageously meet these obstacles with the energy and spirit of peace and reconciliation. The commitment of the Catholic Church to unity is one willing to take time to clarify and deal with these issues in a frank and open way. Examples of this have been the dialogues held with the Oriental Orthodox and other Orthodox churches. The former have produced joint declarations clarifying Christological positions, thereby overcoming many misunderstandings that had arisen in the past about the person of Christ and our common, apostolic faith in him. Difficulties that were born at the times of early ecumenical councils have been overcome with a new and fresh expression of our common faith in the Lord.[23] Concerning the question of the Oriental churches united to Rome, there has been much tension and misunderstanding regarding their position and, especially in former Communist territories, many dis-

22. These unpublished reflections entitled "From Where Have We Come — The Ecumenical Pilgrimage: Why I Am a Man of Hope" were given by Jan Cardinal Willebrands at the annual celebration of the Week of Prayer for Christian Unity at the Centro Pro Unione in Rome, on 20 January 1994.

23. See for example the joint Christological declarations between the Catholic Church and the Coptic Orthodox Church (*Information Service* no. 76 [1991/I], pp. 13 and 30-32); the Catholic Church and the Syrian Orthodox Church (*Acta apostolicae sedis* 85, 3 [1993]: 238-41); the Catholic Church and the Malankara Orthodox Syrian Church (*Information Service* no. 73 [1990/II], p. 39); and the Catholic Church and the Assyrian Church of the East (*Information Service* no. 88 [1995/I], pp. 2-3).

putes over church property have arisen. In recent times, clarification has brought about a deeper and better relationship between Orthodox and Byzantine Catholic churches in these countries and even deeper collaboration with Rome, as was expressed by Cardinal Keeler who led the Roman delegation to the Phanar for the Feast of St. Andrew at the end of November in 1998.[24]

In spite of the results of the theological dialogues that show the sincere commitment of the Catholic Church to the ecumenical movement, we need to move on to yet another level, a more profound one that will touch even more radically the lives of our churches. There now needs to be a reception of the dialogue results, so that they can be integrated into the daily lives of our churches — all of our churches. Far too often we do not correctly understand what this means. The term "reception" is a technical term which involves a critical evaluation in light of the apostolic tradition. As the word itself indicates, it involves a process of doing something again. The goal of the search for Christian unity is that of "communion," which does not mean the amalgamation of chunks of ecclesial material from different traditions but rather, as Jean Tillard has said, "an acceptance of conversion[.] *[T]ogether* we are converted to that which *together* we have rediscovered or reaffirmed concerning the apostolic faith and the demands of the Gospel."[25] He continues:

> when ecclesial groups are presented with an agreement formulated by commissions of experts they are not asked to consider as their first question, "can it be seen as complying with our tradition?"; but rather, "is it in harmony with the authentic, i.e., apostolic, tradition?"
>
> When understood in this perspective, it is clear that ecumenical "reception" is wholly dependent upon a re-reading (i.e., a studying afresh), on a re-evaluating and a re-confessing of the apostolic faith itself, the sole norm of an ecclesial communion of faith.[26]

It is at this level that we *together* need to transform our very existence. Words are not enough if they do not bring action with them; that which

---

24. See E. F. Fortino, "Theological Dialogue Must Continue," *L'Osservatore romano,* English edition, no. 11 (17 March 1999): 6.

25. J. M. R. Tillard, "'Reception: A Time to Beware of False Steps," *Ecumenical Trends* 14, no. 10 (1985): 145.

26. Tillard, "Reception," p. 145.

we speak must become enfleshed in the structures of our churches and ecclesial communions. In other words, reception of the results of the ecumenical dialogues in each of our traditions necessarily demands conversion. We should be careful here since we are not talking about converting the other side to our way of seeing things or doing things; we are talking about something that involves both partners. What must prevail is a collective conversion to the apostolic faith itself. This faith is rooted in the very Word of God and hence it is a conversion to that Word spoken once but heard always afresh and new in each generation. It is this Word that must govern our decisions, our mutual understanding of the apostolic faith, and how we seek to make that faith come alive in our ecclesial structures. We need to ask ourselves if these agreed statements represent an authentic reception in the sense that we have been describing above, or if they are merely words that have been multiplied and stockpiled without becoming words of authentic, communal conversion. If they do not lead to a change of heart (which in turn leads to a change in our way of being Christian for the world) then we have every right to consider them words that betray our very existence or, at least, what we say we are and are trying to achieve on this path toward Christian unity.

Again Jean Tillard warns us of these temptations that we can fall into very easily. The first is the "temptation to be content with a union based on what is little more than a triviality held in common . . . and the second . . . is that of the total absorption of the frailest group by the most forceful, without the latter having even acknowledged the prerequisite of personal involvement."[27] What is at the heart of the quest for Christian unity is profound conversion; and conversion is not a matter of words alone!

I believe this is why the Catholic Church taught in its decree on ecumenism that the "concern for restoring unity pertains to the whole Church, faithful and clergy alike. It extends to everyone, according to the potential of each"[28] and that "the Bishops, individually for their own dioceses, and collegially for the whole Church, are, under the authority of the Holy See, responsible for ecumenical policy and practice."[29] One last

27. Tillard, "Reception," p. 146.
28. *Unitatis Redintegratio* 5.
29. *Directory for the Application of Principles and Norms on Ecumenism*, published by the Pontifical Council for Promoting Christian Unity with the express approval of Pope John Paul II, 25 March 1993 (Vatican City: Vatican Press), no. 4.

example of how the Bishop of Rome understands the Catholic Church's commitment to ecumenism is found in the encyclical letter already cited where we read:

> Thus, it is absolutely clear that ecumenism, the movement promoting Christian Unity, is not just some sort of appendix which is added to the Church's traditional activity. Rather, ecumenism is an organic part of her life and work, and consequently must pervade all that she is and does; it must be like the fruit borne by a flourishing tree which grows to its full stature.[30]

Commitment to Dialogue

Very briefly I would like to describe my reasons for believing that a commitment to dialogue is very much a part of the Catholic Church's agenda — both its agenda for ecumenism and its agenda for the search for healing and reconciliation. The French philosopher Paul Ricoeur, though not a Catholic, has an approach toward this topic very similar to the one taken by John Paul II on some of his journeys throughout the world; it is called the approach of the healing of memories.

At the heart of the gospel is the call for forgiveness. Starting from this perspective, Ricoeur understands the model of pardon as a new way of revisiting the past and, through it, also the narrative identity of each person. Seeing these personal histories, stories, and pasts being intertwined is a way of seeing that they must be told mutually. This is where one can see the real fruit of the exchange or healing of memories taking place. Ricoeur says that "pardon is likewise a specific form of this mutual revision from which deliverance of promises not kept in the past is a very precious effect."[31] It is not a question of cancelling the past but, rather, of going beyond those things which perpetuate a state of alienation. In this sense, then, we can talk about changing our common future.

Paul Ricoeur again offers a fresh way of looking at the situation when he writes:

---

30. *Ut unum sint* 20.

31. P. Ricoeur, "Quel éthos nouveau pour l'Europe?" in *Imaginer l'Europe. Le marché intérieur européen tache culturelle et économique,* ed. P. Koslowski, "Passages" (Paris: Cerf, 1992), p. 113.

the exchange of memories required by our second model demands, according to this new model [of pardon], the exchange of the memory of suffering inflicted and experienced. Now this exchange requires more than imagination and sympathy that I have evoked above. This more than anything else has something to do with pardon, to the degree that pardon consists in *"releasing* the debt." . . .

He continues by affirming that

the "poetic" power (of pardon) [that refers both to the 'creativity on the level of the dynamic of action, and to song and hymn on the level of verbal expression'] consists in the breaking of the law of the irreversibility of time, changing, if not the past (referring to the collection of those things which happened) at least its meaning for men and women of the present. It does this by removing the weight of the guilt which paralyzes the relationship of men [and women] who act out and live their own story. It does not *abolish* the debt since we are and remain the inheritors of the past but removes the suffering of the debt."[32]

This process can only be accomplished by a process of dialogue with other Christians and, indeed, with all other human beings. Dialogue founded in a love for truth and deep Christian charity and humility, then, is the path to which the Catholic Church is committed.[33]

Conclusion

The future of ecumenism, in the perspective that I have attempted to present here, really will not depend only on our commitment to the discussion of ideas, concepts, and formulations of doctrinal statements, but also on a deep-rooted desire to obediently respond to Christ's prayer that all of his followers be one for the sake of the gospel and its spread. Being obedient to this wish of Christ means that each of us needs to be converted ever anew to Christ's mind and spirit in order that we might seek, as he did, to do God's will. This will be costly since it is likely that we will need to change the way we do things and the way we live in the world to-

32. Ricoeur, "Quel éthos nouveau pour l'Europe?" p. 113ff.
33. *Ut unum sint* 36.

day, but it is important; it is, in fact, what is what Jean Tillard considers the essential element in the Catholic Church's reception of the dialogue process.[34] At the beginning of this new millennium the churches have a unique opportunity to seize a *kairos* moment, a graced time — a time to renew their individual commitments to receive the gifts of peace and unity from God on God's terms and not on their own. At stake is the very mission of the Church of God to be of service to the world and to bring the light of the gospel to all of God's creation. I have attempted to present how the Catholic Church has committed herself, in the words of John Paul II, *irrevocably* to this task.[35] It is now up to the Catholic faithful to take up this challenge and begin to realize it in the daily living out of its mission.

34. Tillard, "Reception."
35. *Ut unum sint* 4 and 20.

The Peace Testimony of the
Religious Society of Friends

THOMAS D. PAXSON JR.

The Religious Society of Friends (Quakers) has historically opposed war and participation in war, calling on people to live in Christ's peace. Looking to the Spirit acting within the individual and within the community of the faithful, Friends have generally distrusted and avoided systematic theology.[1] The argument that will be developed in this paper rests, significantly, on an appeal to experience.[2]

History

The principal emphasis in early Quakerism was not so much on recovering the early church in an institutional sense as on recovering the life in Christ as lived by the first Christians. Early Friends believed that through

1. Notwithstanding this generalization, several people contributed significantly to the theological framework of Quaker religious thought. These would include George Fox, Robert Barclay, William Penn, Issac Penington, Margaret Fell, George Keith (who eventually left Quakerism for the Church of England), Samuel Fisher, and Lilias Skene.

2. Those who are interested in seeing a Quaker's justification of the centrality of peace witness to the apostolic faith by appeal to the "New Testament" or "Christian Bible" should read Paul N. Anderson's "Jesus and Peace," in *The Church's Peace Witness*, ed. Marlin E. Miller and Barbara Nelson Gingerich (Grand Rapids: Eerdmans, 1994), pp. 104-30.

experiencing the immediate presence of Christ, human beings could attend directly to the holy Master and harken without intermediary to the Teacher. This message produced in many people a tremendous sense of liberation from both (as they saw it) the dry, empty forms of traditional ritual and ceremony and the social and ecclesiastical hierarchies which in their eyes had been discredited. These "masterless" seekers, whose spiritual needs were not being addressed adequately by the established churches or by radical Puritan groups like the Ranters, were led by George Fox and others to find guidance from Christ's inward teaching. They were eager to live in the Light of Christ and to share the good news that Christ was available to all.

Unlike the Ranters, who denied sin on the grounds that God created all, Friends are all too aware of the evil we harbor within us; we all know this evil from our own experiences, not only from suffering evil but also from struggling with temptations in the course of our own spiritual journeys. For Quakers, sin was and is a matter of concrete experience. No eighteenth-century Enlightenment optimism regarding human reason is found in Fox, who, though arguably the most creative and perceptive of early Quaker theologians, distrusted abstract theory and "airy notions." He was especially suspicious of importing philosophical categories and frameworks into theological reflection. After much suffering as a result of sin and the power of evil, Fox came to recognize in his own experience that faithful obedience to the inward promptings of Christ did save him from the sin which part of his nature desired.[3] As a result, he was able to tell those who in 1651 sought to enlist him in Cromwell's New Model Army[4] that he "lived in the virtue of that life and power that took away the occasion of all wars."[5] This belief was an unintended consequence of

3. John Nickalls, ed., *The Journal of George Fox* (Cambridge: Cambridge University Press, 1952), pp. 14-16, 21.

4. In 1642 civil war erupted in England between the forces of King Charles I and the forces of the parliament. Oliver Cromwell, an officer in the parliament's Puritan army, persuaded the parliament to reorganize the army on the basis of performance rather than on social class. This was the "New Model Army," and it won the war. Charles I was executed 30 January 1649. In 1653 Oliver Cromwell named himself Lord Protector of the Puritan republic.

5. Nickalls, *Journal of George Fox,* p. 65. To "live in the virtue of that life and power . . ." is a seventeenth-century English expression which means to live under the sway of that life and power.

his faithfulness, and at that time and for a number of years thereafter he did not preach nonresistance or opposition to war but simply lived out these ideals in his own life.

In the 1650s there were many leaders of the movement which became the Religious Society of Friends: Edward Burrough, Edward Byllinge, Margaret Fell, Mary Fisher, Samuel Fisher, George Fox, Elizabeth Hooton, Francis Howgill, John Lilburne, James Nayler, and Isaac Penington, to mention just a few. Some of these had been active in the Good Old Cause,[6] which brought down the monarchy in the preceding decade. These leaders looked to the New Model Army to bring justice, if not the kingdom of God, to England. Early Friends sought with some success to "convince"[7] soldiers in the army, and newly convinced soldier-Friends often failed to see any problem with remaining soldiers. Indeed, in the mid-1650s Quakers were purged against their will from many military units on the grounds that they undermined military discipline by such actions as refusing to doff their hats to "superiors" and rejecting the use of honorific titles. During this period there is no evidence that either Fox or Nayler, perhaps the most influential of the early "publishers of Truth," tried to talk Quaker soldiers into quitting the military.[8]

From the beginning of the eighteenth century on, Friends tended to

6. The "Good Old Cause" refers to the English revolution and republican government from 1640-1660, an important aspect of which was the effort to "level" English society by reducing, if not eradicating, class privilege.

7. Quakers sought to "convince" others of the truth of their message. As Dean Freiday explains, "In a sense, it was a matter of being convinced, not only intellectually but also in the heart and by the power of the Spirit, of the truth of Christianity," *Barclay's Apology in Modern English* (Hemlock Press, 1967), p. 254, fn. 9. This was regarded as distinct from full conversion or turning one's life to God.

8. See Peter Brock, "Quaker Attitudes to War before the Peace Testimony" (chap. 2), in *The Quaker Peace Testimony 1660-1914* (York, England: William Sessions Ltd., 1990), pp. 9-23. In *The Quakers in Peace and War* (New York: George H. Doran Co., 1923), however, Margaret Hirst notes that in response to an inquiry of 26 January 1660 George Fox forbade Friends from enlisting in a militia or accepting appointment as an officer, as "it was contrary to our principles, for our weapons are spiritual and not carnal" (p. 56) [spelling modernized]. (The date "26 January 1660" reflects today's convention whereby the calendar year begins January 1, rather than the convention of that time whereby the year began March 25. By the reckoning of that age, the date in question was 26 January 1659. Throughout this essay, dates falling within the interval January 1 through March 24 will be given in the new style, that is, the year will be assumed to have begun on January 1.)

assume that Quaker opposition to participation in war was characteristic of the Society from its very inception, but this belief has been challenged by modern historians. One view, that of the British historians Alan Cole, Christopher Hill, and Barry Reay, is that the Peace Testimony[9] did not exist before 1661, though they concede that there were a few pacifists among Friends, such as John Lilburne and the sailor Thomas Lurting.[10] The picture these historians give is that opposition to war or participation in it was, in the 1650s, a matter of individual conscience rather than of corporate commitment. This picture is rooted in the inchoate nature of the movement before the restoration, the absence of formal pronouncements on the topic by the community of Friends, the millennial hopes and apocalyptic utterances of many Friends (including George Fox), and the focus on England. This view is rejected, however, by Hugh Barbour and others, who see the roots of pacifism emerging earlier. These scholars complain that "these historians' Marxist outlook assumes that a revolution is a class struggle and that radicals turn nonviolent only in despair."[11] The Marxists, it is argued, do not give sufficient weight to the religious concerns and experience of the early Quakers. Peter Brock, a non-Quaker historian, is surely right in seeing "the peace testimony slowly emerging during Quakerism's turbulent first decade."[12]

If we look to the colonies in North America we find that already in the latter half of the 1650s Friends (who first arrived in 1656) were caus-

9. Wilmer Cooper explains what a Testimony is, as the term is used by Friends, in this way: "From the beginning Friends believed that they could have direct and immediate communication with God which would enable them to discern right ethical choices. But they soon experienced certain common leadings of the Spirit which became formalized into testimonies. These testimonies served as common principles and standards of behavior and action." See *The Testimony of Integrity in the Religious Society of Friends* (Pendle Hill Pamphlet #296, 1991), p. 7. These testimonies are printed in the books of discipline or faith and practice published by yearly meetings. The point the British historians are making is that at least no formal statement representing Friends corporately which condemned participation in war existed before 1661.

10. Lurting's conscience was aroused against war during a naval attack on Barcelona in 1757, the year in which Lilburne died. See Brock, "Quaker Attitudes to War," p. 19; and Hirst, *The Quakers in Peace and War,* pp. 52, 53.

11. Hugh Barbour, Christopher Densmore, Arthur Mekeel, and Arthur Worrall, "Wars, Revolutions, and the Peace Testimony," in *Quaker Crosscurrents: Three Hundred Years of Friends in the New York Yearly Meetings* (Syracuse, N.Y.: Syracuse University Press, 1995), p. 48.

12. Brock, "Quaker Attitudes to War," p. 24.

ing consternation by refusing to participate in militias. Brock quotes a letter from the Rhode Island General Assembly to Massachusetts (which had opposed Rhode Island's accepting Quakers) stating that if the Quakers refused "to subject themselves to all duties aforesaid, as training, watching, and other engagements," as the Bay Colony had apparently warned, it would have to ask London for instructions.[13] Until the Crown intervened, Massachusetts hanged the unwelcome Quakers who persisted in bringing their message to the colony. Such a warning would have made no sense unless Quakers already had some reputation for refusing to engage in such activities. The same year as the Rhode Island letter, 1658, officials in Maryland had Quakers whipped or chained "for not bearing arms in the militia, if called upon to do so."[14]

Back in England, on January 6 of 1661, a rebellion was staged against the newly restored monarchy. To indicate that Quakers had no part in this rebellion, a Declaration was written by George Fox and Richard Hubberthorne, "in behalf of the whole body of the Elect People of God who are called Quakers," eschewing violence and any attempt to overthrow the monarchy. It was signed by the authors and ten other prominent Friends and delivered to the king on January 21. This is widely regarded as the initial statement of the Peace Testimony. In the following decades, Friends would be challenged to discern what faithful living required in relation to privateering, obeying calls to watch or to muster, conscription, war taxes, mixed taxes, the manufacture of armaments, and transportation of soldiers and military supplies, among other things.[15]

In 1681, William Penn received a grant to be proprietor of Pennsylvania. He set out to establish a colony that would be governed in a manner consistent with the principles of Friends. It was to have no colonial

13. Brock, "Quaker Attitudes to War," p. 49.

14. Brock, "Quaker Attitudes to War," p. 51.

15. In England's efforts to achieve control of the seas, she exercised benign neglect, if not outright encouragement, of private efforts to seize ships under "enemy flags." This was called "privateering," and the goods stolen were called "prize goods." Friends sought to discipline themselves against both privateering and the purchase of prize goods.

"Calls to watch" refers to the practice of assigning men the responsibility to take a turn in the guarding of the community, usually at night.

"Mixed taxes" were taxes which produced revenue, part of which would be used for military expenditures and part for other purposes.

army or militia; the king was to be responsible for protecting Pennsylvania from privateers and European powers, and Penn adopted a policy of friendly relations with the Delaware, the Native American tribe that lived in southeast Pennsylvania. Nonetheless, in accepting the Charter, Penn accepted the title Captain-General. Until Quakers lost control of the Assembly in 1755, some thirty-seven years after Penn's death, the compromise regarding provincial security was that taxes would be paid for the king's (or queen's) use (which all understood would be used for the royal army), but that there would be no formal provincial army, no conscription, and no taxes explicitly for war.

Peter Brock argues, in effect, that Quaker pacifism reached its maturity as a result of the reformation activities of John Woolman and others in Philadelphia Yearly Meetings in the years leading up to the Revolutionary War. The reformers sought to persuade Quakers to withdraw from the Assembly and abandon the Quaker magistracy. They argued that having control of the Assembly had led to compromise of principle, since the Assembly was caught between the demands of the Crown, on the one hand, and of a populace increasingly hostile to Quaker policies, on the other. Under the pressures of the Revolutionary War, Friends were scrupulous in disciplining those whose practice failed to conform to the Peace Testimony as it had become more exactingly understood. Friends could not, among other things, join armies, supply others to serve in their stead, pay war taxes, or transport materials or soldiers for the army. Those who participated in war on either side were "disowned," formally separated from membership. This discipline seems to have held until the Civil War, during which, although Friends corporately held fast to the Peace Testimony, some meetings seem not to have disciplined members who fought. During the twentieth century, this latter pattern became the general practice; the Peace Testimony held corporately, but individuals who fought in the country's wars were not disciplined.

Theological Justifications in the Seventeenth Century

The Declaration of 1661 was written in haste to meet immediate political exigencies. Its principal argument was the one which Fox had used in turning down a position in the New Model Army in 1651, namely, that war proceeds from human lusts as James said (James 4:1-3), but that the meek and faithful are redeemed from these lusts by the Lord and, as a result, are brought "out of the occasion of war." In addition, the Declaration rejected all "outward wars and strife and fighting with outward weapons for any end or under any pretense whatsoever."[16] In more contemporary language, the argument is that the transformation wrought in the faithful by their encounter with and obedience to God would turn them from the desires which support war and lead them to reject war for any purpose. The authors anticipated the objection that the Spirit might just as well on another occasion move them to change their principle and lead them "to fight for the kingdom of Christ."[17] Their reply was that (1) "Christ's kingdom is not of this world" and thus cannot be gained by the weapons of this world, (2) "the spirit of Christ . . . is not changeable, so as once to command us from a thing as evil and again to move unto it," and (3) the faithful cannot desire the kingdoms of this world but rather desire that by God's power "the kingdoms of this world may become kingdoms of the Lord."[18] The Declaration continues: (4) "he that hath commanded us not to swear at all (Matt. [5:]34), hath also commanded us that we shall not kill (Matt. [5:]21), so that we can neither kill men, nor swear for nor against them."[19] These points echo the idea of the two kingdoms — the kingdom ruled by God, to whom the faithful owe absolute obedience, and the kingdom ruled by a mortal monarch, to whom the faithful owe only that obedience appropriate to "caesar." Since war requires obedience to "caesar" over against the claims of the Lordship of God, warfare for kingdoms of this world is idolatrous. The argument is schematic and not worked out in detail.

The classic defense of the Peace Testimony was given by the theologically trained Robert Barclay in his *An Apology for the True Christian Divinity (1675)*.[20] Whereas Fox had appealed principally to the doctrine of James and the transforming power of Christ operating within the meek and faithful disciple, Barclay gave more emphasis to the Sermon on the Mount (Matt. 5), and also cited Paul (Eph. 6:12, 2 Cor. 10:4), the proph-

16. The Declaration is reprinted in *The Journal of George Fox*, ed. John Nickalls, pp. 398-404. Quote on p. 399.

17. Declaration in *Journal*, ed. Nickalls, p. 399.

18. Declaration in *Journal*, ed. Nickalls, pp. 399, 400.

19. Declaration in *Journal*, ed. Nickalls, p. 401.

20. This book is available in the original seventeenth-century English or in a much more readable edition edited by Dean Freiday, *Barclay's Apology in Modern English*, 4th printing (Newberg, Ore.: Barclay Press, 1991), first printed in 1967.

ets, and early church fathers such as Justin Martyr, Tertullian, Origen, Cyprian of Carthage, and St. John Chrysostom. According to Barclay's argument, in support of which he marshaled many biblical texts, "the Spirit and doctrine of Christ" forbid resisting evil, fighting, and avenging oneself on others. In keeping with the Declaration, he argued that Christ brought a new dispensation such that those who receive it and live under it cannot engage in outward war. His interpretation of the Scriptures was defended by appeal to the authority of church fathers who also embraced nonresistance. Peace witness, Barclay argued in effect, is central to the apostolic faith both in obedience to the spirit of Christ's teaching in the Sermon on the Mount, which is echoed by Paul's counsel to the Romans (12:17-21), and in the call to bear the cross (Mark 8:34).

The Centrality of Peace Witness to the Apostolic Faith

The purpose of this volume is not to rehearse theologies of past centuries but to explore how contemporary developments may contribute to "a revision of judgments made centuries ago, a healing of divisions within the church, and the development of a basis for common Christian witness."[21] Toward this end, I offer a Friend's perspective on the centrality of peace witness to the apostolic faith. In the manner of Friends, I need to begin with experience, pilgrim experience.

Pilgrim Experience

A familiar and enduring dimension of Friends' unprogrammed meeting for worship is gathering together, in the presence of God, in silent searching. This searching is as multifaceted as prayer. It may include searching for surcease of sorrow, for spiritual sustenance, for guidance; it may include searching in wonder for the face of God; it may include opening oneself attentively to God's searching scrutiny. These common elements of pilgrim experience bring with them an awareness of, among other things, our foolishness, helplessness, and separation from God, and our inability to direct our own spiritual journey. Each of us knows by experi-

21. From the leaflet announcing the 1995 consultation.

ence that we come upon obstacles along the way. When finally, wondrously, "the way opens," as Friends say, permitting us to surmount or pass through an obstacle, we discover that others have gone before us. What may have appeared to us in the experience as a great and glorious revelation, we often see to be commonplace when put into words. We learn that what rose up as mountains for us has been traversed by some without difficulty, and we become aware of things that have not stopped us though they have caused great difficulty for others. We are conscious in all of this that it is none of our doing. We learn the futility of trying to control God; we learn humility — again, and again. It is our experience that God often speaks to our own condition through other people, through people flawed and mortal like ourselves.

As we travel along the pilgrim path we learn something of what it is to live in the Spirit, however partial and fleeting realization of that life may be. Friends have found that these words — uttered by James Nayler as he lay dying in 1660 after being tortured for blasphemy and later attacked by thieves — resonate with their experience:

> There is a spirit which I feel that delights to do no evil, nor to revenge any wrong, but delights to endure all things, in hope to enjoy its own in the end. Its hope is to outlive all wrath and contention, and to weary out all exaltation and cruelty, or whatever is of a nature contrary to itself. It sees to the end of all temptations. As it bears no evil in itself, so it conceives none in thoughts to any other. If it be betrayed, it bears it, for its ground and spring is the mercies and forgiveness of God. Its crown is meekness, its life is everlasting love unfeigned; it takes its kingdom with entreaty and not with contention, and keeps it by lowliness of mind. In God alone it can rejoice, though none else regard it, or can own its life. . . .[22]

It is the experience of Friends that to the extent to which we live in the awareness of the presence of God, we are called to live under the guidance of that Spirit of which Nayler spoke.

---

22. James Nayler, *Works* (1716), p. 695, as quoted in *Faith and Practice,* Philadelphia Yearly Meeting of the Religious Society of Friends (Philadelphia: PYM, 1972), p. 59.

The Blessed Community

To this point attention has been focused on the *individual's* experience of relationship with God. Often, however, this experience embraces others. The communion with God is often a communion with the faithful community, or at least with those of the community present. To return to Friends' unprogrammed meetings for worship, the experience is typically not that of isolation in which silence walls off each individual from the other worshipers, each in her or his own separate dialogue with God. Were it so, there would be little point in coming together. There are those private conversations with God, to be sure, but there is also the awe-inspiring choir of silent prayer in which together we raise our hearts into God's presence. Sometimes those present are gathered by the Spirit into a palpable and powerful unity, and on such occasions, wrote Thomas Kelly, Christ

> [breaks] down the middle wall of partition between our separate personalities and [floods] us with a sense of *fellowship*. This unity with our fellow-worshipers, such that we are "written in one another's hearts," is in one sense created and instituted in the hour of worship. But in a deeper sense it is *discovered* in that hour that we are together in one body, which is the true and catholic church invisible. But the fact *disclosed* in the meeting, namely, that we *are* one body, hid with Christ in God, remains, secure from the ebb and flow of *feelings* and *emotions*.[23]

In sustaining a visible unity over time, we human beings need institutional structures and processes. Enduring communities need to make corporate decisions. Friends approach all such decisions as occasions for coming into unity in and under the Spirit of God. The unity sought is not coerced, compelled, or commanded, but recognized and acknowledged. By approaching all corporate decisions as occasions for corporate discernment, Friends seek to live in that holy community announced by Christ. This commitment to corporate discernment carries with it an openness to seeing the light of Christ refracted through each and every one present and to hearing the Word in what each says in speaking to the

---

23. Thomas Kelly, "The Gathered Meeting," reprinted in *Reality of the Spiritual World and the Gathered Meeting* (London: Friends Home Service Committee, 1965), p. 44.

issue at hand. The peace of God is in communion; it is available to us today, as we live.

Thus, it is our experience in both worship and corporate decision making that we can become one in Christ; we can participate in the blessed community.

Waging Violent Warfare v. the Lamb's War

The bee lives in a tight and cohesive community, but it gains membership in this community by becoming wholly subordinate to it. The colony is the true organism: it feeds itself; it reproduces; it stores honey to survive the winter. The individual bee is a member, a digit, as it were. As social animals, human beings are susceptible to following the way of the bee, but to do so is dehumanizing. War calls on participants to subordinate themselves to one human community, such as a nation, tribe, or ethnic group. It thus exhibits the triumph of that way of thinking according to which we decide what to do by appeal to the consequences we expect our actions to have, rather than by appeal to absolute moral principles. War also exhibits the triumph of human willfulness over humble attendance to the guidance of the Spirit. From this perspective, "just war" theory rationalizes people's collective assumption of responsibility for justice on earth. But it is not the case that *we* are sovereign. We cannot, acting collectively or individually, make one another just. When I disregard my own limitations (and the limitations of the groups and social institutions I embrace), disregard the teaching and example of Jesus, and assume responsibility for the just behavior of others, attempting to exact justice violently upon them "if necessary," I am supplanting God's judgment with my own. There are elements of willfulness and *hubris* in taking up the sword or gun to impose justice on other human beings, elements quite incompatible with that life in the Spirit to which we are called.

The approach to the centrality of peace witness to the apostolic faith sketched here appeals to an apocalyptic vision that provides support for nonviolence, on the one hand, and for a prophetic calling, on the other. It is suggestive that apocalyptic hopes were high in the first two centuries of the church, among Anabaptists in the sixteenth century, and among radical Puritans and Friends in the seventeenth century. Douglas Gwyn, building on the pioneering work of Lewis Benson, has brought out convincingly the apocalyptic dimensions of George Fox's teaching.[24] His is not the vision of the end of days, but that of realized eschatology: the kingdom is come, though not yet in its fullness. The first Quakers experienced Christ's teachings as so revolutionary as to turn the world upside down. As Gwyn has put it, the Quakers proclaimed "that the vivid apocalyptic expectations of the people were now being fulfilled: *Christ had come* to lead the faithful in new paths, thus setting up a new order and government . . . [which] superseded all existing Church orders, governments, teachers, and ministers."[25] The real authority and touchstone was the Word of God, Christ himself, the Teacher, not the ancient words of Scripture which had been inspired by the *Logos,* the Word. As Dean Freiday has put it, "the Friends felt called both to proclaim and to demonstrate that Christ has indeed inaugurated the reign of God on earth."[26] The focus was, and is, not doctrine or theory, but the living presence of Christ whose power gathers us together. We are gathered together to join the "Lamb's war," a prophetic struggle against the powers of darkness using weapons not our own, carnal or otherwise, but weapons of the Spirit. Fox's writings are filled with martial language, often misinterpreted today. The struggle requires great humility and meekness in order that the continuing revelation be received. Dean Freiday cautions, in this regard, that this is revelation "in the sense of *new applicational insights, not new doctrine.*"[27] The apocalyptic nature of Fox's teaching is characterized by Douglas Gwyn as follows:

> The experience of Christ . . . is the revelation of history — not only the history *recorded* by scripture but also the end of history *foretold* by scripture. Christ first reveals one's alienation from God, giving an understanding of Adam's Fall in Genesis. If one remains in the light of this revelation, Christ will empower one to enter the city of New Jerusalem, as envisioned by John at the end of Revelation. . . . History, as the vast realm of human activity carried out by men and women alienated from

24. Douglas Gwyn, *Apocalypse of the Word: The Life and Message of George Fox (1624-1691)* (Richmond, Ind.: Friends United Press, 1986).

25. Gwyn, *Apocalypse of the Word,* p. 30.

26. Dean Freiday, "Apostolicity and OrthoChristianity," in *Apostolic Faith in America,* ed. Thaddeus D. Horgan (New York: Commission of Faith and Order, NCCCUSA, 1988), p. 44.

27. Freiday, "Apostolicity and OrthoChristianity," p. 45.

God and from one another, is *ended* as they hear and obey the voice of Christ, who reconciles them to God and one another. . . . Thus, men and women are brought to the end of history by revelation of Christ.[28]

It is fair to say, I think, that this apocalyptic vision has dimmed among Friends and yet, however they might shrink from the terminology employed by theologians, there remains among Friends an abiding hope in the coming of God's holy peace and order to this earth and the desire and endeavor to live in that peace and order.

The impulse toward nonresistance found in the words of Nayler quoted earlier is balanced by the prophetic imperative "the Lamb's war," the call to work against the forces of darkness. Early Friends suffered non-violently the physical abuse to which their opponents subjected them. While they practiced nonviolent disobedience to those demands of civil authority seen as incompatible with the leadings of the Spirit, they were careful that this disobedience be open, and they accepted the sanctions civil authority levied for that disobedience. In this way the authority of civil government was recognized and respected. The first Friends denounced the evils of their day and engaged actively in lobbying parliament, protector, and then king to change laws and policies seen as unjust. They tried to adopt for themselves practices which they believed to be more in accord with the kingdom of God than were those of the society at large, while at the same time seeking to extend the reality of the blessed community beyond the meeting house and beyond the meeting into the world. This prophetic stance has never died among Friends, though it has waxed and waned.

Toward Reconciliation Regarding Peace Witness

Augustine of Hippo would be unimpressed, very likely, by these efforts on behalf of justice. The Christian pacifist appeared to him to abdicate responsibility for innocent neighbors. In responding to this familiar criticism, I wish to highlight two developments within the Religious Society of Friends in particular, and the Historic Peace Churches in general, which seem to be facilitating a dialogue that may lead to reconciliation re-

28. Gwyn, *Apocalypse of the Word,* p. 209.

garding peace witness: (1) the willingness to participate, however critically, in the civil state, and (2) the realization that the third way, between responding to evil with violence and responding to evil with submission to the will of the evildoer, can be much more robust than the unyielding nonresistance of martyrdom. Both of these points warrant some comment.

The Anabaptist proscription against entanglement in civil government concerned principally entanglements that would implicate the Anabaptist in acts of violence or idolatry. Nevertheless, refusal to participate in civil affairs was once a major ground of contention between the established churches (especially Lutheran and Roman Catholic) and the Anabaptists.[29] In light of this history, it is noteworthy that in her essay Dr. Barrett, the Mennonite theologian, invokes the notion of the holy nation of faithful Christians in order to ground involvement as peacemaker in the civil states in which the church finds itself scattered; she does not, as Anabaptists once did, advocate withdrawal. The Brethren have also moved in this direction, as documented by Donald F. Durnbaugh: "No longer were the Brethren thinking in terms of two separate realms or kingdoms, that of the church and that of the world. They began to think of the church as co-responsible with the government for the solution to the world's problems."[30] Of the three Historic Peace Churches, Quakers have been more willing, historically, to become involved in civil governance, though on occasion this has caused major problems for the Religious Society of Friends. For all three Historic Peace Churches, indeed for all churches in the United States, there must remain a tension between, on the one hand, a prophetic approach to civil government which calls it to account in Christian witness, and, on the other, a democratic approach which accepts the political validity of majority opinions with which the church must disagree. Neither theological nor moral questions are answered by votes.

The second point of movement is a greatly increased appreciation of the fact that a third way exists; one does not have to choose between violent resistance to evil, on the one hand, and nonresisting submission to it,

29. Marlin Miller, "Toward Acknowledging Together the Apostolic Character of the Church's Peace Witness," in *The Church's Peace Witness,* ed. Miller and Gingerich, pp. 198, 199.

30. Donald Durnbaugh, p. 75.

on the other. As Miroslav Volf has noted, "the option for nonviolence in reaction to violence should not be confused with that self-effacing attitude in which I completely place myself at the disposal of the others to do with me as they please."[31]

Although instances of nonviolent *resistance* can be found throughout history, much has been learned about the efficacy of intentionally nonviolent strategies and techniques for combating evil. Whether or not we accept, as Lois Barrett does, Walter Wink's argument in *Engaging the Powers*[32] that Jesus practiced and taught the "third way" of nonviolent action to secure both peace and justice, the Historic Peace Churches have all been influenced by what has been learned about the power of nonviolent direct action for peace and justice. This is a significant shift. In the face of determined evil, nonresistance left the matter of justice almost entirely in God's hands; this was part of the faithful's humble service to God. Nonviolent direct action opened up the possibility of working diligently for justice without violating the proscription against warring with carnal weapons. Indeed, peacemaker teams have been created in the last several years to intervene nonviolently in trouble-spots like Chiapas and Bosnia so as to forestall violence while working for justice.

No one thinks that nonviolent strategies can *guarantee* justice, but neither does anyone think that violent strategies can. The calculations involved in decisions made in the course of nonviolent campaigns include, though they are not limited to, assessments of consequences. This opens up additional areas of common ground between the Historic Peace Churches and others, regardless of whether deontological considerations or those of character also and importantly inform the churches' ethical decisions.

Concluding Remarks

Every person has within, like Saul of Tarsus, that which can respond to divine love, harken to the movement of the Holy Spirit, and hear and re-

31. Miroslav Volf, "The Suffering Messiah and the Rider on the White Horse: On Christian Faith and Violence in the Modern World," delivered at the Faith and Order NCCC/USA Consultation, "The Fragmentation of the Church and Its Unity in Peacemaking," University of Notre Dame, South Bend, Ind., 14 June 1995, p. 11.

32. Walter Wink, *Engaging the Powers* (Minneapolis: Fortress, 1992). Cf. Barrett, p. 169.

spond to God. To say this is not to deny that there are those who refuse to attend and to heed.

It was this faith which led Friends to deal with the Delaware Indians with respect. It is this faith which today underlies the Alternatives to Violence Project (AVP). Just one example of a program that reflects a commitment to peacemaking, AVP was begun in 1974 in response to a request to Quakers from inmates at Greenhaven prison in Stormville, New York; the inmates wanted help persuading teenagers in trouble to abandon violence. The project, as it turned out, focused instead on the adult convicts. It runs workshops to help them discover in themselves irenic alternatives in the sorts of circumstances which otherwise would trigger their acting violently. So successful has the project been in transforming lives that it has spread across the United States and to many other countries throughout the world.

The World Council of Churches has launched a "Programme to Overcome Violence" designed to "challeng[e] and [transform] the global cultural of violence in the direction of a culture of just peace." The even deeper imperative, however, is for the churches to acknowledge the centrality of peace witness to the apostolic faith. In this essay I, as a Friend, have drawn on the experience of Friends, but the intent has been to point to experience which will be familiar in content, if not in context, to Christians generally; it is the experience of the Prince of Peace calling us to rise up and follow, calling us to the Peaceable Kingdom, calling us to live in the Spirit.[33]

33. I am grateful to the following persons for their reactions to earlier versions of this paper: Martha Grundy, Melissa Meyer, Heather Paxson; my colleagues Sheila Ruth, Clyde Nabe, and Carol Keene; and especially for his detailed, thoughtful, and helpful comments, Dean Freiday.

Some Reformed Approaches
to the Peace Question

ALAN P. F. SELL

For the purposes of this paper, "Reformed" refers to that Christian tradition which claims continuity with the apostolic faith of the ages, but which takes its empirical shape from the side of the Reformation in which Zurich and Geneva were prominent, and which, especially in ecclesiology and church polity, was informed by the English and Welsh pedobaptist dissent. That is to say, the reference is to a Christian communion whose early roots were nourished by a number of reformers who worked in a variety of political contexts and developed their understanding of the Church accordingly. "Reformed" thus stands here for the traditions embraced within the World Alliance of Reformed Churches (1970) — the harbingers of which were the World Presbyterian Alliance (1875) and the International Congregational Council (1891) — a family which now includes a number of united churches in whose polity are blended Presbyterian and Congregational ecclesiological insights and convictions.[1]

Traditionally, the Reformed family has not focused on peace. Hence my modest title. I cannot describe *the* Reformed theology of peace, for

---

1. For the history see Marcel Pradervand, *A Century of Service. A History of the World Alliance of Reformed Churches* (Edinburgh: The Saint Andrew Press, 1975); for the theology see Alan P. F. Sell, *A Reformed, Evangelical Catholic Theology. The Contribution of the World Alliance of Reformed Churches 1875-1982* (1991; Eugene, Ore.: Wipf & Stock, 1998). There exist smaller international groupings of Reformed churches, but the focus here is upon the most widely representative body.

there is no such thing. Moreover, insofar as the Reformed have made statements on peace and peacemaking, they have not been noticeably different in tone or content from similar pronouncements of other Christian traditions. Nevertheless, the following general claims would, I think, command widespread assent throughout the communion. First, the Reformed, following Calvin and their other early leaders, stand broadly in the line of Augustinian just war theory.[2] Second, since the advent of nuclear power, many in the Reformed family (as elsewhere) have questioned the degree to which just war criteria apply to situations in which there might well be no clear winners or losers and almost certainly will be devastation of the health and land of many innocents. Third, the Reformed have not regarded specific stances on peacemaking (especially concerning the pacifist/non-pacifist question) as terms of church fellowship. Rather, the view has been that differing views are permissible, and that peace should not (paradoxically) become a church-dividing issue. Fourth, during the past forty years, individual and corporate statements on peace have frequently made reference to the biblical concepts of *shalom/eirene*, which are seen as entailing the quest for societal wholeness, justice, and the removal of disruptive economic inequalities. Fifth, the rise and fall of communism, the Vietnam War, tribal and civil wars, and occurrences of terrorism, in addition to the development of nuclear technology, have all had a bearing on Reformed thinking on peace, peacemaking, and violence in the second half of the twentieth century.

Against this background it is possible to exemplify, in a necessarily selective way,[3] the contributions to the witness for peace of some Reformed individuals, churches, and larger bodies. The illustrations presented, I shall offer some concluding reflections.

2. See, for example, John Calvin, *Institutes,* IV.xx.10-12, where Augustine is quoted with approval; *Belgic Confession,* XXXV; *Westminster Confession,* XXIII.i.

3. The selectivity here is the product not only of space restrictions, but of the fact that many Reformed peace testimonies have yet to be gathered. I can only illustrate the types of contribution made from the branches of the family to whose materials I have access. Since the points made in the available sources are remarkably similar, we may have some confidence that they will be reiterated elsewhere within the Reformed communion.

I

Among the early Congregational pacifists[4] we find Edward Williams (1750-1813), principal of the denominational theological college at Rotherham.[5] His most illustrious student was John Pye Smith (1774-1851), also a pacifist, who was principal of Homerton College from 1806 until his death, and who became vice president of the London Peace Society, founded in 1816.[6] When Henry Richard (1812-88) became secretary of the Society in 1848, he broadened its horizons and, in the context of the Crimean War and the American Civil War, urged governments to seek international and peaceful solutions to their disputes. Richard secured a further platform for his views upon becoming Member of Parliament for Merthyr in 1868, a position he held until his death.[7] Alexander Mackennal (1835-1904), who had earlier found the Crimean and American wars to be justifiable, reached a different conclusion regarding the Boer War. This put him at odds with a number of members in his fashionable Bowdon Downs congregation, though they took no steps to remove him.[8]

Congregational pacifists of the twentieth century have included William E. Orchard (1877-1955), the prominent minister of London's King's Weigh House until his departure for Rome, whose war-time book *The Outlook for Religion* (1917) prompted questions in Parliament;[9] Albert D. Belden (1883-1964) of Whitefield's Central Mission, author of

4. For many of the details in this and the next two paragraphs I am indebted to R. Tudur Jones, *Congregationalism in England 1662-1962* (London: Independent Press, 1962).

5. For Williams see *Dictionary of National Biography* (hereinafter, DNB). See also Joseph Gilbert, *Memoir* (1825); W. T. Owen, *Edward Williams, D.D.* (Cardiff: University of Wales Press, 1963); and K. W. Wadsworth, *Yorkshire United Independent College* (London: Independent Press, 1954), pp. 76-86.

6. For Smith see DNB. See also John Medway, *Memoirs* (1853); *Congregational Year Book* (hereinafter CYB), 1851, p. 233; and Alan P. F. Sell, *Commemorations, Studies in Christian Thought and History* (1993; Eugene, Ore.: Wipf & Stock, 1998), pp. 201-6.

7. For Richard see DNB. See also C. S. Miall, *Henry Richard, M.P.* (1889).

8. See Clyde Binfield, *So Down to Prayers* (London: J. M. Dent, 1977), p. 239. For Mackennal see DNB; see also D. Macfadyen, *Alexander Mackennal, B.A., DD. Life and Letters* (London: James Clarke, 1905).

9. For Orchard see Elaine Kaye and Ross Mackenzie, *W. E. Orchard, A Study in Christian Exploration* (Oxford: Education Services, 1990).

The Strategy of Christian Pacifism (1958), who, with Orchard, was in fellowship with Pax Christi, the Roman Catholic peace movement founded in France in 1945 and reorganized internationally in 1950;[10] H. C. Carter (1875-1954) of Emmanuel Church, Cambridge;[11] and Leyton Richards (1879-1948), a successor of Mackennal at Bowdon Downs who resigned his charge following his protest against the Conscription Act of 1916 — for which protest he was fined £100.00, a sum reimbursed by three of his deacons. He later published *Christian Pacifism after Two World Wars* (1948).[12] Nathaniel Micklem (1888-1976) held views so out of accord with those of the majority of his Withington, Manchester, church that he had little option but to resign his charge. Subsequently, however, he became principal of Mansfield College, Oxford,[13] where he found that pacifism was one of relatively few stances he shared with his colleague, the learned C. J. Cadoux (1883-1947), whose *Christian Pacifism Examined* (1940) remains a valuable study of its subject.[14] Among those of this tradition still living may be noted the distinguished church historian Geoffrey F. Nuttall, author of the brief but stimulating book, *Christian Pacifism Through History* (1958), and the hymn writer Fred Kaan.[15] A number of those mentioned were members of the Congregational Pacifist Crusade (later Fellowship) founded in 1926, while Orchard, Richards, the Cambridge mathematician Ebenezer Cunningham, and others were members of the interdenominational Fellowship of Reconciliation, which was founded in 1914. A survey of 1959 revealed that 40 percent of Congregational ministers were pacifists.[16]

A number of leading Congregationalists stood on the other side of the pacifist/non-pacifist argument, among them P. T. Forsyth (1848-1921), principal of Hackney College, who pulled no punches in *The Jus-*

10. For Belden see CYB, 1965-66, p. 439.

11. For Carter see CYB, 1955, pp. 509-10.

12. For Richards see CYB, 1949, p. 503; Edith Ryley Richards, *Private View of a Public Man, The Life of Leyton Richards* (London: Allen & Unwin, 1950).

13. For Micklem see *United Reformed Church Year Book*, 1978, 266; N. Micklem, *The Box and the Puppets* (London: Geoffrey Bles, 1957).

14. For Cadoux see CYB, 1948, pp. 489-90. See also Elaine Kaye, *C. J. Cadoux: Theologian, Scholar and Pacifist* (Edinburgh: Edinburgh University Press, 1988).

15. See F. Kaan, "Covenanting for peace," *Reformed World* XXXIX, no. 4 (December 1986): 617-24.

16. See Stephen Mayor, *Beliefs of Congregational Ministers* (privately circulated transcript, 1959), p. 5.

tification of God (1916),[17] and W. B. Selbie (1862-1944),[18] principal of Mansfield College. Forsyth and Selbie were by no means hostile to conscientious objectors, but the same cannot be said of Arthur Pringle (1866-1933), whose scathing remarks at the autumn meeting of the Congregational Union in 1914 brought "a great crash of approving cheers."[19] Among ministers in pastoral charge, Sidney M. Berry[20] and R. F. Horton were prominent non-pacifists.[21] By the time he had become Secretary of the Congregational Union of England and Wales in 1945, however, Berry, together with the Union's chairman, A. M. Chirgwin, urged the banning of the atom bomb and of poison gas.[22] Like all the Reformed churches I have examined on this matter, the Congregational Union of England and Wales, while respecting the convictions of its pacifist members, nevertheless reluctantly concluded that in time of war the government's course must be followed.[23]

Among Scottish Reformed pacifists — some of whom were associated with the London Peace Union early on and all of whom remained ever a minority group — we find James Barr (1862-1949). Barr was raised in the Free Church but became the leader of the remnant of the church that declined to unite with the Church of Scotland in 1929. Committed to evangelism and possessing an acute social conscience, he felt that the "Church of the nation" was, by its social and political allegiances, alienating itself from many. From 1924-1931 he was Labor M.P. for Motherwell and Wishaw. In addition to promoting pacifism, he espoused the cause of temperance and strove for the abolition of capital punishment.[24] George

17. For Forsyth see, among others, Trevor Hart, ed., *Justice the True and Only Mercy* (Edinburgh: T. & T. Clark, 1994).

18. For Selbie see CYB, 1945, p. 441.

19. *The British Weekly,* 5 October 1916, pp. 4, 6. For Pringle see CYB, 1934, pp. 273-74. This obituary paints a quite different picture of Pringle, under whose leadership the church at Purley, Surrey, became one of the largest and most prominent in the Congregational Union ("the Purley gates" to the *cognoscenti!*).

20. For Berry see CYB, 1962, pp. 449-50.

21. For Horton, minister at Lyndhurst Road, Hampstead, for fifty-five years, see CYB, 1935, pp. 278-79. See also Albert Peel and J. A. R. Marriott, *Robert Forman Horton* (London: Allen & Unwin, 1937).

22. See *The British Weekly,* 16 August 1945, p. 264.

23. See CYB, 1916, p. 4.

24. See A. C. Ross in Nigel M. de S. Cameron et al., eds., *Dictionary of Scottish Church History and Theology* (Edinburgh: T. & T. Clark, 1993).

MacLeod (1895-1991) is another striking case; a captain in the Argyll and Sutherland Highlanders during World War I who received both the Military Cross and the Croix de Guerre, MacLeod subsequently became a pacifist, founded the Iona Community in 1938, and became president of the International Fellowship of Reconciliation.[25] Also from Scotland came Professor G. H. C. MacGregor's careful examination of *The New Testament Basis of Pacifism* (1936) and his critique of Niebuhr's anti-pacifist reading of Scripture entitled *The Relevance of the Impossible Ideal* (1941).[26] On the other side, albeit in uncharacteristically restrained fashion, was the theologian James Denny (1856-1917), in whose *War and the Fear of God* (1916) the perceived obligation to defend the right is related to the gospel concepts of compassion, hope, and victory.[27]

Many Reformed individuals in America were among early supporters of the American Peace Society (1828) and, later, of the Fellowship of Reconciliation. Between the two World Wars the Presbyterian Peace Fellowship was constituted within the United Presbyterian Church in the United States (UPCUSA), and in 1949 the Southern Presbyterian Peace Fellowship was organized within the Presbyterian Church in the United States (PCUS). These fellowships worked together from 1978 on and were united when the UPCUSA merged with the PCUS in 1983.

Individual members of the Reformed Church in America gave particularly strong leadership in the field of peace and international order during the 1930s. Among them were Lawrence French, chairman of the Committee on International Justice and Goodwill; Bernard Mulder, editor of the *Intelligence Leader;* A. J. Muste, secretary of the Fellowship of Reconciliation; and Broer D. Dykstra, staunch opponent of any notion of a holy war. On the other hand, Albertus Pieters, in *The Christian Attitude Toward War* (1932), argued that since war, in the hands of God, could restrain and punish sin, the Reformed Church should not publish unrealistic and irresponsible statements absolutely repudiating war.[28]

25. For MacLeod see R. Ferguson in *Dictionary of Scottish Church History and Theology.*

26. For MacGregor (1892-1953) see *Who Was Who,* 1961-1970.

27. For Denny see DNB. See also Alan P. F. Sell, *Defending and Declaring the Faith. Some Scottish Examples 1860-1920* (Exeter: Paternoster Press and Colorado Springs: Helmers & Howard, 1987), ch. 9.

28. See further John De Jong, "Social Concerns," in *Piety and Patriotism. Biennial*

Contributions by individuals from other branches of the Reformed family within the United States include *The Gift of Shalom* (1976) by Paul L. Hammer of the United Church of Christ and Presbyterian Arthur C. Cochrane's deeply thoughtful study *The Mystery of Peace* (1986). A symposium on peace and peacemaking by teachers and others connected with Austin Presbyterian Seminary, interesting for its balance of theoretical and practical studies, was published in the *Bulletin* of that institution in October 1983.

On the issue of pacifism, one must also examine the intellectual pilgrimage of Reinhold Niebuhr (1892-1971), who was raised in the Evangelical and Reformed tradition but whose pilgrimage took him in a direction opposite to that of MacLeod of Iona. At first, Niebuhr was a somewhat uneasy pacifist; indeed, for a period of time he was national chairman of the Fellowship of Reconciliation. His realistic Christian ethics, however — developed in his *Moral Man and Immoral Society* (1932) and further propounded in *An Interpretation of Christian Ethics* (1935) and *Why the Christian Church Is Not Pacifist* (1940) — led him to argue that in the sinful world as it exists, force may, on occasion, need to be met with a return of force. He also argued that justice necessitates coercion and that many pacifists — that is, those who prescribe pacifist solutions for political strife, not those who maintain a peace testimony in sectarian groupings — are seriously at fault in reducing Christianity to the law of love.[29]

Before turning from this highly selective record of some of the Reformed individuals who have been active in pursuing the peace question, mention should be made of those who, in the climate of the cold war, contributed to the Christian Peace Conference (CPC) based in Prague, the first meetings of which were held in 1958. Prominent here was Josef Lukl Hromádka (1889-1970) of the Evangelical Church of Czech Brethren. By no means limited to participants from Central and Eastern Europe, the conference included delegates from many parts of the world. The strife which followed the invasion of Czechoslovakia by five commu-

---

Studies of the Reformed Church in America 1776-1976, ed. James W. Van Hoeven (Grand Rapids: Eerdmans, 1976), pp. 122-24.

29. The literature is vast, but see Charles W. Kegley, ed., *Reinhold Niebuhr, His Religious, Social and Political Thought* (1956; New York: The Pilgrim Press, 1984). See also Gordon Harland, *The Thought of Reinhold Niebuhr* (New York: Oxford University Press, 1960), ch. 7.

nist nations in 1968 led to the resignations of Hromádka and the general secretary, and the work of the Conference was viewed with increasing suspicion by many from that time onwards.[30]

II

We turn now to a few examples of actions taken and declarations made by Reformed churches, proceeding chronologically. In 1917 the General Assembly of the Presbyterian Church in Canada set up a Commission of the War which produced a reported entitled *The War and the Christian Church*. They regarded the war as a product of sin and a judgment on Western culture.[31] In 1921 the National Council of Congregational Churches requested the United States Government to convene an international conference to advance the cause of world disarmament. The Congregational General Council went so far in 1934 as to say that "The Church is through with war!" — precisely the kind of utterance that, as we saw, Pieters of the Reformed Church in America seriously questioned. The rise of Nazism, however, moderated the Congregationalists' anti-war stance, and in 1940 (and again in 1942 and 1944), in resolutions on "Christian Attitudes in a Warring World," the General Council recognized both the Niebuhrian and pacifist positions. It also sought the humane treatment of conscientious objectors.[32]

The concern for justice and peace is clearly expressed in the 1967 *Confession of Faith* of the United Presbyterian Church in the U.S.A. and in *A Declaration of Faith* (1976) of the Presbyterian Church in the United States.[33] These inspired a paper entitled *Peacemaking: The Believer's Calling*, which was endorsed by the two churches in 1980 and 1981 respec-

30. See further Milan Opocensky, "Christian Peace Conference," in *Dictionary of the Ecumenical Movement*, ed. Nicholas Lossky et al. (Geneva: WCC, 1991). For Hromádka see Ans J. Van Der Bent, *Dictionary of the Ecumenical Movement*.

31. See Brian A. Fraser, *The Social Uplifters. Presbyterian Progressives and the Social Gospel in Canada,* 1875-1915 (Waterloo, Ont.: Wilfrid Laurier University Press, 1988), p. 162.

32. See John Von Rohr, *The Shaping of American Congregationalism* (Cleveland: The Pilgrim Press, 1992), pp. 398-401.

33. For the relevant paragraphs see Lukas Vischer, ed., *Reformed Witness Today* (Bern: Evangelische Arbeitsstelle Oekumene Schweiz, 1982), pp. 214, 259.

tively. For its part, the Reformed Church in America decided in 1980 to publish a paper by its Theological Commission on (and against) the nuclear arms race.[34] In 1982, the General Synod urged all congregations to study the issue, and in the same year a study guide, *Christ is Our Peace,* was published to assist the process. During the same decade the United Church of Christ produced a discussion document on "The United Church of Christ as a Just Peace Church," while one of its theologians, M. Douglas Meeks, enquired, *Is the United Church of Christ a Peace Church?* (1980).[35]

Turning finally to the United Kingdom, we find that in 1937 the General Assembly of the Church of Scotland produced a report on Christian attitudes toward war and peace, in the preparation of which the pacifist stance was staunchly represented by G. H. C. MacGregor, and in 1983 the General Assembly took a stand on moral and theological grounds against nuclear weapons. Meanwhile, in 1954 the report of a Congregational Union of England and Wales Commission on "The Christian Gospel and the Use of Force" was published; it demonstrated that, although commonly accepted principles could be affirmed, there were divergent views concerning the appropriate course of action in particular circumstances. More recently, in 1994, a declaration on "The Church's Peace Vocation" was adopted by the General Assembly of the Presbyterian Church in Ireland.[36] In Wales, in 1995, the General Assembly of the Presbyterian Church of Wales heard a debate on the question, "Should the Presbyterian Church of Wales become a Peace Church?" Pacifists spoke strongly in favor of the idea, but the proposal was narrowly defeated, largely on the ground that no consultation had taken place to ascertain the views of church members on the peace question, that it would therefore be premature for the church to declare itself in this way on that occasion, and that nothing undermines the integrity of a church's national assembly more than the subsequent discovery that what it had

---

34. See James I. Cook, ed., *The Church Speaks. Papers of the Commission on Theology, Reformed Church in America 1959-1984* (Grand Rapids: Eerdmans, 1985), pp. 165-82.

35. Apart from opening references to Augustine and the Reformers, the scope of the article on "Peace" in Donald K. McKim, ed., *Encyclopedia of the Reformed Faith* (Louisville: Westminster/John Knox, 1992), is confined to the United States and, within that, almost entirely to Presbyterianism.

36. For the text see *Reformed World* XLVI, no. 1 (March 1996): 35-36.

proclaimed as "the mind of the Church" on a given issue was in fact no such thing.[37]

III

We come finally to the contribution of the World Alliance of Reformed Churches and its predecessor bodies.[38] At the very first meeting of the International Congregational Council the Honorable J. W. Patterson advocated disarmament as the "logical sequence to the teaching of both natural and revealed religion." Nevertheless, he added, "disarmament is impossible if not general"[39] — a conviction which has been echoed from his day to ours. The General Council of the Presbyterian Alliance addressed the peace question on a number of occasions, and at its fifteenth session (1937) it pronounced on "The Church and War" in the following terms:

> We believe that recourse to war by the nations of the world is a heinous evidence of the sin of man's heart and an offence to God and to man. . . . The way of Christ is the way of love and reconciliation. . . . War can neither establish justice and security, nor reconcile enemies. . . . While, in accordance with the Reformed tradition, we do not deny that war may lawfully be waged in defense against unjust and violent aggression, yet we recognize that among sincere Christians there is a divergence of opinion as to whether war can any longer find sanction in the Christian ethic. . . . We call upon the nations of the world to support their professions and pledges of peace by mutual reductions in their armed preparations for war. . . . Finally, we call upon Christian people everywhere to work unremittingly for the removal of injustices and antagonisms between the nations, and, above all, to seek by the

37. See Alan P. F. Sell, "Should the Presbyterian Church of Wales Become a Peace Church?" *Reconciliation Quarterly* (Autumn 1996): 25-27. This is the speech arguing for restraint which I was invited to make, and which I managed to accomplish without divulging whether or not I was a pacifist. It seemed to me that that was not the point. The question was whether the PCW is a peace church.

38. In this paragraph and the next but one I draw on my *A Reformed, Evangelical Catholic Theology,* pp. 209-11.

39. *The International Congregational Council* (London: James Clarke, 1891), p. 238.

practice of Christian forgiveness, reconciliation, and love, to create lasting goodwill.[40]

The theme of the 1970 General Council, at which the World Presbyterian Alliance and the International Congregational Council celebrated their union, was, appropriately enough, "God Reconciles and Makes Free." A collection of introductory papers edited by Allen O. Miller was published under the title *Reconciliation in Today's World.* Among these is one by Charles C. West on "Reconciliation and World Peace" which touches on political, social, and economic questions and emphasizes the fact that "the ground of peace in this world is Jesus Christ."[41]

Perhaps the most striking of the World Alliance's actions in pursuit of peace was the call of its Executive Committee in 1983 for a "Covenant for Peace and Justice." The statement declares that questions of peace and justice do not belong exclusively to the realm of politics, finds no moral or theological justification for the use of nuclear weapons, denounces the folly of the nuclear arms race, pledges support for trust- and peace-building initiatives, notes the destabilizing influence of poverty and the denial of human rights, and invites Alliance members to covenant to work together for peace and justice. It suggests that the World Council of Churches take up the cause — which it did through its program on "Justice, Peace and the Integrity of Creation."[42]

It is interesting to note that in contrast to its 1937 predecessor, the 1983 statement makes no reference to just war theory. Whereas the former thinks in terms of an aggressor nation opposing other nations, the latter emphasizes the underlying socioeconomic causes of strife and discord. In a word, it closely associates the quest for peace with that for justice. Reflections by Reformed church leaders on the subject were published by the Alliance in *Covenanting for Peace and Justice* (1989), and the theme was renewed in the preparations for the twenty-second General Council in 1989, where references were made to such matters

---

40. *Proceedings of the Fifteenth General Council of the Alliance of Reformed Churches Holding the Presbyterial System* (Edinburgh: Office of the Alliance, 1937), pp. 226-27.

41. Allen O. Miller, ed., *Reconciliation in Today's World* (Grand Rapids: Eerdmans, 1969), p. 115.

42. See "A Covenant for Peace and Justice," *Reformed World* XXXVII, no. 6 (June 1983): 179-82.

as the greenhouse effect, deforestation, acid rain, and unbridled bio-technology,[43] all within the understanding of the covenant as embracing the created order.[44] The Council's "Statement on Peace" included the following declaration: "The churches today can no longer subscribe to the traditional doctrine of the 'just war.'" This doctrine, the statement went on, laid down rules for the declaring and the conducting of war when no other way of resolving conflicts seemed possible; today, however, we are in an entirely different historical situation, one in which these rules are even less likely to be observed than in the past, when their observance was rare enough.[45] Having thus appeared to dispense with just war theory, the Council nevertheless instructed its Department of Theology to give further consideration to it.[46]

In addition to Alliance work at the international level, the Caribbean and North American Area Council has on a number of occasions tackled the issue of peace and related topics. Among the fruits of this labor are two collections of papers: *A Covenant Challenge to Our Broken World,* in which the Church's global context and pressing challenges are viewed in the light of its covenant calling; and *Peace, War and God's Justice,* in which the biblical foundations of the theology of peace, historical understandings of peace and war, and contemporary interpretations are discussed.[47]

Not the least important aspect of its work over the past thirty years has been the Alliance's program of dialogues with other Christian world communions. Of these, the one which has been most directly concerned with peace is that with the Mennonite World Conference — the Alliance's first dialogue with one of the Historic Peace Churches. Like other Christian world communions (though they must speak for themselves) the Reformed have not always found it easy to live at peace with their Christian neighbors — or even with one another, as demonstrated by the

---

43. See *Reformed World* XL, no. 5 (March 1989): 83-89. Even if, as some scientists now suggest, global warming is caused primarily by geological factors rather than the emission of gasses on earth, the case for reducing such emissions based on health and other grounds would still be strong.

44. See *Proceedings of the 22nd General Council* (Geneva: WARC, 1989), passim.

45. *Proceedings of the 22nd General Council,* p. 277.

46. *Proceedings of the 22nd General Council,* p. 277.

47. The former was published by the Area Council in 1982, the latter by The United Church Publishing House, Toronto, in 1989.

numerous secessions which have marked the history of the Reformed family. Though their English and Welsh Separatist harbingers were persecuted, in some cases even to the point of martyrdom, in the sixteenth century, the Reformed have on occasion become the oppressors when in the majority themselves. The execution of Anabaptists in Zurich and the banishment of Roger Williams in New England are only two examples of this. What is more, in some of their most formal utterances, their confessions of faith, the Reformed anathematized the Anabaptists, forebears of today's Mennonites. The memory of such Reformed cruelty and anathemas clearly had to be addressed before dialogue with Mennonites could proceed with integrity. Hence, at a service in Zurich Cathedral on 5 March 1983, the Reformed lamented the cruelty and disowned the anathemas. This paved the way for the first joint consultation between the two families[48] in Strasbourg on July 17-18, 1984, the findings of which were published under the title *Mennonites and Reformed in Dialogue* (1986). The two families presented accounts of their respective heritages and their current situations, and the historic anathemas were further considered.

It was clear, however, that, the ice now being broken, further work was needed. Accordingly, the then Theological Secretary of the Alliance was asked to consult with leaders of the Mennonite World Conference with a view to further conversations. He reported to his Executive Committee that there was agreement that the three major "neuralgic" issues between the two traditions — baptism, peace, and the state — should be discussed in a second phase of the dialogue.[49] This was done at a consultation held at the University of Calgary on October 11-14, 1989. Papers from both sides were presented on the three main issues, and participants from other traditions presented their responses. The papers on peace were by Max L. Stackhouse of the United Church of Christ and Howard John Loewen of the Mennonite Brethren Church. In the concluding report of this phase of the dialogue the Reformed and Mennonites challenged one another on the peace question. These challenges are summarized in the following two of nine appended recommendations:

48. For a fuller account of the background to the dialogue, and an introduction to its second phase, see Alan P. F. Sell, "Introduction" to *Baptism, Peace and the State in the Reformed and Mennonite Traditions,* ed. Ross T. Bender and Alan P. F. Sell (Waterloo, Ont.: Wilfrid Laurier University Press, 1991).

49. WARC Executive Committee Minutes, 1987, pp. 166, 169.

6. That the Executive Committee of the Mennonite World Conference initiate a discussion among Mennonites on the possibility of a theological understanding of revolution, and the application of the peace principle in face of economic, institutional, military, and cultural violence.

7. That the Executive Committee of the World Alliance of Reformed Churches initiate a discussion among Reformed churches on the possibilities in, and applications of, just war theory, and on Christian participation in the responsible use of coercive power.[50]

Suggestions for further dialogue were made and reaffirmed, and appropriate action was sought, at the Alliance's consultations on bilateral dialogues in 1992.[51] At the time of writing there is, sadly, nothing further to report.[52]

IV

Having pondered the Reformed contributions to peace and peacemaking that it has been possible to gather, and having lived through some of the formal and informal conversations on the subject, I offer tentatively the following personal reflections.

First, while I could not within the compass of this paper demonstrate that the evidence presented above is on a par with that from many other Christian world communions, I should be very surprised indeed if non-Reformed readers of my essay did not feel that at many points their own communions echo the Reformed witness and experience where peace and peacemaking are concerned. The briefest perusal of dictionary articles on "Peace" will make it clear that just war theory is under review in many quarters. Moreover, it is well known that most if not all Christian communions contain both pacifists and non-pacifists and do not fall

---

50. Sell, *Baptist, Peace and the State in the Reformed and Mennonite Traditions*, p. 238.

51. See H. S. Wilson, ed., *Bilateral Dialogues. The papers and findings of the WARC Consultation held from April 21-25, 1992, at Princeton Theological Seminary, Princeton, New Jersey, U.S.A.* (Geneva: WARC, 1993), p. 68.

52. A series of consultations on the first and second Reformations has, however, taken place. See *Towards a Renewed Dialogue* (Geneva: WARC, 1986).

prey to a version of the Galatian heresy by elevating either position to a condition of membership. On the contrary, it is recognized by most Christian communions that peace should not be a church-dividing issue (though tolerance of pacifists in war-time has not been universal). Finally, the broadening of the peace question to include the consideration of those socio-political-economic factors which yield strife between people and nations is not peculiar to Reformed thinkers.

Second, it must be noted that pacifism comes in a variety of styles. At the risk of oversimplifying, there are those who regard pacifism as a positive alternative to war and are politically active in making their case, and there are others who draw a distinction between the kingdoms of this world and the kingdom of God, believing that their witness for peace can be coherently made only over against "the world" and its systems. Hence, they believe Christians should not engage in "the world's" political activity. Sometimes such pacifists think more in terms of peace with God than in terms of peace as the healing of the nations. My hunch is that a higher proportion of these are to be found among the Historic Peace Churches than among the Reformed.

However that may be, a deeply theological question arises to which, so far as I am aware, the Reformed family has as yet given no clear answer. (It might in fact be asked, has anyone?) What are the implications, in a pluralist culture, of Charles West's assertion, quoted earlier, that "the ground of peace in this world is Jesus Christ"? Is war, then, an unavoidable occurrence until all are "in Christ"? If so, what are the implications for Christian mission? On the other hand, if the immediate dangers and responsibilities are such that we cannot wait until what is perhaps an eschatological hope is realized, how are we to proceed in the interim? How far can this Christian claim cohere with the different claims of people of other faiths or of none? If we are not in accord on the fundamental principle, are there lesser grounds upon which we may stand with others of good will? Shall we need to revivify the old natural law doctrine — and modify it so that its deliverances are not, in circular fashion, ecclesiastically predetermined? Or should we take our cue from the philosopher Bernard Williams and advocate a rationalistic as distinct from a moralistic approach to the difficult questions of arms possession, deterrence, and the like?[53] What is

53. See Bernard Williams, "How to Think Sceptically about the Bomb," *New Society* (18 November 1982): 288-90.

the relationship between that peace which those "in Christ" know, and the call to mitigate strife in a multi-religious, variously secularized world?

Third, the related concepts of power, coercion, and nonviolence require careful analysis. It must be confessed that Christian thought upon all of these is frequently muddled, and (dare one say it?) the muddles sometimes flow from notions of political correctness. One thinks of hymnbook editors who tremble at what "fighting pacifists" will do to them if they propose to include the hymn "Fight the good fight" — even though the allusion is biblical, the reference being to the "good" fight against the "principalities and powers," the very phenomena which, on other occasions, the same pacifists wish to counter by nonviolent means. Indeed, the report on "The Fragmentation of the Church and Its Unity in Peacemaking" declares that "All churches must pit themselves against the forces of a fallen world where evil manifests itself in ever more insidious ways."[54] On the other hand, even committed pacifists will join Charles Wesley in singing lustily of the Christ who "breaks the power of canceled sin, He sets the prisoner free." But this takes a certain force, albeit a force for good. Then there are pacifists who appear to be selectively nonviolent. They profess general nonviolence but, for example, they wish to invoke the force of that law which in England and Wales requires religious worship in state schools.[55] Some of these pacifists are heirs of a tradition sprinkled with martyrs to the cause of conscientious worship who, to be consistent, ought to respect the conscientious convictions of those who do not wish to worship at all. Again, what of those forms of violence which can be experienced in regions where there is a legally established church (whether Reformed, Lutheran, or Anglican), or a majority folk church, and "the rest"? It is not unknown for participants in international dialogues to make all the right ecumenical noises, while at the same time continuing to place obstacles in the path of those at home whom their dialogue partners represent.

Fourth, with the querying of just war theory and the growing realization that the quest for peace entails urgent attention to the manifold causes of strife in the world, the importance of competent empirical anal-

---

54. See *Ecumenical Review* LXVIII, no. 1 (January 1996): 122.

55. There is, of course, an "opt-out" clause, but the separation of a child from his or her peers on grounds which are likely to be seen as odd by others is not the happiest of positions in which to place a young person.

ysis is highlighted. In the absence of this, moralistic platitudes or partisan rhetoric may well replace credible testimony. The dangers are never closer than when pressure groups from the church, advocating their sometimes contradictory party lines, are at work.

Fifth, what of the moves in a few Reformed churches to announce themselves as peace churches? The Historic Peace Churches — the Mennonites, the Brethren in Christ, and the Quakers — have made their peace witness over many years and they have experienced tension in times of war when some of their members felt conscience-bound to take up arms. This raises the question of church discipline. As the 1995 consultation report asks, "How meaningful can a church's testimony be if it goes unheeded by its members?"[56] But suppose a Reformed church were to become a peace church in the sense of a (largely) pacifist church — what of church discipline then? As it happens, the Historic Peace Churches do not practice infant baptism, and it is therefore unproblematic for a baptized church member (who must be competent to profess faith in Christ) to also make the pacifist position his or her own; the Reformed, however, welcome baptized infants into the Church. What, then, would be the position of a baptized infant who grew up to become an Admiral of the Fleet? Would such a person be asked to resign church membership, or be excommunicated? To pose such questions is to indicate the nature of the theological and pastoral minefield into which an unwary church might stumble.

Finally, it seems to me that all Christian talk of peace and peacemaking will ring hollow until Christians repudiate those divisions over ministry and sacraments which prevent those not of their tradition but nonetheless, like themselves, at peace with God through Christ, from joyfully witnessing to this fact at the Lord's table. This point has theoretically been taken in some of the bilateral dialogue reports, but consequent action is too often slow to follow.

In some cases any action will presuppose the reconciliation of memories. The Reformed and the Mennonites have action on this matter, but steps in other directions and from other quarters need to be taken. In taking these steps due regard must be paid to the philosophical, liturgical, and pastoral complications that will ensue if the idea of covenant, for example, is abused in such a way that an individual today is seen as objec-

56. *Ecumenical Review* LDXVIII, no. 1 (January 1996): 124.

tively morally responsible for the actions of a person in the sixteenth century. (The converse is that individuals may not justifiably plead that "the sinfulness of the race" or "sinful structures" release them from culpability for their voluntary sinful acts.)[57] That is not to say, however, that peace between communions is all that needs to be sought. To return to my opening remarks, the Reformed have not always lived at peace among themselves either locally or in their wider expressions of churchly fellowship. There is much work to be done at all foci of church life — not least in the local church. Bernard Lord Manning's challenge has lost none of its force with the passage of the years:

> You say you love Christ's Church. Well, here it is: Tom, Dick, Harry, and the rest; a funny lot of lame ducks. . . . They are not very good. But they have all in their own odd ways, heard Christ's call. . . . They have made a covenant with God, and so joined themselves in the saved society with Him. It is little use your feeling mystical sympathy with St. Francis who is dead, with St. Somebody Else who never existed, with men of goodwill all over the world whom you are quite safe from meeting. If you do not love your brothers whom you have seen . . . you cannot, in fact, love those brothers . . . whom you have not seen.[58]

What is worse, such persons do not love God, and hence cannot be at peace with him either (1 John 4:20-21).

57. See further Alan P. F. Sell, *Aspects of Christian Integrity* (1990; Eugene, Ore.: Wipf & Stock, 1998), ch. 3.

58. Bernard Lord Manning, *Why Not Abandon the Church?* (London: Independent Press, 1939), pp. 37-38. For a thoughtful article on peacemaking in relation to the local church see Paul Flucke, "The Pastoral Task in a Peacemaking Church, a Theological Perspective," *Prism,* Introductory Issue (Fall 1985): 72-86.

Pacifism in Pentecostalism:
The Case of the Assemblies of God

MURRAY W. DEMPSTER

The year 1914 witnessed both the beginning of the Great War and the formation of the Assemblies of God. News of the war hit the headlines of *The New York Times;* the formation of the Pentecostal denomination in Arkansas elicited two small notices in the regional *The Hot Springs Sentinel.* At the time, these two events had no relationship to one another, or so it seemed. Yet in the short span of three years the global impact of the war would reach even the fledgling Pentecostal denomination.

By April 28, 1917, only about three weeks after the United States had declared war on Germany, officials of the denomination's governing body, its General Council, formulated a resolution on military service. They got the church's Executive and General Presbytery to approve it and prepared to send it to President Wilson. A cover letter accompanying the resolution requested the right of conscientious objection for Assemblies of God members, and the resolution itself read as follows:

> While recognizing Human Government as of Divine ordination and affirming our unswerving loyalty to the Government of the United States, nevertheless we are constrained to define our position with reference to the taking of human life.
>
> WHEREAS, in the Constitutional Resolution adopted at the Hot Springs General Council, April 1-10, 1914, we plainly declare the Holy Inspired Scriptures to be the all-sufficient rule of faith and practice, and

137

WHEREAS the Scriptures deal plainly with the obligations and relations of humanity, setting forth the principles of "Peace on earth, good will toward men" (Luke 2:14); and

WHEREAS we as the followers of the Lord Jesus Christ, the Prince of Peace, believe in implicit obedience to the Divine commands and precepts which instruct us to "Follow peace with all men," (Heb. 12:14); "Thou shalt not kill," (Exod. 20:12); "Resist not evil," (Matt. 5:29); "Love your enemies," (Matt. 5:44); etc., and

WHEREAS those and other Scriptures have always been accepted and interpreted by our churches as prohibiting Christians from shedding blood or taking human life;

THEREFORE we, as a body of Christians, while purposing to fulfill all the obligations of loyal citizenship, are nevertheless constrained to declare we cannot conscientiously participate in war and armed resistance which involves the actual destruction of human life since this is contrary to our view of the clear teachings of the inspired Word of God, which is the sole basis of our faith.

April 28th, 1917[1]

In August of 1967, five decades after formulating the denomination's policy on military service, the General Council of the Assemblies of God gathered in Long Beach, California, and changed its official statement from one of pacifism to a position that enshrined "the principle of individual freedom of conscience as it relates to military service." Adopted when many Americans were agonizing in conscience over the continued involvement of the United States in the Vietnam war, the statement read:

As a movement we affirm our loyalty to the government of the United States in war or peace.

We shall continue to insist, as we have historically, on the right of

---

1. "Resolution Concerning the Attitude of the General Council of the Assemblies of God Toward Military Service Which Involves the Actual Participation in the Destruction of Human Life," printed in *Weekly Evangel,* 4 August 1917, p. 6. Each biennium from 1927 to 1965 a slightly modified version appeared in published, official minutes of the denomination's General Council. See *Minutes of the Thirty-First General Council of the Assemblies of God* (1965), p. 134 (such minutes hereafter cited as "General Council *Minutes,*" with year).

each member to choose for himself whether to declare his position as a combatant, a non-combatant, or a conscientious objector.[2]

The 1967 statement simply codified a change in the church's position on military service that had occurred much earlier. Various attempts have been made by scholars to understand the nature and the demise of pacifism in the Assemblies of God as well as in the larger pentecostal movement.[3] By far the most comprehensive and insightful study is Jay Beaman's book, *Pentecostal Pacifism: The Origins, Development and Rejec-*

2. General Council *Minutes* (1967), p. 35. This statement continues verbatim through the most recent meeting of the General Council, 6-11 August 1991, in Portland, Oregon; see 1991 *Minutes*, p. 220.

3. Lack of knowledge about pacifism in classical pentecostalism began with omissions in the first histories written by academically trained historians: Carl Brumback's *Suddenly from Heaven* and Klaude Kendrick's *The Promise Fulfilled: A History of the Modern Pentecostal Movement* (both Springfield, Mo.: Gospel Publishing House, 1961). Their omissions are puzzling since by 1954 Irvine John Harrison's Th.D. thesis, "A History of the Assemblies of God" (Berkeley Baptist Divinity School, Berkeley, Calif.), had treated military service as an early "theological storm." Nils Bloch-Hoell, *The Pentecostal Movement: Its Origins, Development and Distinctive Character* (Oslo, Norway: Universitetsforlaget; London: Allen & Unwin; and New York: Humanities Press, 1964), is also silent on pacifism. John Thomas Nichol's *Pentecostalism* (New York: Harper & Row, 1966) did mention pacifism in the International Pentecostal Assemblies but treated it as merely isolated and aberrational. The first histories to recognize early pentecostalism's pacifism were: William W. Menzies, *Anointed to Serve* (Springfield, Mo.: Gospel Publishing House, 1971); Walter J. Hollenweger's *The Pentecostals: The Charismatic Movement in the Churches* (Minneapolis: Augsburg, 1972); and Vinson Synan, *The Holiness-Pentecostal Movement in the U.S.* (Grand Rapids: Eerdmans, 1975). Robert Mapes Anderson, in *The Vision of the Disinherited: The Making of American Pentecostalism* (New York: Oxford University Press, 1979), broke fresh ground by developing its significance and offering the interpretation that it grew out of pentecostals' socioeconomic disenfranchisement. See also Roger Robins, "Our Forgotten Heritage: A Look at Early Pentecostal Pacifism," *Assemblies of God Heritage* 6 (Winter 1986-1987): 3-5; Robins, "A Chronology of Peace: Attitudes Toward War and Peace in the Assemblies of God: 1914-1918," *Pneuma: The Journal of the Society for Pentecostal Studies* 6 (Spring 1984): 3-25; James R. Goff Jr., *Fields White Unto Harvest: Charles F. Parham and the Missionary Origins of Pentecostalism* (Fayetteville: The University of Arkansas Press, 1988); Edith Blumhofer, *The Assemblies of God: A Chapter in the Story of American Pentecostalism*, vol. 1 (to 1941) (Springfield, Mo.: Gospel Publishing House, 1989); Mickey Crews, *The Church of God: A Social History* (Knoxville: The University of Tennessee Press, 1990); and above all Jay Beaman, *Pentecostal Pacifism: The Origins, Development and Rejection of Pacific Belief Among the Pentecostals* (Hillsboro, Kans.: Center for Mennonite Brethren Studies, 1989).

tion of Pacific Belief Among the Pentecostals.[4] Beaman's work, though largely focusing on pentecostalism in the United States, sought to establish the fact that the pentecostal movement worldwide was almost entirely officially pacifist during World War I until certain events and developments of the 1940s and 1950s triggered a basic shift in pentecostal belief about Christians bearing arms in military service. Beaman took care to describe the diversity of positions on military service that existed among pentecostals even during World War I. Even though the pentecostal movement was not a monolithic group of individual pacifists, however, Beaman demonstrated that at the official level the Pentecostal church was a pacifist church.

The predominant "rejection of pacific belief among the pentecostals," according to Beaman, can be traced to their assimilation into the cultural and religious mainstream during and following World War II. The "moral" interpretation of World War II, the institutionalization of the pentecostal chaplaincy, the leadership role of the Assemblies of God and its membership in the National Association of Evangelicals, and the social and economic mobility experienced by pentecostals since World War II are the factors Beaman identified to account for the movement's cultural accommodation and the corresponding demise of pacifism among pentecostals.[5]

Given the sectarian profile that characterized much of early pentecostalism, and pentecostalism's transition over time into a denomination, Beaman's sociological explanation for the loss of pacifist belief among pentecostals makes good sense. As I have stated elsewhere, however, "something is not quite kosher in this portrayal of a majority pacifist movement shifting to a non-pacifist movement within such a short period of time, especially in light of the intensity with which the pacifists held their convictions on this matter."[6] What Beaman's thesis presupposes is that during World War I and through the interwar years pacifism among early pentecostals was caused by the movement's anti-worldly sectarianism and eschatological mind-set. With that assumption intact, the

4. See publication information at end of note 3. The book, drawing on Beaman's 1982 M.Div. thesis, argues that pentecostals lost their pacifism due to assimilation into the American mainstream.

5. Beaman, *Pentecostal Pacifism,* pp. 107-21.

6. Dempster, Review, *Pneuma: The Journal of the Society for Pentecostal Studies* 11 (Fall 1989): 59-64.

cultural assimilation theory gives an intelligible explanation for the loss of pentecostal pacifism. Certainly the link that Beaman assumes to exist between pacifism, the sectarian character, and the eschatological mind-set of early pentecostalism does rest on readily demonstrable facts. The question is whether or not alongside of the anti-cultural expression of pacifism other justifications for pacifism can also be found.

From my own research into North American pentecostal pacifism, particularly within the Assemblies of God, I have found that the arguments used by those pentecostals who were absolute pacifists reflected a variety of theological and ethical convictions. Arthur S. Booth-Clibborn, his son Samuel H. Booth-Clibborn, Frank Bartleman, and Stanley Frodsham were four of the most important absolute pacifists influential in cultivating pacifist sentiment and shaping pacifist belief among early North American pentecostals. More specifically, during World War I their writings were the ones that were most often advertised for purchase, reprinted, or solicited by the leadership of the Assemblies of God in promoting pacifism in the periodicals of the newly-formed denomination.[7] Despite the different justifications for pacifism that can be found in their writings, all agreed that a pacifist ethic was compatible with the option of noncombatant service in a time of war. Three discrete arguments for pacifism recur regularly in the popular writings of these pentecostal absolute pacifists. Although these arguments did promote an anti-cultural "come out from the world" justification for pacifism, they also connected pacifism to the church's redemptive witness to the world.[8] Without question,

---

7. These absolute pacifists were influential in promoting and shaping pacifist sentiment within the Assemblies of God. Notable writings were Arthur Booth-Clibborn, *Blood Against Blood*, esp. 2nd ed. (Springfield, Mo.: Gospel Publishing House, 1914); Samuel H. Booth-Clibborn's writings in the *Weekly Evangel*, esp. "The Christian and War," serialized in issues of 28 April and 5 and 19 May 1917, with some of the same content reappearing in his booklet *Should a Christian Fight? An Appeal to Christian Young Men of All Nations* (Swengal, Pa.: Bible Truth Depot, no date [ca. 1917-1918]); and Frank Bartleman's pieces in the group's official *Weekly Evangel* (June, July, August 1915). See n. 23 for more articles by Bartleman. Stanley H. Frodsham was an influential spokesman for Assemblies of God pacifism, through both a *Word and Witness* article critical of neutrality early in WWI and his role as Executive Secretary of the denomination. Frodsham wrote and sent the letter of 28 April 1917 to President Wilson accompanying the resolution on military service.

8. See my "Reassessing the Moral Rhetoric of Early American Pentecostal Pacifism," *Crux* 26 (March 1990): 23-36; my thesis is that pacifism gave pentecostals the rudi-

the pacifism of Bartleman and Frodsham represented a more narrow sectarian strain of world-denying pacifism, whereas the two Booth-Clibborns related pacifism more positively to the global character and witness of the church; that typification seems too arbitrary to maintain categorically, however, in light of the fact that all four pacifists formulated arguments that at times embodied an anti-cultural attitude and at other times reflected a pro-Christian rationale for pacifism. Although classifying the variety of theological and ethical convictions in a way that makes sense remains a task to be done, one point has become obviously clear: The absolute pacifists did not share in common a single cohesive social philosophy of pacifism. Another salient factor becomes evident when these arguments are set over against the denomination's own practices, at least at the leadership level. The Assemblies of God was a pacifist denomination at the official level during World War I, but at the practical level pacifism was a controversial position among Assemblies of God denominational officials and pastors, at times even generating a divisive spirit. Diversity of opinion on military service was often marked by heated controversy. The official statement on pacifism and the three major arguments used to support pacifism in the popular literature seem at odds with the intense sparring that was revealed at times in the denominational politics surrounding the war issue.

To make sense out of these disparate details in the story of pentecostal pacifism within the Assemblies of God, and to indicate how these details may shed fresh light on understanding the demise of pacifism in the denomination, are the purposes of my essay. First, I will examine three of the principal pacifist arguments put forward to convince North American

---

mentary principles of a social ethic and disclosed a pentecostal social conscience. I argue further that with the loss of pacifism, pentecostals also lost a holistic conception of the church's mission in the world. Such arguments appear also in a paper I read in 1991 in Switzerland, "'Crossing Borders': Arguments Used by Early American Pentecostals in Support of the Global Character of Pacifism," later published in *EPTA Bulletin: The Journal of the European Pentecostal Theological Association,* 10/2 (1991): 63-80. My analysis offers a revision of Jay Beaman's cultural assimilation thesis as an explanation for the demise of pentecostal pacifism. Critics have noted that at least four of the five pacifists I treated — Bartleman, Frodsham, and the Booth-Clibborns — were influential primarily in the Assemblies of God and may not have been very important influences on the pacifism of other pentecostals. The present essay demonstrates my appreciation for that criticism. I wish also to thank Professors Augustus Cerillo and Lewis F. Wilson for helpful criticisms based on expertise in pentecostal history.

pentecostals, particularly those affiliated with the Assemblies of God, during the period of World War I and shortly thereafter. I will analyze these arguments to reveal the dual effects of pacifism within the pentecostal worldview, showing how pacifism both expressed the moral requirement of believers to separate from the dominant values and practices of human culture and expressed the moral value that God places on all members of the human family. After examining the content of the three arguments used by the pentecostal pacifists, I will demonstrate that, as the war progressed, some influential Assemblies of God leaders developed a growing aversion to pacifism. Based on my analysis of the arguments and on identification of factors influencing the denominational politics of the time, I will propose a revision of the cultural assimilation thesis as an interpretive framework to explain the demise of pacifism within the Assemblies of God.

Restoring the Apostolic Faith: Pacifism as the Moral Sign of a Restored New Testament Apostolic Church

The leaders of the pentecostal movement chronicled its "restorationist" character from its inception.[9] In 1912 Charles Parham recollected his

9. In *The Apostolic Faith,* Charles F. Parham wove restorationism through many of his articles — see esp. "The Apostolic Faith Movement," *The Apostolic Faith* 1 (December-January 1912-1913): 1-2 — and he linked his restorationism with pacifism. The present paper does not include Parham because, due to his doctrinal excesses, his racist attitudes, and questions about his sexual conduct, he was anathema to the Assemblies of God from its inception; see Goff, *Fields White Unto Harvest,* esp. pp. 128-46. For other restorationist interpretations, see Frank Bartleman's "God's Onward March Through the Centuries," *The Latter Rain Evangel* 2 (July 1910): 2-8, and his later *How Pentecost Came to Los Angeles — How It Was in the Beginning* (1925), reprinted as *Asuza Street* (Plainfield, N.J.: Logos International, 1980); D. Wesley Myland, *The Latter Rain Covenant and Pentecostal Power* (Chicago: The Evangel Publishing House, 1910), and B. F. Lawrence, *The Apostolic Faith Restored* (St. Louis: The Gospel Publishing House, 1916), both reprinted in *Three Early Pentecostal Tracts* as vol. 14 of the Garland Series, *"The Higher Christian Life": Sources for the Study of the Holiness, Pentecostal, and Keswick Movements,* ed. Donald W. Dayton (48 vols.; New York and London: Garland Publishing, Inc., 1985); and Elizabeth Sisson, "Acts — Two-Four — Past and Present," *Weekly Evangel,* 1 December 1917, pp. 2-3. For analysis of restorationism in early pentecostalism, see Grant Wacker, "Are the Golden Oldies Still Worth Playing? Reflections on History Writing Among Early Pentecostals," *Pneuma: The Journal of the Society for Pentecostal Studies* 8 (Fall 1986): 81-100.

own restorationist vision: "My first position, given July 4th, 1900, was a God-given commission to deliver to this age the truths of a restored PENTECOST, during which time I was called the Projector of the Apostolic Faith Movement."[10] Pentecostals proclaimed the modern-day, worldwide outpouring of the Holy Spirit, commonly associated with Azusa Street, Los Angeles, to be the restoration of the Baptism of the Spirit and the supernatural work of the Spirit from New Testament times to the twentieth-century church. Azusa Street was the Day of Pentecost revisited, a new rain of the Spirit that portended the imminent return of Jesus Christ. A code phrase within early pentecostal discourse that symbolized this restorationist interpretation of the twentieth-century outpouring of the Spirit was "Bible days are here again." "This reversion to the New Testament," B. F. Lawrence told his readers, "was directly responsible for the Movement." Only in order to highlight his claim did Lawrence recognize that the church had a history: "The Pentecostal Movement," he wrote, "has no such history; it leaps the intervening years, crying 'Back to Pentecost.'"[11]

In contrast to Lawrence's denigration of church history, some early pentecostal leaders actually employed an apologetic construction of church history to support their restorationist claim. Frank Bartleman and some others delineated the historical scenario of restoration as follows: The early church was a vital organism that proclaimed the apostolic faith of the New Testament through the first three centuries of church history. The *Pax Romana* that eventually joined church and state in the common cause of promoting Christian civilization culminated in the Dark Ages, during which the light of the gospel finally flickered out. The once-vibrant organism had become "a backslidden" organization, using holy water to baptize the world and its ways. Nevertheless, the argument ran, God by grace intervened in the church's history in order to restore New Testament Christianity. Starting with the Reformation, God used Martin Luther to restore to the church the reality of justification by faith. Later, in the Great Awakenings, God used John Wesley to restore the reality of sanctification through consecrated holy

10. Charles Parham, "Leadership," *The Apostolic Faith* 1 (June 1912): 7.

11. Lawrence, *Apostolic Faith Restored*, p. 12. Pentecostalism sometimes appears quite ahistorical; for an analysis, see Grant Wacker, "A Profile of American Pentecostalism," in *Pastoral Problems in the Pentecostal-Charismatic Movement*, ed. Harold D. Hunter (Cleveland, Tenn.: Society for Pentecostal Studies, 1983), esp. pp. 24-36.

living. In the twentieth century, God acted sovereignly again, this time to restore to the church the reality of Spirit baptism and the supernatural gifts that come through the outpouring of the Holy Spirit. This latter-day outpouring of the Spirit, which pentecostals called the "Latter Rain," was sent by God to empower Christians to gather the harvest of lost men and women into God's kingdom before the impending return of Jesus Christ.[12]

Variations on the restorationist theme were present among pentecostal leaders; however, all shared the view that the pentecostal movement was God's means of restoring the full gospel of the New Testament proclaimed by Jesus and the apostles. Moral commitment to pacifism among early pentecostals has to be appreciated in light of this restorationist understanding of church history. From the pentecostal perspective, militarism entered the church's life when the church backslid and forged a political alliance with the Roman state. In this context, pacifism represented the restoration of the Christian ethic found in the apostolic church of the New Testament to the twentieth-century church.

As a consequence of this logic, one of the apologetic features of the pentecostal argument was to demonstrate that pacifism was the normative position on military service within the early church. "For the first three centuries," according to Samuel Booth-Clibborn, "Christians abstained totally from carnal warfare."[13] To provide evidence for such an assertion, both Booth-Clibborns listed pacifist quotations from the church fathers and gave anecdotes about Roman soldiers being converted and immediately casting their weapons to the ground.[14] According to the younger Booth-Clibborn, early church history "simply swarms" with such accounts of soldiers' conversions to a pacifist outlook.[15] Meanwhile, Bartleman claimed that until the fifth century Roman soldiers were de-

12. For an analysis of Frank Bartleman's view of this "process of restoration" see "Introduction" in Cecil M. Robeck Jr., *Witness to Pentecost: The Life of Frank Bartleman*, vol. 5 of the Garland Series, "The Higher Christian Life": *Sources for the Study of the Holiness, Pentecostal, and Keswick Movements*, ed. Donald W. Dayton (48 vols.; New York and London: Garland Publishers, Inc., 1985), esp. xviii-xxi.

13. Samuel H. Booth-Clibborn, *Should a Christian Fight?* p. 32.

14. Arthur Sydney Booth-Clibborn, *Blood Against Blood* (New York: Charles C. Cook, no date [reprint of preface in the 2nd ed. is dated 1914]), pp. 106-10; S. Booth-Clibborn, *Should a Christian Fight?*, pp. 32-35.

15. S. Booth-Clibborn, *Should a Christian Fight?* p. 33.

nied Holy Communion because they engaged in the immoral practice of killing other human beings.[16]

Arthur Booth-Clibborn clearly drew out the moral implications of this apologetic for pacifism as the normative position in the early church in light of a restorationist interpretation of church history. He made the point in his culminating argument in *Blood Against Blood:* "Wherever there is a revival of the spirit of Apostolic Christianity," he wrote, "there also appears a revival of the conviction and the testimony that war is anti-Christian."[17] From this pentecostal restorationist perspective, pacifism was the concrete moral practice that signaled the recovery of the original, eschatological apostolic faith of the New Testament. The key phrases pentecostals used most often to portray the eschatological character of Christian life that pacifism encapsulated were "the heavenly citizenship of the Christian" and "the pilgrim role of the church." Shortly after the war began Frank Bartleman orchestrated these themes together in his forthright challenge to the pentecostal readership of *Word and Work:*

> War is damnation in the end to all concerned. . . . The present nations at war declare they will fight to a finish. . . . The hopelessness of all such efforts for peace should cause every true Christian to separate himself from it, confessing themselves [*sic*] but "strangers and pilgrims" in this world. . . . We are not of this world, but "our citizenship is in heaven" from whence we await our Savior. We must be separate from "nationalism." . . . The early church occupied a position of separation from nationalism completely separated unto God, and so must the church of the end.[18]

Based on the believer's heavenly citizenship and pilgrim role, Stanley Frodsham in the October 1915 issue of *Word and Witness* criticized the viewpoint of fellow pentecostals who argued in *The Evangel* that "the children of God should preserve an attitude of strict neutrality to the warring nations in Europe." In Frodsham's view, to remain neutral on the war issue was to support the patriotism that fired up the war spirit. Such national pride was an "abomination in the sight of God." Moreover, according to Frodsham, "one of the old things that pass away when one becomes

16. Frank Bartleman, "Christian Preparedness," *Word and Work* (ca. 1916), p. 114.
17. Booth-Clibborn, *Blood Against Blood,* p. 146.
18. Frank Bartleman, "War and the Christian," *Word and Work* (ca. 1915), p. 83.

a new creature in Christ" is such "cultural love for the nation where one happened to be born." To be translated into the kingdom of God's dear son meant that "loyalty to the new King should swallow up all other loyalties." Frodsham argued that this new center of loyalty eliminated the possibility that a Christian could remain neutral on the war. A pentecostal who sang "this world, this world is not my home" should not remain neutral toward "the nations who have drawn the sword to kill those of the same blood in other nations . . . with their policy of 'War on earth and ill will toward men.'" Because the bellicose rulers of this world denied the truth that God "hath made of one blood the nations of men," Frodsham claimed that they had set themselves "against the Lord and against His anointed." The options were clear: "Is any child of God going to side with these belligerent kings? Will he not rather side with the Prince of Peace under whose banner of love he has chosen to serve?"[19]

Some aspects of Frodsham's argument are enigmatic and their meaning difficult to track. But one clear idea was his conception that an eschatology which "made this world not his home" required a pacifism that resisted compliance with the world's pugnacious ways and witnessed to the universal values of the gospel. This grounding of Christian pacifism in a restorationist understanding connected closely with the notion that the church had a prophetic mission to unmask the sinful pretensions of the world. During the war, that second line of argument recurred with rhythmic frequency.

Unmasking the Reality of Social Evil: Pacifism as the Moral Critique of the Existing Sinful Social Order

The prophetic indictment of the first world war by pentecostal pacifists also was based on a fundamental conviction about fallen human nature. War was both rooted in and an expression of human sinfulness. As the Apostle James had declared in his epistle, war arose from "the lusts of man" (cf. James 4:1-2). That was why war bore all the features of human sin: cheating, greed, hatred, hypocrisy, lying, murder, pride, spying, vengeance, and so on. Marked by such vices, war explicitly ex-

19. Stanley H. Frodsham, "Our Heavenly Citizenship," *Word and Witness* 12 (October 1915): 3.

ploited the victim while it subtly dehumanized the victor. Thus, for Bartleman, war was "insanity, madness." It was "a great insane asylum turned out of doors."[20]

According to Bartleman and other absolute pacifists, war was more than individual human sinfulness on the loose. It was institutionalized evil which reflected the sinful power structure of the world system. "Men's laws of destruction," "organized iniquity," and "systematized sinning" are some of the phrases Arthur Booth-Clibborn used against war in *Blood Against Blood*.[21] "The Scripture shows us," he wrote, "that organized sin is much worse in the sight of God than are the sins of individuals." To its shame, he went on, the church has at times been complicit in legitimizing "the organized slaying of millions in the wars" through an "unholy alliance" with emperors and governments.[22]

Pacifist pentecostals targeted two groups within the power structure, the ruling politicians and the upper class, because the political policies and practices of those groups revealed the structural evil that war represented and perpetuated. The ruling politicians, Bartleman believed, used the war machine to consolidate their power. Weaker nations were blamed for the failed domestic policies and misguided international relations of stronger nations, and thus were cast into the role of enemy. Military conscription of civilians provided the soldiers needed to fight the enemy and, as a consequence, to ameliorate the unsolvable social problems of the respective countries.[23] Sounding like Old Testament prophets, the pacifist preachers catalogued the warring nations, unmasking the sins each tried to cover and pronouncing the war to be God's judgment on the nations for their "brazen hypocrisy."[24] Samuel Booth-Clibborn,

20. Bartleman, *War and the Christian* (tract, ca. 1922), p. 4.

21. A. Booth-Clibborn, *Blood Against Blood*, pp. 39, 82, 73.

22. A. Booth-Clibborn, *Blood Against Blood*, pp. 87-88.

23. These indictments were repeated by Bartleman in a variety of articles: "Present Day Conditions," *Weekly Evangel*, 5 June 1915, p. 3; "The European War," *Weekly Evangel*, 10 July 1915, p. 3; "What Will The Harvest Be?" *Weekly Evangel*, 7 August 1915, p. 1; "The War — Our Danger," *Word and Work*, November 1915, pp. 300-301; "Christian Preparedness," *Word and Work* (ca. 1916), pp. 114-15; "Not of This World," *Word and Work* (ca. 1916), pp. 296-97; "The World War," *Word and Work*, July 1916, pp. 296-97; "The World Situation," *Word and Work* (ca. 1916), pp. 344-45; "The Money God," *Word and Work* (ca. 1916-1917), pp. 274-75; "A Time of Trouble," *Word and Work* (April 1917), pp. 185-86.

24. S. Booth-Clibborn, *Should a Christian Fight?* p. 19. Frank Bartleman also used

for example, listed the social sins which generated "the present cataclysm":

> *England* is being punished for her increasing and overbearing pride, coupled with wretched hypocrisy in trying to cover such sins as her cowardly Boer War, her Chinese opium scandal, her drunkenness and oppression of the poor. . . .
>
> *Germany* for her military pride and greed of conquest, her boastful and blasphemous philosophies which have developed unbelief in numberless young minds, and for her subtle and clever higher criticism which has been Satan's best weapon for undermining man's faith in God's Holy Word as being true and inspired.
>
> *France* for her blatant infidelity and unspeakably vile morals . . . trying hard to beat Sodom's record for disgusting immorality, [while] making frantic but useless efforts to cover it all up with an outward show of art, architecture and science.
>
> *Belgium* for her recent Congo atrocities, her widespread immorality and drunkenness. . . .
>
> *Russia* for her continual and cruel treatment of God's chosen people, the Jews, not to speak of her over-bearing tyranny on her own subjects.
>
> *Italy* for her general wickedness and anarchy, which sins have been encouraged rather than reproved by the Roman Catholic Church, the "harlot" of Revelation (see Rev. 17:5, 9).[25]

The pentecostal pacifists saw the United States as also under divine judgment, charging it with blatant idolatry. The war was God's judgment on America for "her degrading and long-continued worship of the golden calf — the almighty (?) dollar."[26] War camouflaged these national sins and provided a mechanism under the guise of patriotism for the stronger nations to compete for "the spoils" of the weaker ones.[27] Drawing a clear distinction between civilian populations and government officials, Bartleman unhesitatingly blamed government bureaucrats for the carnage of war:

---

this rhetorical technique; see esp. "Present Day Conditions," p. 3; "What Will the Harvest Be?" p. 1; and "The War — Our Danger," p. 300.

25. S. Booth-Clibborn, *Should a Christian Fight?* pp. 19-20.

26. S. Booth-Clibborn, *Should a Christian Fight?* p. 20.

27. Bartleman, "War and the Christian" (article), p. 82; S. Booth-Clibborn, "What Will the Harvest Be?" p. 1.

Crimination and recrimination among politicians . . . proves to us beyond the shadow of doubt that human governments are simply rotten. Men in public office and ruling positions rule their fellow-men, produce wars or avoid them, according to their own fancies and welfare. . . . The souls of men are used up as so much fodder for their own wills and wishes.[28]

Even though politicians used the military system for the accumulation of power, economic expansion, and amelioration of social problems at home, the pacifists considered the beneficiaries of this material production to be the rich classes of the world's nations. They thought this was especially true in the United States. An American "'money bag' despotism," as Bartleman labeled it,[29] of the ruler and the capitalist exploited the poor and working classes in at least two ways. Economically, war increased the disparity between rich and poor: the rich got richer and the poor got poorer until finally "the rich man's dog gets more meat than the poor man's family."[30] The capitalist viewed the war as a commercial enterprise which produced profits. Reprehensibly, the profits came from exploiting the misfortune of others. In a wartime economy the prices for munitions as well as for wheat and other staples of life were driven up for profit. And who received the profits? Bartleman listed the recipients as "Wall Street interests, Pork Barrel administration, Brewer's Corporation, Syndicate and Monopoly, Steel Trust and Armor Plate, Powder Trust, etc. without end."[31] Meanwhile, Bartleman noted, "the poor must live on half rations. The sick must die. We cannot buy new clothes. We cannot buy good food. We cannot travel. Rent prices are criminally high." In Bartleman's view the most galling part of this hypocrisy was that the politicians who had enough power to "commandeer a nation" into war did nothing about this "handful of exploiters."[32] "Human leeches" is how he characterized such monopolists.[33]

Observing the shrewd way the wealthy used the government's promotion of patriotism for their own benefit, Bartleman chided the rich for their ingenuity in finding schemes to rip off the common worker:

28. Bartleman, "War and the Christian" (article), p. 83.
29. Bartleman, "The War — Our Danger," p. 301.
30. Bartleman, "In the Last Days," p. 393.
31. Bartleman, "War and the Christian" (article), p. 83.
32. Bartleman, *War and the Christian* (tract), p. 4.
33. Bartleman, "In the Last Days," p. 393.

> Patriotism in most cases has proven to spell "Graft." "Dollar" patrio-
> tism. War bonds are reduced in price until the poor man is either
> forced or frightened into unloading. Then they suddenly soar above
> par. Stung again! They are now in the hands of the patriotic Broker.[34]

Individual greed, the capitalist free-market system, and the politicians
who made public policy coalesced together to institutionalize the unequal
distribution of wealth. In Bartleman's judgment, the distance between the
classes in wartime constituted such an egregious criminal act that it
"crie[d] to heaven." "Think of Charlie Chaplin, the popular movie actor,
getting around a half million dollars and over, for one year's salary while
millions are starving."[35]

Economic exploitation of the poor by the rich was only one aspect
of the evil social functions of war. The other area that the pacifists dwelled
on was the cost in human life. From the war's outset, they emphasized
that the American upper class was profiting financially from the bloody
transaction of human killing. For example, Samuel Booth-Clibborn recalled how the rich profited without regard to human suffering when the
Allies looked to U.S. firms for millions of tons of munitions.

> Did these millionaires "stand by the president" by keeping strictly neu-
> tral??? No!!! Not while there was a chance of piling up dollars, even
> though every one of them was dripping with the blood and tears of tor-
> tured Europe.[36]

After America entered the war, a new pool of the poor and working class
helped to revitalize this "blood money" exchange of human lives for
profit. Bartleman saw in this killing the ultimate irony: "the innocent are
sent to do the killing, and be killed" while "those responsible for the wars
are generally beyond its reach."[37]

Arthur Booth-Clibborn recalled a personal incident that made him
see with extraordinary clarity the systemic evil involved in this exchange
of life for money. He had visited a dock at Cork in Ireland where a ship

---

34. Bartleman, *War and the Christian* (tract), p. 4.
35. Bartleman, "Christian Preparedness," p. 114.
36. S. Booth-Clibborn, *Should a Christian Fight?* p. 42.
37. Bartleman, *War and the Christian* (tract), p. 4; cf. "The War — Our Danger,"
p. 301.

was en route to war and saw firsthand the "organized inequity" which, in his words, used "human flesh as 'food for cannon.'"

> As I looked at a mass of . . . factory lads from Lancashire packed on the forward deck of a great transport ship . . . and talked to them from one ship to the other, there was a horrid squeezing at my heart. The scene reminded one of slavery, or the Irish cattle market preceding the shambles. Poor lads! How hollow their laughter sounded. How shy they looked when I passed them across some religious literature. A shilling a head was their price. The Queen's shilling, taken perhaps outside some corner saloon. And some widow's prodigal boys were probably among them. My heart felt like bursting.[38]

The Booth-Clibborns and Frank Bartleman were absolute pacifists who shared the belief that war was institutionalized violence under the cover of law. For them, a Christian resisted complicity in the social evil called war through the practice of pacifism. Living by the principles of Christian pacifism was a way to critique the power structure of the world order and to do so with definite moral action.

For such pacifists, an essential part of the church's moral witness was to remind the world and its military, economic, and political systems of God's judgment on human sin, both individual and corporate. Moreover, resisting cultural assimilation into the world's power structure was the only way for the church to maintain its loyalty to Jesus Christ and keep its true identity as an eschatological community. Early pentecostal pacifism built on these theological and ethical convictions. Bartleman succinctly expressed such ethics without pulling any punches: "The war church is a harlot church," he wrote, persecuting its pacifists in order to sell its own members for blood money — to sell them in exchange for the favor of the powerful and the rich.[39] For him, a commitment to pacifism was the moral way to express the truth that "the 'body of Christ' is not the Body of 'a harlot'."[40] Pacifism was a way to remind the world, in practical behavior, that the church and its moral conscience were not for sale to the highest bidder.

The church was called to do more than stand against the world; it

38. A. Booth-Clibborn, *Blood Against Blood,* p. 83.
39. Bartleman, *War and the Christian* (tract), p. 4.
40. Bartleman, "War and the Christian" (article), p. 83.

was called also to witness proactively for the fundamental value of human life.

Affirming the Value of Human Life: Pacifism as the Certification of the Universal Value of Humanity

The decision of whether to participate in war's killing or in making peace made clear what were the Christian's ultimate loyalties, values, and dispositions. To kill another human being in war was to demonstrate through one's conduct that one's ultimate loyalty was to what Arthur Booth-Clibborn called "the Earth Empire." The earth empire "selfishly cuts up humanity as a whole in the supposed interest of a part . . . [and] places kings and countries between the soul and Christ." It disseminated propaganda for "the organized discouraging of any good and kind information about 'the hereditary enemy' or rival nationality," and it willfully cultivated a "blind and narrow spirit" which was "the seed of war."[41] In contrast, Christians were people who gave their ultimate loyalty to Jesus Christ after experiencing a genuine conversion to God. In Booth-Clibborn's words, this life-changing transformation, in which all Christians share, lifted their minds "above the fogs of prejudice or party, of politics or nationality." It made them into "overcomers, whose spiritual stature makes their heads come over little partitions which separate nations and organizations — enabling them to examine universal truths in a spirit of universal love, and recognize fellow men everywhere and brethren in those born again."[42]

Intentionally or not, the brand of pacifism that the Assemblies of God leaders promoted among early pentecostals through Arthur Booth-Clibborn's book *Blood Against Blood* was, in the author's words, "pro-Christian." Ultimately, Booth-Clibborn's pacifism was a pacifism rooted not in a spirit of anti-militarism but in an attempt to actualize the way of Christian peacemaking in the world. The practice of Christian pacifism necessarily required the transforming power of the gospel. In Booth-Clibborn's view, any effort to build international harmony without a true spiritual life led only to the delusion of a false peace; the real war could be

41. A. Booth-Clibborn, *Blood Against Blood*, p. 26.
42. A. Booth-Clibborn, *Blood Against Blood*, p. 31.

won only by killing "the war spirit" within, through spiritual transformation. "In the trans-Calvary empire alone," he wrote, "can peace be found either for a world or for an individual soul. But those who have been born again alone dwell there. The words 'enemy' and 'foreigner' are not in their language." The ultimate distinction between "the Earth Empire" and the "trans-Calvary Empire" was "an essential difference in *spirit and disposition* and *in the means employed to remedy the evils in the world*." For the unregenerate "it is carnal power and worldly war, expressed in hatred and ending in death; to the Christian, it is spiritual power and gospel war, expressed in love and ending in life."[43]

For these men, Christian pacifism not only reflected a pursuit of peace based on a spiritual foundation; in a very explicit way it also certified the gospel that the church proclaimed to a war-ridden world. For instance, Bartleman stated flatly that the Christian who went to war against fellow human beings thereby betrayed "the principles of the Christ who died for all men."[44] "God's grace and Gospel are international," he declared; "Christ died for all men."[45] In the same vein, Samuel Booth-Clibborn expressed disbelief at the dehumanizing effects of war. War caused people to become calloused toward the very human lives Jesus came to save: reading about "thousands upon thousands of precious souls *for whom Christ died*' being blasted into eternity or sunk in the ocean, causes the average person no more feeling than as if they were so many swatted flies or drowned rats."[46] In the view of these pentecostal pacifists, those spent lives had value — a value placed on them by Jesus Christ in his redemptive death.

It was not only the redemptive death of Jesus Christ that certified the value God places on all people. Redemption only disclosed that which God had deemed of value in creation itself; all people were part of a common humanity already in Adam, a humanity God loved. Killing humans in war therefore denied a central truth of natural law: by definition, it denied that all people are a part of a common humanity. Arthur Booth-Clibborn expressed the point eloquently: "Those persons who died out yonder belonged, after all, to no empire, to no church, to no organization

---

43. A. Booth-Clibborn, *Blood Against Blood*, pp. 125, 99, 95, 14 (his emphasis).
44. Bartleman, *War and the Christian* (tract), p. 3.
45. Bartleman, "Christian Citizenship," p. 2.
46. S. Booth-Clibborn, *Should a Christian Fight?* p. 18.

or sect. They belonged to God, to humanity, to each of us, as we belong to them." According to Booth-Clibborn, the truly converted person recognizes that in belonging to Christ he also belongs "to humanity and not to any nation." This, wrote he, "will settle the question of war for him forever."[47]

According to this logic, when a Christian believer kills his fellow Christian in war, the act creates a double moral evil. In the words of the elder Booth-Clibborn: "In war the worldling denies one kind of tie in killing his fellow-creature; the Christian denies two kinds — he kills his *fellow-creature* and his *fellow-Christian*."[48] Bartleman agreed. The very idea of "converting men by the power of the Gospel, and later killing these same converts, across some imaginary boundary line," he wrote, "is unthinkable."[49]

These men saw Christians killing Christians as a violation both of natural law and of Christ's law; moreover, such actions violated the church's identity as the community who made visible the new humanity that exists in Christ. Samuel Booth-Clibborn emphasized this principle from Paul's teaching, quoting or citing 1 Corinthians 12:13, "For in the one Spirit we were all baptized into one body — Jews or Greeks, slaves or free"; 1 Corinthians 12:27, "Now you are the body of Christ and individually members of it"; Colossians 3:11, "In that renewal there is no longer Greek and Jew, circumcised and uncircumcised, barbarian, Scythian, slave and free; but Christ is all and in all"; and Romans 12:5, "so we, who are many, are one body in Christ, and individually we are members one of another." From these biblical affirmations Booth-Clibborn adduced that the Body of Christ is composed of people of different national identities united into "one mystical Body of which Christ is the Head." He claimed that "as a member of that Body," a Christian "must love its members irrespective of their nationality." In the younger Booth-Clibborn's mind, Paul's portrayal of the church was inconsistent with the practice of Christians from different countries fighting, hating, and killing each other. Therefore, in saying a "Yes" to Christ, the Christian as a member of Christ's Body must say a "No" to the wars of the world.[50]

47. A. Booth-Clibborn, *Blood Against Blood,* p. 30.
48. A. Booth-Clibborn, *Blood Against Blood,* p. 32.
49. Bartleman, "Christian Citizenship," p. 1.
50. S. Booth-Clibborn, *Should a Christian Fight?* pp. 14-15.

Thus the pacifist pentecostal writers put forward three major arguments against killing in war: the value of a common humanity created by God, the value of a humanity headed toward redemption in Christ, and the value of a new humanity already existing as the Body of Christ. But Arthur Booth-Clibborn thought that, however argued, the ethical question boiled down to the same basic moral value. "And so, as in all such questions of right and wrong," he reflected, "everything comes finally to a point, and that point is *life* — human life."[51] In this theological context pacifism was moral because it valued all people created by God for whom Christ died, and because it gave visible expression to this pro-life witness in its own transnational community of regenerated believers.

In light of the three salient arguments used by early pentecostals to justify their pacifism, and in light of the pacifist Assemblies of God statement of 1917, it seems justifiable to infer that the Assemblies of God was "officially" a pacifist church during World War I. We may also infer that the Assemblies of God was "officially" a pacifist church from the fact that a majority of its members held a pacifist belief in concert with the denominational statement and in keeping with the arguments that the leaders marshaled to support pentecostal pacifism. The official denominational statement and the way the denominational literature promoted the writings of the absolute pacifists support these inferences. And so, it would seem perspicacious and convincing to use the cultural assimilation thesis to explain the later demise of pacifism which was codified in a denominational statement on military service in 1967. The cultural explanation is all the more plausible in light of the upwardly mobile membership of the Assemblies of God during the 1940s and 1950s.

Nonetheless, the pacifist confession contained in the statement of 1917, and the content analysis of the pentecostals' arguments for pacifism, tell only the conceptual part of the story of pacifism within the Assemblies of God. When the "official" statement and the pacifist rationale are interpreted within the denominational and political contexts in which they were written and distributed, another part of the story becomes significant for understanding this demise of pacifism. The definite contextual features of the story suggest that the "official" pacifist statement and the pacifist arguments may not have represented a position held by a majority of members in the denomination after all; if this is the case, the cul-

51. A. Booth-Clibborn, *Blood Against Blood,* p. 16.

tural assimilation thesis needs to be modified in order to explain the loss of pentecostal pacifism, particularly in the case of the Assemblies of God.

Pentecostal Pacifism, Denominational Dealings, and Political Pressure: Revising the Thesis of Cultural Assimilation

After the Executive Presbytery of the Assemblies of God sent the pacifism statement of 1917 to President Woodrow Wilson, officially declaring the denomination to be a pacifist church, the *Weekly Evangel* published the statement with an explanation to readers. The explanation justified the action of the denomination's leaders on three grounds: (1) pacifism represented the movement's "Quaker principles"; (2) pacifism represented "every branch of the movement, whether in the United States, Canada, Great Britain, or Germany"; and (3) some part of the pentecostal movement needed to take responsibility to speak for the movement as a whole in light of the United States's conscription law.[52]

The first justification, alluding to the movement's Quaker principles, is enigmatic in light of the theological roots of pentecostalism;[53] the second, that pacifism pervaded all branches of the pentecostal movement, is somewhat supported by the documentation. For example, in his study of pacifism, Jay Beaman noted that for the twenty-one pentecostal groups that had formed by 1917, he had found evidence that thirteen of them adhered to pacifism.[54] To some degree, however, the fact that pacifism pervaded all sections of the movement is logically discrete from the num-

52. "The Pentecostal Movement and the Conscription Law," *Weekly Evangel,* 4 August 1917, p. 6.

53. Quaker principles may have been brought into the everyday discourse of pentecostals through influential leaders. Frank Bartleman's mother had nurtured him in the Quaker faith. Arthur Sydney Booth-Clibborn in the third edition of *Blood Against Blood* traced his own pacifist heritage back to the conversion of John Clibborn to the Quaker faith in 1658 (Appendix C, pp. 166-76). Arthur of course passed on his Quaker-based pacifism to his son Samuel. Nonetheless, given the theological roots of the pentecostal movement, the allusion to the movement's "Quaker principles" remains puzzling. For a comprehensive analysis of the theological roots of the broader movement, see Donald W. Dayton, *The Theological Roots of Pentecostalism* (Grand Rapids: Zondervan, 1987); and, for a more specific analysis of the origins of pentecostalism that bear on the formation of the Assemblies of God, see Blumhofer, *The Assemblies of God,* esp. vol. 1, pp. 17-64.

54. Beaman, *Pentecostal Pacifism,* p. 30.

ber of pacifists within each branch or section of the movement. The issue of representation is sticky. In fact, from the time discussions on the subject first began, pacifism appears to have been controversial among North American pentecostals. That was true especially within the ranks of the Assemblies of God. From 1914 on — that is, as much as three years prior to the statement of 1917 — the *Christian Evangel* and its successor the *Weekly Evangel* carried exchanges, sometimes rather pointed ones, on the pacifism versus military service issue. Although from 1915 on the editorial policy of these magazines moved cautiously but deliberately toward pacifism, a backlash of reaction clearly indicated that not all Assemblies of God preachers agreed with their church's official magazine.[55] The 1917 statement brought additional reactions from the clergy. In its 1917 session, for example, the Texas District Council (one of the strongest regional powers in the denomination at the time) resolved to cancel the credentials of any preacher who spoke against the government. Such a resolution, of course, applied very directly to pacifists. The Texas delegation was taking a firm stance against the anti-government statements being made by some pacifists, and, in response to this pressure, the General Council in 1917 concurred with them. "Such radicals," it said, "do not represent this General Council."[56]

This antipathy toward pacifists within the Assemblies of God from their non-pacifist fellow members was not restricted to Texas. As the war progressed, some of the denomination's leaders tried to restrict explicit pacifist expression among the church's preachers. This occurred especially after the government established conscription in May of 1917 and even more following the Espionage Act of 1917 and the Sedition Act of 1918. When some pentecostal preachers were numbered among a half-dozen clergy jailed by U.S. marshals for violating wartime laws, for example, E. N. Bell, editor of the *Weekly Evangel* and himself not an absolute pacifist, used the occasion to address the Assemblies of God clergy. In the January 5, 1918, issue of the magazine he sternly warned the clergy to register for the draft in order to make their exemption legal, and told them not

55. This pacifist-militarist exchange is analyzed by Roger Robins, "A Chronology of Peace," pp. 3-25.

56. General Council *Minutes* (1917), pp. 17-18, reported the Assemblies of God reaching a consensus on loyalty to government and honoring the flag, and reported their agreement that those with radical opinions on such matters did not represent the General Council's views.

to push their pacifist convictions into the political arena. Bell told the clergy that if they were arrested for making what the government regarded as treasonous remarks, he doubted that the pentecostal movement would stand with them. Bell wrote not only as editor of the denomination's paper; he also had been the first to serve as Chairman of the General Council, in 1914. He concluded in a foreboding tone: "So let all our preachers be duly warned not to do anything rash, like these other preachers, that will land them in a Federal Penitentiary, or up before a shooting squad for Treason to the Country."[57]

Only seven months after Bell had issued his warning, he urged his paper's readers to destroy one of Frank Bartleman's tracts on pacifism.[58] Part of his motive may have been a quarrel within the pentecostal movement, for as the war progressed Bartleman and his fellow pacifist Samuel H. Booth-Clibborn had come to associate more closely with a faction known as the Oneness Pentecostals. As the oneness branch splintered off from the Assemblies of God, it sustained the radical restorationist vision of the early movement without compromise even under the pressures of the war.[59] In calling upon readers to destroy Bartleman's tract, Bell was no doubt concerned that the content of the pamphlet might invoke the government's reprisal under the Espionage Act. Whatever his intent, the effect of Bell's action was to marginalize Bartleman's influence within the Assemblies of God. Ironically, only three years earlier, in 1915, the *Weekly Evangel* had carried a reprint of Bartleman's tract in its columns; now the editor of the same *Evangel* called the Assemblies of God faithful to destroy the pamphlet.[60] An influential voice whom the denominational leaders had earlier used to provide the rationale for pacifism within the Assemblies of God was now being muted.

With the proverbial mighty pen, Bell kept up his campaign. In October of 1918, two months after calling for Bartleman's tract to be de-

57. E. N. Bell, "Preachers Warned," *Weekly Evangel*, 5 January 1918, p. 4. Interestingly, the resolution on pacifism was formulated during a brief period when E. N. Bell was not serving as an officer within the Assemblies of God. Bell seemed to conform to the pacifism of the movement upon his return to the ranks of denominational leadership; yet as time passed his own unease with pacifism came more and more to the surface.

58. E. N. Bell, "Destroy That Tract," *Weekly Evangel*, 24 August 1918, p. 3.

59. Blumhofer, *Assemblies of God*, vol. 1, p. 434 n. 16.

60. The tract was Bartleman's *Present Day Conditions;* the *Weekly Evangel* had printed it in its 5 June 1915 issue.

stroyed, he went on record flatly opposing the pacifists' contention that killing in war was murder. "When a soldier obeys his country in executing just punishment on the criminal Hun," he wrote, that soldier was not a murderer so long as his motive was not personal hatred of the enemy.[61] The fault line on the pacifist issue was widening. Many denominational leaders, Bell included, had become increasingly disaffected with the pacifist position after the United States entered the war. Pacifists such as Frank Bartleman and Samuel H. Booth-Clibborn had apparently become disenchanted with the Assemblies of God, preferring to associate with more radical restorationist pentecostal groups.

Along with the growing strain in relations between certain denominational leaders and leading pacifist spokespersons, both the government's concerted effort to clamp down on both pacifist activity and the patriotic spirit that swept through the country after America entered the war caused many pentecostal Christians to break ranks with those who were conscientiously opposed to the war. When the war was over, Frank Bartleman, reflecting on pacifism within the Pentecostal church from a global perspective, stated bluntly that during the war "the Pentecostal failed to stand by the Lord."[62] It was clear to Bartleman that World War I had robbed "the church of her sacred calling and 'pilgrim' role" and plunged her headlong "into the vortex of world politics and patriotism, with all its fallen prejudices and preferences, avarices, cruelties, hates and murders."[63] In a two-part article published in the *Pentecostal Evangel* in 1930 Donald Gee concurred with Bartleman's assessment. Like Bartleman, he concluded that the church as a whole had imbibed the patriotic spirit during World War I and betrayed its own pacifist principles.[64] Seen in the light of history, the denomination's second justification for its pacifist statement of 1917 (that pacifism pervaded all branches of the pentecostal movement) turns out to have been hyperbole.

The third and final justification the Assemblies of God executives used to register the denomination as a pacifist church (the idea that someone had to speak for all pentecostals in response to the conscription law)

61. E. N. Bell, "Question and Answers," *Weekly Evangel,* 19 October 1918, p. 5.
62. Bartleman, *War and the Christian* (tract), p. 4.
63. Bartleman, *Christian Citizenship,* p. 2.
64. Donald Gee, "War, the Bible and the Christian," *Pentecostal Evangel,* 8 November 1930), p. 6.

is really a disguised confession. It was in the context of the press of dead-lines imposed by the United States government and the conditions established by Congress for religious denominations to qualify their members for conscientious objector status that the Assemblies of God leadership registered the denomination as a pacifist church;[65] in other words, the action was politically necessary to give draft protection to those pentecostals who were indeed pacifists. Only if the church as a whole registered as a pacifist denomination could its pacifist members — whatever their number — receive official status as conscientious objectors. Accordingly, the statement itself and the rationales developed to justify it simply do not provide reliable measures of how deep or broad pacifist belief was in the Assemblies of God movement as a whole. The official position adopted by the church was not necessarily based on a majority consensus of the church's membership; it was an action that the denomination's leaders (by their own confession) took in order to protect those members who wanted to claim conscientious objector status. Moreover, for the denomination's clergy the "official" position provided a way to secure ministerial exemptions. That was true both for preachers who were principled pacifists and for those who were not but who nonetheless believed that the clergy as a class should not be involved in combatant service and the taking of human life.

Considered in its context, the denomination's pacifist statement of 1917 does not point to the uncritical conclusion that the Assemblies of God was a pacifist movement during World War I. Officially, the denomination did register itself as such with the government. At a practical level, however, the Assemblies of God was made up of regional District Councils, some of whose leadership expressed explicit sympathy for the American war effort, and of individual members, many of whom chose as a matter of personal conscience to participate in military service. The official action taken by the Assemblies of God leaders protected those pentecostal believers who wished to be conscientious objectors, but by no means all church members chose this position.

The political context also casts fresh light on the significance of the three arguments we analyzed in interpreting pacifism within the Assemblies of God. The theological and ethical arguments for pacifism demonstrated that within the thinking of pentecostals a variety of justifications

65. "The Pentecostal Movement and the Conscription Law," *Weekly Evangel*, p. 6.

existed for pacifism as a normative moral position. Pacifism was tied to the idea of restoring a vibrant apostolic faith, to resisting assimilation into an exploitive, war-ridden world, and to affirming the value of human life. Accordingly, for some pentecostals, pacifism became the moral sign of a restored New Testament faith, the moral critique of the existing sinful social order, and the moral certification of the universal value of humanity — a humanity that was created by God, redeemed by Jesus Christ, and was now finding visible expression in the church. All of these arguments reflect the dissonance that early pentecostals as a whole felt toward the world of human culture. According to the pentecostal absolute pacifists, a pacifist way of life was an expression of a sojourner's mentality which made it clear that this world was not the pentecostal pilgrim's home.

The arguments to support the normativeness of pacifism indicate just as clearly that pentecostalism's absolute pacifists viewed a pacifist way of life as a positive expression of the truth of the gospel. Pacifism was understood as a way of life that both resisted accommodation to the world and expressed the truth of God's love for all human beings. It validated the church's proclamation that God was the creator of human life, that Jesus died to save all people, and that the church was a multinational community.

Given the sturdy theological and ethical content of these arguments (whatever their sense of ambivalence between anti-cultural and pro-Christian sentiments) and the intensity with which the pacifists presented them, it seems almost incredible that the denomination could lose its pacifism as rapidly as it did. It seems doubly incredible if a majority of pentecostals within the Assemblies of God were pacifists and believed in this rationale.

Our investigation, in fact, reveals something different: the absolute pacifists' arguments had a definite quality of advocacy to them. The arguments were written by pentecostals to other pentecostals, and their goal was persuasion. They were not intended to describe an established denominational position. To be sure, the popular literature functioned to express and consolidate some already-existing sentiment; but its main function, or at least the hope, was quite clearly to bring more pentecostals into the pacifist fold.

*   *

When the theological and ethical content and the persuasive functions of these arguments are coupled with other factors of the time, it seems that the cultural assimilation theory needs to be nuanced in an important way. Only then can the theory account for the demise of pentecostal pacifism, at least in the case of the Assemblies of God. Given the advocacy character of the pacifist literature, the theological and ethical content of the pacifist arguments, the political nature of the 1917 statement, the disaffection as the war progressed between the denominational leaders and some of the spokespersons for pacifism, and the eyewitness appraisal of pacifists like Bartleman and Gee — given all of these, the change that took place within the Assemblies of God between 1917 and 1967 regarding the view toward military service needs a religious as well as a cultural explanation. This religious explanation is not hard to find, and can be traced back to the denomination's loss of its prophetic pacifist minority. These minority pacifists, holding some overlapping ideas and common arguments, used a variety of theological frameworks and ethical principles to justify Christian pacifism,[66] but before they had an opportunity to cultivate a pacifist *tradition,* history had overtaken them and the nation's patriotic war spirit had invaded the house, never to leave. Without a theologically-informed ethical tradition to sustain the pacifists' numbers and to hand down their beliefs to new generations, the demise of pentecostal pacifism within the Assemblies of God was only a matter of time. That demise would become all the more apparent in World War II, the Korean War, and the Vietnam War; but the unraveling of the pacifist tradition within the Assemblies of God Church was already in motion by the end of World War I.[67] The loss

66. Even a cursory examination of representative pacifist literature suggests to the reader that early pentecostals did not set forth a unified set of theological convictions and ethical principles to justify Christian pacifism. A typology of the North American pentecostal pacifism examined in this essay might be characterized as follows: "sectarian" pacifism (Frodsham); "dispensationalist" pacifism (S. Booth-Clibborn); "prophetic" pacifism (Bartleman); and "ethical-humanitarian" pacifism (A. Booth-Clibborn). Including other pacifists in addition to the four examined in this paper might expand the database within each of these types or expand the variety of types.

67. Writing in 1954 when the church was still officially pacifist, Irvine John Harrison observed that Assemblies of God people had radically changed their practice by World War II. He noted that the Executive's 1917 statement was still held officially, and that "at least theoretically the Assemblies of God are still a church which holds in common with Quakers, Mennonites and others their refusal to bear arms even to resist aggression." But he also noted that in World War II only an "infinitismal [*sic*]" fraction of members had

of the prophetic strain of pacifists within the movement grew out of theological and ethical conditions which allowed for the subsequent cultural accommodation of the denomination.

Ironically, the statement on military service adopted in 1967 put into denominational policy the truth as it had been *practiced* within the Assemblies of God even in 1917: "We shall continue to insist, as we have historically, on the right of each member to choose for himself whether to declare his position as a combatant, a non-combatant, or a conscientious objector."[68] When the pluralism of pentecostal conscience was moved from the level of practice to "official" policy, however, the 1967 statement forfeited the opportunity of the denomination's youth to claim conscientious objector status. The Selective Service Act of 1967 (like U.S. conscription laws ever since 1917) granted conscientious objector status only to those whose conscience was grounded in a pacifism nurtured by religious conviction and teaching.[69] The truth of the matter, however, is that since 1917 both the conscription laws and the court decisions interpreting them have made conscientious objection more and more a matter of individual conscience and less a matter of membership in a church officially recognized as pacifist. Therefore, from a legal standpoint, the Assemblies of God had far less need in 1967 (as opposed to 1917) to maintain an official statement of the denomination's pacifism in order to protect their pacifist minority; the need to be sensitively inclusive of conscientious objectors within their ranks by keeping the pacifist statement at the "official" level of the denomination's Constitution no longer existed as it had in World War I.

Nonetheless, the change in the "official" statement adopted during the agony of the Vietnam war did indeed reveal that pacifism was past

---

chosen conscientious objection; and he expressed personal support of the U.S. war effort in grandiose rhetoric (Harrison, "A History of the Assemblies of God," pp. 156-57). No doubt a great majority of Assemblies of God members shared Harrison's patriotism; yet vestiges of the earlier pacifism remained. Jay Beaman has noted that of approximately 12,000 World War II objectors in Civilian Public Service, pentecostals numbered about 131; and that of the 131, about 20 can be identified as Assemblies of God. For the period from World War II through 1967, the time of the change in the official statement, Beaman chronicled various developments (including some behind-the-scenes maneuvering) that culminated in that change; see *Pentecostal Pacifism*, pp. 103, 107-18.

68. General Council *Minutes* (1967), p. 35.

69. *Selective Service Act of 1967* (PL 90-40), 81 Stat. 100.

history within a culturally accommodated Assemblies of God. Sad to say, the accommodation left believers with only an individual right of conscience and no church teaching, one way or the other, to inform the exercise of that right in a morally responsible manner.

The Fragmentation of the Church
and Its Unity in Peacemaking:
A Mennonite Perspective

LOIS Y. BARRETT

That peace has been a cause of division among the Christian churches has been amply illustrated in history as it relates to the Anabaptist-Mennonite movement. In sixteenth-century Europe, for example, both the Augsburg Confession and the Second Helvetic Confession explicitly condemned the Anabaptists, in part, because of their refusal to take up arms in defense of the state. In Strasbourg, many Anabaptists refused to swear oaths of allegiance to the city, required by law every January, because part of that oath was a commitment to defend the city militarily if necessary.[1] Anabaptists refused to be magistrates, with the power of life and death over others; for this they were condemned by both the Roman Catholic church and the churches of the magisterial Reformation, and governmental powers were engaged to hunt down, torture, burn, or drown thousands of them during the sixteenth century. Many of the martyr stories are recounted in the seventeenth-century book known as the *Martyrs Mirror*,[2] which continues to be reprinted. A re-

---

1. See, for example, description of the hearing of Anabaptist Michael Ecker and the arrests of forty others in *Quellen zur Geschichte der Täufer*, vol. 7, *Elsaß, 1. Teil, Stadt Straßburg*, 1522-1532, ed. Johann Adam, Manfred Krebs, and Hans Georg Rott (Gütersloh: Gerd Mohn, 1959), Nos. 128 and 130, March 31, 1528, and April 22, 1528, pp. 153-54.

2. Thieleman J. van Braght, *The Bloody Theater, or, Martyrs Mirror of the Defenseless*

cent Mennonite joke book claims that you're really a Mennonite when "you think that a book describing 4,000 grisly executions might make a nice wedding gift."[3] The joke is an illustration of the continuing impact of the sixteenth-century martyrdoms on the Mennonite psyche. The distrust on the side of the sixteenth-century Anabaptists is evident in the first written Anabaptist confession of faith, the Schleitheim Confession of 1527. There, one of the ways in which Anabaptists agreed to be separate from the evil of the world was to avoid attendance at the state churches.[4]

Menno Simons, a second-generation Anabaptist leader in the Low Countries for whom the movement came to be named, put Jesus Christ at the center of all interpretation of Scripture. Thus, he argued, Christians should follow Christ's example in rejecting violence as a means of dealing with enemies.

> If Christ fights his enemies with the sword of His mouth, if he smites the earth with the rod of his mouth, and slays the wicked with the breath of his lips; and if we are to be conformed to his image, how can we, then, oppose our enemies with any other sword?[5]

On the strength of this conviction, Mennonites have migrated to the Americas and to eastern Europe in search of freedom from military service, which would compromise their beliefs. The memory of the dangers of being a people of peace has been reinforced by later martyrdoms: of two Hutterite young men in an American military prison during World War I, of hundreds of church leaders in the Soviet Union under Stalin. Within the memory of some living Mennonites in the United States are the images of attempted lynchings, barn burnings, the burning of church buildings, and other forms of harassment of nonviolent Mennonites during World War I, many times carried out by persons who

---

Christians, 13th English ed., trans. Joseph F. Sohm (Scottdale, Pa.: Herald Press, 1982). First published in Dutch in 1660.

    3. Craig Haas and Steve Nolt, *The Mennonite Starter Kit* (Intercourse, Pa.: Good Books, 1993), p. 6.

    4. "Brotherly Union of a Number of Children of God Concerning Seven Articles," in *The Legacy of Michael Sattler,* ed. John H. Yoder (Scottdale, Pa.: Herald Press, 1973), p. 38.

    5. *The Complete Works of Menno Simons,* trans. Leonard Verduin, ed. John Christian Wenger (Scottdale, Pa.: Herald Press, 1956), p. 44.

called themselves Christians.[6] The General Conference Mennonite Church early in this century thought it would be possible to cooperate with other denominations in the United States. In 1908 it became a charter member of the Federal Council of Churches of Christ, optimistic that the peace position would soon be adopted by Protestants as a whole. But it withdrew from the Federal Council in 1917, in large part because it had adopted a supportive stance toward U.S. involvement in World War I. After 1917, the General Conference began to focus on making more contacts with other Mennonite groups, with the Friends, and with the Brethren, and these Historic Peace Churches held joint conferences beginning in 1922.[7]

Mennonite denominations and service agencies continue to staff peace offices and provide congregational peace materials. During World War II, the Korean War, and the Vietnam War, Mennonites provided service programs as alternatives to the military for conscientious objectors, Mennonites and others. Mennonite delegate bodies continue to pass statements on peace and nonviolence, the most recent being "'And No One Shall Make Them Afraid'; A Mennonite Statement on Violence" (1997).

My own personal history includes leaving the mainline Protestant denomination in which I was raised to become a Mennonite at the age of twenty-three, in the midst of the Vietnam War. I had become repulsed by the war, by the senseless killing. During my year as a volunteer with Mennonite Voluntary Service, I was attracted to the Mennonite church precisely because of its unapologetic stance against the war (in fact, against all wars) and because of, as I phrased it then, the sense of community I found there.

The issue of peace has not only been a cause of the separation of Mennonites from other church bodies, however; it has also been an opportunity for dialogue. During the time I was a Mennonite pastor in Wichita, Kansas, I was part of an organization called Churches United for Peacemaking, a coalition of more than a dozen congregations who had

6. See James Juhnke, *A People of Two Kingdoms: The Political Acculturation of Kansas Mennonites* (Newton, Kans.: Faith and Life Press, 1975), p. 105; see also Gerlof D. Homan, *American Mennonites and the Great War, 1914-1918* (Scottdale, Pa.: Herald Press, 1956), p. 44.

7. Lois Barrett, *The Vision and the Reality: The Story of Home Missions in the General Conference Mennonite Church* (Newton, Kans.: Faith and Life Press, 1983), p. 147.

taken official action to stand and work for peace. These congregations included not only Historic Peace Churches, but also mainline Protestant churches and two Catholic religious orders.

In recent months I have been more deeply convinced that we in the various denominations need to have dialogue with each other on theological issues, including peacemaking, because we live in the midst of, or perhaps in the shadow of, the same dominant culture; we are influenced by many of the same trends of that culture. We are also influenced by each other. Renewal movements in one church group affect other groups. Renewed interest in spirituality, house churches, the charismatic movement, various forms of Pietism, and liturgical renewal — all these have had an effect across denominational lines. In a sense, we are a means of renewal for each other. To some extent, the same has been happening with regard to peacemaking, and it is important to continue that dialogue.

There are several forces pushing that dialogue forward. In previous conferences and in peace meetings related to the World Council of Churches the changing nature of modern warfare has been noted. Christians of many denominational backgrounds are questioning whether it is possible for a modern war, particularly one involving nuclear weapons, ever to satisfy the just war criteria. A second force encouraging interchurch dialogue is the increasing secularization of modern society. All the denominations are faced with the same questions because the same forces are pushing us to the edges of society; we face questions of relevance in a time when it is deemed possible to teach history in the schools without reference to religion, to make moral decisions without reference to the church, and to schedule children's hockey games on Sunday morning. This secularization is related to the third force pushing us toward dialogue on peacemaking: the disestablishment of the mainline churches and the attempts at establishment of the churches of the evangelical right. We see on the one hand the political efforts of the Christian Coalition, and on the other the Episcopal bishop who complained to a group of us, "I just don't have access to the governor's mansion the way I used to." Is it possible to have new dialogue between churches that are becoming disestablished and those that have lived that way for centuries? Is it possible to have new dialogue with churches that are trying as hard as they can to gain the status of the twenty-first-century versions of establishment?

Because I believe that interchurch dialogue on peacemaking can be fruitful, I enter into that dialogue today. True dialogue involves each party being clear about its own identity and understandings. So I offer a Mennonite perspective on peacemaking. This perspective understands the gospel of peace in the context of the broader theological issues, because the claim is that peace is not a peripheral issue, but is central to the gospel. Peace is not just one of the Mennonite "distinctives," an option that can be added to the Christian faith like the parsley with which one garnishes a casserole. Peace, instead, is an essential ingredient of the gospel. Thus, I intend to look at a number of central theological topics and the way in which peace plays a role in understanding each of them.

The Reality of Evil and Sin

The issue of peacemaking is at the core of our faith because it relates to what we are to do in the face of evil and sin. It is difficult enough to endure accidental suffering or the suffering that comes from natural disasters or death in old age. But a theology of peacemaking is related to how we deal with sin, with evil that was intended. In other words, it attempts to answer the question, How do we deal with enemies?

The context of Jesus' teaching and practice of peacemaking was systemic and intentional evil. His first-century hearers knew about Roman occupation armies, popular uprisings, debtors' prisons, poverty, and death. Anabaptist peace theology in the sixteenth century was likewise developed in the context of the lords' ever more restrictive practices and laws, an increasing number of peasants becoming serfs bound to the land, peasant uprisings, poverty, debt, and martyrdom.[8] In both the first and the sixteenth centuries, a theology of peace developed in relation to the need to confront evil and sin.

A biblical peace theology is not overly optimistic about the nature of the world in which we live. It recognizes the reality of evil, both individual and corporate. Evil is not an illusion; it is not merely the absence of good as shadow (so Plato would say) is the absence of light. Evil is real, and enemies are real. The question is, how do we treat enemies? Are enemies people for whom Christ died? Is there any enemy beyond Christ's

8. See the *Twelve Articles* (Memmingen) in Peter Blickle, *The Reformation of 1525: The German Peasants' War from a New Perspective,* trans. Thomas A. Brady Jr.; see also H. C. Erik Midelfort (Baltimore: Johns Hopkins University Press, 1981), pp. 195-201.

salvation? Even more importantly, what does the way we treat our enemies have to do with our spirituality? In his book *Engaging the Powers,* New Testament scholar Walter Wink includes a chapter called "On Not Becoming What We Hate."[9] There he argues that, when we return hate for hate, violence for violence, we become like our enemies. He says, "[w]hen we resist evil with evil, when we mirror it, when we lash out at it in kind, we simply guarantee its perpetuation."[10] The Allies who hated Hitler and the Holocaust became the ones who dropped the first atomic bombs. Those who refuse to forgive are themselves destroyed in the process. Wink says that, when confronted with evil people, we have three choices: passive acquiescence (flight), violent or aggressive retaliation (fight), or Jesus' third way, a nonviolent way, of overcoming evil, taught in the Sermon on the Mount. Both fight and flight are a way of giving in to evil. The fight option does not get rid of evil; at best, it only creates a new evil. There is no such thing as redemptive violence, Wink writes. Violence cannot redeem us from violence; it only turns us into violent people. *The Return of the Jedi* illustrates this fact; in the movie, Luke Skywalker (the hero) and The Emperor (the embodiment of evil) face each other alone in a spaceship as the battle rages outside. Knowing he must resist the emperor, Luke Skywalker is unsure what to do. The emperor taunts him: Go ahead and hate me; if you hate me, then I have won. You will have become like me.

If I believed in original sin, I would identify it as the desire to have ourselves and everyone connected to us be just alike. For infants and small children, this desire is not sin; it is absolutely necessary in order to grow up and learn a culture and language and to be part of family and community. Children must have the desire to be just like those they love in order to be socialized. But, as we get older, it is easy for that good desire to be distorted. We find it difficult to stay connected with people who are different from us, and often hate those who are not like us. Fighting a common enemy may create community for a while, but, pushed to the extreme, it causes progressive alienation and separation from everyone else, because no one else is exactly like us. Then, of course, there is no way to love God, because God is not just like us.

This sin, this separation from God and from each other, is what

---

9. Walter Wink, *Engaging the Powers* (Minneapolis: Fortress, 1992), pp. 195-207.
10. Wink, *Engaging,* p. 207.

peace theology addresses. Overcoming evil with good, loving enemies, praying for them, using peaceful means to bring about peace, confronting enemies without letting oneself become like them in violence or hate — these are the ways that Christian peacemakers deal with evil and sin.

Jesus Christ and Peace

Our christology also affects our understanding of peacemaking. The plain sense of Jesus' teaching, especially in the Sermon on the Mount, is a call to peacemaking, love of enemies, showing mercy, and forgiving. In fact, the only part of the Lord's Prayer on which Matthew comments is the sentence on forgiveness. There Jesus says that, if we do not forgive those who sin against us, it is not possible for God to forgive our sin.[11] When we love those who do not love us in return, then we are acting as God does.[12]

But peace is not only at the center of Jesus' teaching; it is at the center of the story of his life, death, and resurrection. When faced with enemies who wanted to take his life, Jesus responded without violence. He told Peter, the headstrong disciple, to put away his sword rather than defend him with violence.[13] When Pilate asked Jesus if he were the king of the Jews, Jesus replied, "If my kingdom were from this world, my followers would be fighting to keep me from being handed over to the Jews."[14] Even Judas, the betrayer, is greeted with the title "friend."[15] Jesus died forgiving his enemies.[16]

Although it would be possible to view Jesus' nonviolent response to torture and death as part of his unique mission as the Son of God and therefore not binding on his followers, that option is not given in the biblical texts. Instead, Jesus told his followers to take up their cross and fol-

---

11. Matt. 6:14-15. The only ethical element of the Nicene Creed is the phrase "the forgiveness of sins." This is usually interpreted to mean God's forgiving our sins through Jesus Christ. However, in the context of Matthew 6:14-15, this Nicene phrase must also be interpreted to mean our forgiving the sins of those who have sinned against us.

12. Matt. 5:43-48.

13. Matt. 26:52; Luke 22:49-51; John 18:10-11.

14. John 18:36.

15. Matt. 26:50.

16. Luke 23:34.

low him,[17] assuring them that they also would be persecuted as he would be.[18] The Johannine commission of the risen Lord to his disciples says "Peace be with you. As the Father has sent me, so I send you."[19] Jesus' mission, his death, and his way of meeting his death in the hope of the resurrection are all commended to his disciples as well.

The Pauline Epistles and other books of the New Testament also view Jesus' death and resurrection as paradigmatic for his followers. The same Spirit that empowered Jesus has now been poured out on the believers. Believers are being transformed into the image of Christ. They share in Christ's sufferings, that they might also share in his glory. First Peter specifically connects nonviolent responses to evil with following Jesus:

> But if you endure when you do right and suffer for it, you have God's approval. For to this you have been called, because Christ also suffered for you, leaving you an example, so that you should follow in his steps. . . . When he was abused, he did not return abuse; when he suffered, he did not threaten; but he entrusted himself to the one who judges justly. He himself bore our sins in his body on the cross, so that, free from sins, we might live for righteousness; by his wounds you have been healed.[20]

> For it is better to suffer for doing good, if suffering should be God's will, than to suffer for doing evil. For Christ also suffered for sins once for all, the righteous for the unrighteous, in order to bring you to God.[21]

Thus it is impossible to separate ethics from theology, or discipleship from salvation. To *believe,* to *have faith,* to *be faithful,* is covenant language. It means not only to think, but to behave in ways that are consistent with the covenant, in ways that maintain or improve the covenant relationship. In the biblical language, *belief* or *faith* never means simply inner assent or an inner attitude. This divorce of love as an inner attitude from outer acts, by Augustine and, later, the magisterial reformers, made

17. Mark 8:34-38 and parallels.
18. John 15:18-25.
19. John 20:21.
20. 1 Pet. 2:20-21, 23-25.
21. 1 Pet. 3:17-18.

possible the established churches' approval of capital punishment and warfare. Augustine wrote (and was quoted thus by Calvin):

> In the next place, these precepts of nonresistance to evil according to Matt. [5:38-40] relate to the internal affection of the heart more than to the external actions; in order that in the secrecy of our minds we may feel patience and benevolence, but in our outward conduct may do that which we see tends to the advantage of those to whom we ought to feel benevolent affections.[22]

Against such statements, sixteenth-century Anabaptist evangelist Melchior Hofmann used the analogy of the marriage of the church to the heavenly Bridegroom, arguing that words and actions must be congruent:

> For what kind of faith would that be in the case of a woman with her husband, to whom she publicly adhered and confessed to be her lord and bridegroom, and nevertheless continuously went out to commit adultery and illicit love-making with others?[23]

One cannot talk about "believing" in Jesus without doing what he said and as he did, in the grace and power of the Holy Spirit. Like many other Anabaptists, Hutterite leader Peter Riedeman started his confession of faith by writing a commentary on each sentence or phrase of the Apostles' Creed. But he did not stop there because, for him, the Apostles' Creed did not say enough. Riedeman continued with a commentary on faith in relation to various issues of Christian ethics; ethics was a part of his theology.

Moreover, the cross of Christ has brought social peace to people who were formerly enemies. In the New Testament, this is illustrated most clearly in the new relationship between Jewish Christians and Gentile Christians, to whom Jesus brought his peace, breaking down the dividing wall between them and creating one new humanity.[24] In fact, part of Romans 12 sounds like a commentary on the Sermon on the Mount:

---

22. Augustine, Epistle 5, *ad Marcellinum,* quoted by John Calvin in "On Civil Government," *Institutes of the Christian Religion,* in *On God and Political Duty,* 2nd ed., ed. John T. McNeill (Indianapolis: Bobbs-Merrill, 1956), p. 70.

23. Melchior Hofmann, "The Ordinance of God," in *Spiritual and Anabaptist Writers,* ed. George Huntston Williams, The Library of Christian Classics (Philadelphia: Westminster, 1957), p. 202.

24. Eph. 2:11-22.

Bless those who persecute you; bless and do not curse them. . . . Live in harmony with one another. . . . Do not repay anyone evil for evil. . . . so far as it depends on you, live peaceably with all. Beloved, never avenge yourselves, but leave room for the wrath of God. . . . Do not be overcome by evil, but overcome evil with good.[25]

Salvation thus becomes not only reconciliation with God, but also reconciliation with our former enemies in the church. Believers are saved not only from the sins they commit but also from the sins others commit against them. The latter salvation sometimes comes in this life, but certainly in the resurrection; just as God raised Jesus from the dead, so God will also raise believers when the final victory against evil has been won. Through his death and resurrection, Jesus inaugurated a new covenant. Much like the older covenant — with its emphasis on dependence on God alone, salvation from enemies, the boomerang effect of evil on evildoers, the suffering servant, and the prophetic visions of peace in the Day of the Lord — the new covenant shows how to depend on God to deal with evil. But this time God's covenant offers salvation and a new way of life, a new way of confronting evil — peacefully, trusting God for salvation, and anticipating the Day when evil is fully overcome.

Church as Holy Nation

Few Christians dispute that peacemaking should be the norm for one's personal life. Most could agree that followers of Jesus should not commit murder within a society and could agree on reconciliation as the goal in personal relationships. Where consensus often breaks down over peacemaking is in the church's relation to civil authority.

It is no accident that the shift in the church's attitude toward military service coincided with the beginnings of Christendom, the belief that the empire and the church had common goals and were to support each other, and the privatization of things spiritual. This shift is usually associated with the emperor Constantine, although it took place over a longer period of time and was not complete until toward the end of the

25. Rom. 12:14-21.

fourth century. One fact that dramatically illustrates this transition is that, while at one time Christians did not serve in the Roman army at all, by the end of the fourth century only Christians were allowed to serve. Part of what made this shift possible is not only a change in attitude toward the government, but a change in the understanding of the church.

The early church understood itself as a political entity, as the political language used in the Bible shows. Jesus is *Lord* (the title also used for Caesar). The *kingdom* of God is at hand. At the Last Supper, Jesus confers *a kingdom* on his disciples. Believers' *citizenship* is in heaven. The church is a *holy nation, God's own people,* the same language previously used for Israel.[26] Even the Greek word for *church (ekklesia)* is a political word; in its most general sense, it means simply "assembly," but in the ancient Greek world it was often used in the sense of a political assembly, a town meeting. The Hebrew word for *worship,* in its most concrete sense, means to fall down flat on one's face in front of one's ruler.

This political understanding of the church as holy nation is not confined to the Bible but is present in other early writings as well. The *Letter to Diognetus* (perhaps from the second century) describes Christians as a nation scattered among the nations:

> For Christians are not differentiated from other people by country, language, or customs; you see, they do not live in cities of their own, or speak some strange dialect, or have some peculiar lifestyle. . . . They follow local customs in clothing, food, and the other aspects of life. But at the same time, they demonstrate to us the wonderful and certainly unusual form of their own citizenship. They live in their own native lands, but as aliens; as citizens, they share all things with others; but like aliens, suffer all things. Every foreign country is to them as their native country, and every native land as a foreign country.[27]

Several things distinguish this holy nation from the other nations: It claims God alone as its ruler, through Jesus Christ and the Holy Spirit, and it has no geographical boundaries forcing those within its borders to be citizens of the nation whether they like it or not — its citizenship is

26. Compare 1 Pet. 2:9 with Exod. 19:5-6.
27. *Letter to Diognetus,* quoted in *Eerdmans' Handbook to the History of Christianity,* ed. Tim Dowley (Grand Rapids: Eerdmans, 1977), p. 69.

voluntary. Because it has no involuntary boundaries, the holy nation has no need to maintain these boundaries by violence or the threat of violence. In fact, the only nation that can fully practice peace and nonviolence is the church, because a geographical nation of people, some of whom are not there by choice, will at some point rely on violence to maintain order.[28] The economics of the Christian nation are those of aid to any who have need. Its justice does not model itself on the Aristotelian concept of each getting what he or she is due, but on the biblical understanding of restoring right relationships. The Christian nation is not the Roman Empire or the United States of America. The only possible Christian nation is the church of Jesus Christ. It is with that holy nation that the Christian's primary loyalty must lie.

What then is the relationship of the church to civil government and to the dominant culture? It is not one of revolt, nor of fusion of church and civil government, nor of absorption of one by the other, nor of mutual uncritical blessing of the other's activities. The attitude of the church as nation toward the civil authorities must be that of critical participation; that is, participation in those areas of civil life that do not conflict with loyalty to God and critical dissent in those where believers must obey God rather than human authorities.

Mennonites have traditionally seen state-sponsored lethal violence, whether in the form of warfare and military service or of capital punishment, as a key point of dissent from civil government. This dissent is not based on the belief that a nation-state should not have a military — although it would be better if nations behaved more justly, and it is appropriate to petition governments to act in more peaceful ways, pursuing negotiations rather than surprise attacks, for example. It is also not based on ethical systems guided by the question, "what if everybody did it?" or "what if the king or the president did it?" — although if everybody acted peacefully there would be no more war. Instead, the Mennonite-Anabaptist understanding of nonparticipation in warfare grows out of giving primary allegiance to God and to the holy nation, the people of God. If the people of God are called to love their enemies and to resolve conflict

28. In *Theology and Social Theory: Beyond Secular Reason* (Cambridge, Mass.: Blackwell, 1990) John Milbank argues, in fact, that the only Christian social theory is ecclesiology, and that theology is a social science. Greco-Roman and Enlightenment social theories, he says, are all grounded in violence. Only the church has the possibility of a social order without violent power over others.

through the rule of Christ,[29] then they are to reject calls to other allegiances and other ways of dealing with enemies.

To say it another way, at a point of critical dissent such as participation in warfare and military service, the question of loyalties is raised. Whom do we worship? To whom do we pledge our allegiance? To what body of people do we feel most "responsibility"? Whose bidding will we give priority? Who is our Lord: Caesar, or God? If living in covenant relationship with God and God's people demands love of enemies, then to follow another master's call to kill enemies is to worship that master. It is idolatry. This is why it is a moot point whether the early Christians opposed military service because of an opposition to warfare itself or because of opposition to idolatry; the two issues cannot be separated.

It is only possible to relegate Jesus' teachings on peace to the realm of individual relationships or inner attitudes if we also restrict the church to the private realm and give our public allegiance to the nation-state. When the church understands itself as a holy nation, albeit often scattered and in exile, then it is free to seek the shalom of the civil entity in which it finds itself and, at the same time, to practice critical dissent when the demands of the state conflict with loyalty to God. This dissent is to be understood not so much in the Enlightenment terminology of individual rights of conscience, but as a matter of allegiance to God and the people of God.

The Community That Makes Peacemaking Possible

Peacemaking is not sustainable as an individual ethic; it requires a community. The church is the community where believers learn the culture, if you will, of the holy nation, the practices that make peacemaking a possibility. In this way peace becomes realistic rather than simply a far-off ideal.

Peacemaking is thus a communal ethic, and it is such an ethic, in part, because it springs from an allegiance to God and to the holy nation. A "national" identity is, by definition, communal. In addition, community is the setting for learning the practices that are necessary for following Jesus in peacemaking. These practices include

29. Matt. 18:15-20.

— forgiveness — learning to love the antagonist close at hand, the one who has sinned against us

— church discipline — disciplining the erring brother or sister with the hope of reconciliation and re-incorporation into the body of Christ. In the sixteenth century, the Anabaptist practice of excluding erring, unrepentant persons from the church was a nonviolent alternative to the state church's execution or imprisonment of unrepentant "heretics."

— truth telling and truth living. Truth, like belief, is also a covenant word and a faith word. It means not only being true to the facts, but true to relationships as well.

— sharing, simplicity of lifestyle, and not becoming too attached to money and the things over which some people fight[30]

— humility, poverty of spirit, and knowing that without God none of us has it all together. If the Beatitudes can be seen as progressive, this poverty of spirit is the first step in the spiritual life that culminates in peacemaking and rejoicing in persecution for righteousness' sake.

— love of the enemy, praying for and doing good to persecutors. Sometimes it seems that there is a continuum of love. On the one end, the less intense end, is staying connected with people who are different from us. That is difficult enough. But on the other end of the continuum is love of the enemy, the person who is not only different, but who has intentionally done evil against us. One can only learn to love enemies in community, in a network of relationships. One begins by practicing staying in relationship with people who are simply different.

All of these practices are the outcomes of what the New Testament calls growing up into Christ[31] or being transformed into the image of Christ.[32] In addition, the New Testament frequently tells us to imitate the peace practices of Jesus, particularly what is often translated as having "patient endurance." Even when there is no room for creative nonviolent confrontation of the enemy, one can still practice patient endurance in

30. Cf. James 4:1-4.
31. Eph. 4:15.
32. Rom. 8:29; 2 Cor. 3:18.

the face of maltreatment by enemies. In Psalm 37, the faithful are to be still before God and wait patiently, not fretting over evildoers but leaving vengeance up to God, because it is the meek, the gentle, and the nonviolent who will receive an inheritance and delight themselves in the plenty of shalom. In many New Testament passages, this patient endurance appears in the context of suffering and persecution.[33] Be patient in suffering; do not repay anyone evil for evil; overcome evil with good, we read.[34] The same concept can be found in Hebrews, where we are exhorted to "run with perseverance [or patient endurance] the race that is set before us, looking to Jesus the pioneer and perfecter of our faith, who for the sake of the joy that was set before him endured the cross."[35] John the writer of Revelation tells his readers that he shares with them "the persecution and the kingdom and the patient endurance"; in the face of the Beast of the Roman Empire, the call is for the patient endurance of the saints.[36]

This practice of patient endurance — of calmness before persecution from the enemy, of trust that God will act on our behalf, of overcoming evil with good nonviolently — cannot be learned without a community of people. Peacemaking is practiced not by the lone individual, but by the individual in community, who works through the conflicts in community and is strengthened and encouraged by the community of others who have also suffered evil and who also have hope in God's ultimate victory over evil.

Eschatology and Peacemaking

Not every eschatology is compatible with a theology of peacemaking. A theology of the gradual coming of the reign of God on earth would seem, at first glance, to support working for peace, but unfortunately human history has not been one of continuous progress, human beings by their own efforts have seldom brought about peace, and discouragement has usually set in. For more obvious reasons, a theology that postpones most

33. Rom. 5:3; 2 Cor. 1:6, for example.
34. Rom. 12:12, 17, 21.
35. Heb. 12:1-2.
36. Rev. 1:9; 13:10.

180

social ethics until the millennium does not need a theology of peacemaking in the present. Equally lacking in support for Christian peacemaking is a theology which limits God's action to the past or which views God as detached from the world and unwilling or unable to act in human affairs.

The political shifts of the fourth century were accompanied by a shift in eschatology. As John Howard Yoder wrote,

> Before Constantine, one knew as a fact of everyday experience that there was a believing Christian community but one had to "take it on faith" that God was governing history. After Constantine, one had to believe without seeing that there was a community of believers, within the larger nominally Christian mass, but one knew for a fact that God was in control of history.[37]

Augustine believed that the millennium had arrived now that the empire and the church were supporting each other. His theology kept a general resurrection at the end of time, but it was not logically necessary in his theological system. God's viceroy, in the form of the emperor, was already in control on earth; no drastic changes were needed. God's judgment became primarily a private matter which took effect for each individual at the time of his or her death.

In contrast, the eschatology necessary to sustain a peace ethic in the early church included hope in a cataclysmic change in the state of affairs, nothing less than a new heaven and a new earth, a dramatic shift not only in the spiritual realm but also in the physical realm. There would be a new kingdom, a new government with God as ruler. God would win the victory over evil. Persecution and oppression would disappear. The ethic of Jesus and his followers would be vindicated.

Those in power would not have seen this as good news; they did not want the present state of affairs upset. For those who were persecuted, however — for the church already living now according to the pattern of the age to come — a new heaven and a new earth was good news. For those practicing critical dissent from the dominant culture and from the authorities in charge, there was hope that God would again act in history and vindicate the way of peace.

If it were not for hope in the future fulfillment of the reign of God,

37. *The Priestly Kingdom: Social Ethics as Gospel* (Notre Dame, Ind.: University of Notre Dame Press, 1984), p. 137.

it would be difficult to sustain a life of Christian peacemaking. Attempting to overcome evil with good does not always turn out the way we want it to; loving enemies does not always result in enemies becoming friends; confronting an antagonist with love sometimes brings about the conversion of the antagonist, and we hope for that possibility, but it does not always happen. Why should we expect that it always happen that way for us, when it did not work that way for Jesus? His love and forgiveness for his enemies did not prevent his crucifixion. Jesus' hope did not lie solely in the conversion of enemies, but in God, who was able to raise him from the dead. His resurrection thus became a kind of first fruits sign of God's ultimate victory over evil.

This assurance of God's final victory gives hope to the church, living now as if to provide a preview, a foretaste, of the coming reign of God. If in the age to come there will be peace, an absence of hunger and thirst, then God's people should start living that way now. Because God has acted in the resurrection, because Jesus has sent the Holy Spirit to continue to act in the world, the church can expect that God will act again in the future. A lifestyle of peacemaking thus becomes possible in spite of the way things look now, in spite of suffering, in spite of the prevalence of evil in the world. Indeed, peace is not only possible, but the way of the future, the sign of the nature of the coming reign of God.

Conclusion

This paper has not attempted to address all of the theological themes related to peacemaking. The five themes we have looked at here, however, are illustrative of how peace theology intersects with major theological topics. We will find it easier to come to unity on peacemaking when we look at it in the context of the whole of theology, and not just as an optional add-on or as a subtopic of ethics unconnected to the central issues of theology.

Peacemaking is a response to intended evil and to enemies, those who sin against us. It is a participation in the life and death of Christ, a part of the social ethic of the church as holy nation. Peacemaking is made possible by a community that teaches and practices peace, and it is sustainable in a community that places its hope in the present and the future reign of God.

These affirmations are a challenge to contemporary Mennonite churches as well as to other Christian communions. May the God of peace grant us the grace, the ability, and the courage to grow even more in the image of Jesus Christ and to find our unity in him.

Baptists as Peacemakers

GLEN H. STASSEN

When you read the first Baptist confessions of faith from seventeenth-century England, as well as those from subsequent centuries in various countries, you are struck by the recurrence of several themes that are easily remembered by the acronym, **A Bible Discipleship:**

> **A**uthority of Scriptures, not traditions, with Christ as norm for interpretation
>
> **B**aptism of believers who profess their faith and commit themselves as disciples of Jesus
>
> **I**mmersion baptism into the death, burial, and resurrection of Christ (Rom. 6:4; Col. 2:12)
>
> **B**orn-again, regenerate, visible disciples in the church
>
> **L**iberty of religion and conscience and liberty of church from the state
>
> **E**fficacy of God's grace manifest in Christ's life, death, and resurrection, received by faith for salvation; baptism as obedience to Christ, not for salvation
>
> **D**iscipleship, obedience to the commands of Jesus, and the sovereignty of God and lordship of Christ over all of life.

When you examine Baptist history, you also see that not all Baptists have been peacemakers. Some are infamous for engendering fights among fellow Baptists, and some have had decidedly hawkish attitudes toward the enemy. But there have also been many outstanding Baptist peacemakers, foremost among them Martin Luther King Jr. The American Baptist Convention regularly gives the Dahlberg Peace Award to an outstanding Baptist peacemaker, and it is seen as an extraordinarily high honor — the Baptist Nobel Peace Prize. Paul Dekar has written a book that tells the story of Baptist peacemakers through the centuries. We call them our "Baptist saints." Baptists don't literally claim to have saints, and some may say we do not have peacemakers either, but Dekar identifies about two hundred historic Baptist peacemakers, not even counting those still living.[1]

In our search for Baptist peacemakers, it is important to understand that some of them were pacifists, but not all by any means. More of them supported some wars while strongly advocating peacemaking initiatives. All of them, however, did much for peacemaking.

The Stream that Nourishes Baptist Peacemaking

Dekar asks what "life-giving forces have guided and energized Baptist peacemakers," what biblical passages or beliefs and what traditions have nourished them? Is there a stream running through Baptist life that encourages the faithful to become one of those witnesses to peacemaking that pop up regularly, sometimes where they are least expected? He cannot answer this question in depth, his vignettes being necessarily brief since his peacemakers are many. Nevertheless, a number of themes recur in these short descriptions, and what strikes me most is the recurrence of precisely the central Baptist themes enumerated earlier.

Clearly, the most central theme for the Baptist peacemakers is following Jesus. Throughout Dekar's stories, the theme of following Jesus keeps recurring. We read of his teachings, life, and whole ministry; of the Sermon on the Mount and the spirit of Jesus Christ; and of his fulfillment of the words of the Hebrew prophets. Baptists become peacemakers when they take the way of the incarnate Jesus Christ seriously.[2]

Similarly, identifying with Jesus' death, burial, and resurrection, ex-

1. Paul Dekar, *For the Healing of the Nations: Baptist Peacemakers* (Macon, Ga.: Smyth and Helwys Press, 1993).

2. Dekar, *For the Healing of the Nations.* Some of the many locations where emphasizing the way of Jesus Christ seemed important to Dekar as described by different Baptist peacemakers are pp. 34-35, 49, 52-54, 58-59, 72, 97, 112, 185, 187, 199, 203, 207, 213, 216, 236, 248, 259, 264-65.

perienced as one's own death to sin and rising to live in Christ (Rom. 6:4 and Col. 2:12), is a way of taking up the cross and following Jesus and of dying to the ways of the world and the ways of selfishness and hate. This can nurture a sense of independence from the worldly ways of hate, nationalism, racism, and economic injustice. Dekar finds the way of death and resurrection — the way of the cross, suffering and dying — to be important for some Baptist peacemakers.[3] It is often expressed in repentance for the ways of injustice and war. In his conclusion, he reports that during the Persian Gulf war against Iraq, he and his wife, along with many members of the Baptist Peace Fellowship of North America, engaged in a discipline of prayer and fasting:

> This was a time for repentance and renewal of our experience of the love of Jesus. Feeling helpless in the face of the enormity of the evil at work in the world, we found that the disciplines of prayer and fasting helped us to focus on the love of Jesus as he prepared to be crucified, on the suffering of those who can not choose not to eat, on the wider community of believers with whom we shared the experience, and on the potential power of these spiritual disciplines for transforming initiatives. . . .
>
> Repentance, prayer, and fasting enable one to experience forgiveness and healing. . . . The fast God requires is to loose the fetters of injustice, to untie the knots of the yoke, to snap every yoke and set free those who have been crushed, to share food with the hungry and to take into my home the homeless poor (Isa. 58:6-7).[4]

The theme of the search for religious liberty is also prominent in the stories of these individuals. It is well known that Baptists were pioneers in the push for religious liberty and liberty of the Church from the state — following the Anabaptists, who had advocated these two liberties for a century prior to the Baptist movement in the face of their own sufferings under religious persecution. What is not so well known is that Baptists, including pioneers Roger Williams, Richard Overton, and Gerrard Winstanley, advocated religious liberty as a peacemaking practice. They argued that religious persecution had caused most of the wars in history, and that religious liberty and liberty of the churches from the state were therefore needed if peace were to prevail. Roger Williams titled his book

3. Dekar, *For the Healing of the Nations*, pp. 229, 237, 273.
4. Dekar, *For the Healing of the Nations*, pp. 276-77.

The Bloudy Tenent of Persecution, making the point that religious persecution causes wars and bloodshed. Richard Overton's *The Arraignement of Mr. Persecution* made twelve accusations against Mr. Religious Persecution, ten of which demonstrated the great number of wars caused by such persecution. We can see evidence of this in our own time as well: Catholics and Protestants in Northern Ireland continue to struggle against religiously entwined violence; Orthodox Serbs fight Catholic Croatians and Muslim Bosnians; Muslims in Pakistan and Hindus in India threaten nuclear war; the Hindu party in India advocates discrimination against other religions, causing conflicts which boil over into violent clashes. In our own day, when the Muslim Sudanese government makes war against Christian and animist southern Sudan and the Middle East seems stuck in vicious cycles of religious hostility, the peacemaking initiatives of religious liberty and liberty of churches from the state are desperately needed to disentangle fear of religious persecution and religious privilege from the forces of hate and violence.

The Baptist saints described by Dekar were often motivated by their commitment to religious liberty.[5] They asserted not individualistic autonomy but the sovereignty of God, whose will is above the state and above the laws government makes. This provides a strong foundation upon which to criticize the government when it makes wars — especially unjust ones — or fails to take initiatives to prevent wars. It gives a basis for independence from the actions of government and the ideology of the nation.[6] Too often, of course, Baptists and other Christians give away their religious liberty and live in captivity to the powers and authorities of the state and the warlike spirit of the nation. Here, however, we seek to identify those streams in Baptist life that do occasionally produce peacemaking saints. Martin Luther King Jr., the chief of those saints, made the classical case for obeying God rather than the segregationist laws of the state in "Letter from a Birmingham Jail" in his book, *Why We Can't Wait.* In his struggle against segregation and discrimination by the state, King drew on a tradition of nonviolent resistance; for example, an earlier Baptist campaign of nonviolent, passive resistance (against unfair privilege given to the established church and discrimination in the British school system) influenced Gandhi's development of

5. Dekar, *For the Healing of the Nations,* pp. 83, 91, 94, 103-15, 121, 248, 273.
6. Dekar, *For the Healing of the Nations,* pp. 108 and 121.

the method of nonviolent direct action, and this in turn influenced Martin Luther King.[7]

Baptist peacemakers struggled for the liberty of conscientious objectors, who refused to fight in wars (or in a particular war). The best known case was Baptist Yale Professor D. C. Macintosh, whose application for U.S. citizenship was blocked because he was a selective conscientious objector. He said he would "put first allegiance and obedience to God," second allegiance to country, and third his own private interests. Macintosh put allegiance to God above individual autonomy, but the justice system did not approve; despite fighting his case all the way to the Supreme Court, Macintosh lost by a 5-4 vote in 1931. Baptist Chief Justice Charles Evans Hughes wrote the minority opinion, calling the case "the battle for religious liberty" and saying that "there is abundant room for enforcing the requisite authority of law . . . without demanding that either citizens or applicants for citizenship shall assume by oath an obligation to regard allegiance to God as subordinate to allegiance to civil power." The Supreme Court finally reversed its stand in 1946, a remarkable fact since the court rarely directly reverses a previous ruling. Justice William Douglas wrote the majority opinion, declaring that the 1931 ruling against Macintosh did "not state the correct rule of law." The decision established the right of conscientious objection against participation in war.[8]

Puritan and Anabaptist Sources of the Stream

Baptist scholars debate whether the Baptist themes described in this essay arose as the logical outcome of Puritan piety and Bible study, without influence from Anabaptists or Mennonites, or whether Menno Simons' *Foundation of Christian Doctrine* and other Anabaptist witnesses influenced Baptist origins and persuaded the Baptists of the truth of these beliefs. My own contribution to that debate can be found in *Baptist History and Heritage*.[9] I believe it serves historical accuracy and present-day clarity about the heart of Baptist identity to give thanks for the contributions of both Puritan and Anabaptist traditions.

7. Dekar, *For the Healing of the Nations*, pp. 69-71.
8. Dekar, *For the Healing of the Nations*, pp. 87-99.
9. See *Baptist History and Heritage* (Spring 1998), pp. 34-54.

Whatever position one takes on that debate, all agree that present-day Baptists descend from British Congregationalists, i.e., free-church Puritans. One group was non-Calvinist (the General Baptists) and the other was Calvinist (the Particular Baptists). The Puritans, even more than other groups, emphasized grace, the sovereignty of God over all worldly authorities, and social justice. The Anabaptists emphasized a Christ-centered understanding of the Christian life, baptism of believers into the life, death, and resurrection of Jesus, religious liberty, and liberty of the church from the state. Both Puritans and Anabaptists emphasized biblical authority, a church of visible discipleship, God's grace manifest in Christ's life, death, and resurrection, and seriousness about living a moral life of obedience to God's will as revealed in the scriptures, with Jesus Christ as Lord.

It is clear that the original Baptists, and Baptist confessions since, have emphasized these themes. One can therefore bypass the question of historical origin, and simply agree that the Baptists emphasize both the sovereignty of God and Christ-centered discipleship. Additionally, the emphasis on the experience of repentance and conversion, evangelism, personal commitment to Christ as Lord and Savior, and Sunday School classes and accountability groups came with the Whitefield revivals and the Great Awakenings. The theme of going into all the world and making disciples (Matt. 28:18-20) was emphasized by Menno Simons and became central for Baptists after the world mission movement. All these themes have contributed to the style of Baptist peacemaking. Martin Luther King Jr. emphasized God's providence and rule over the universe as well as his justice, often referring to the Sermon on the Mount and Jesus' way of love, and of the command to follow Jesus.

The Emphasis on Practical Peacemaking Initiatives

Paul Dekar notices a shift across the centuries in Baptist peacemaking emphases. The shift is from a negative peace — avoiding war and participation in war — to positive peace — participation in struggling for justice and creating the conditions of peace. It is not that early Baptists lacked an emphasis on positive peace, or that conscientious objection against participation in war does not exist in recent times, but the emphases on justice, overcoming racism and economic deprivation, and transforming initiatives for creating peace are clearly becoming more prominent. Hope in

God's rule and the promise of Isaiah 2 that swords will be beaten into ploughshares and that God's kingdom is coming have led Baptists to hope for the prospects of peacemaking and to push for practical peacemaking initiatives.[10] The theme of peacemaking as working for justice and human rights thus emerges as a strong theme in Baptist history.[11] Again, Martin Luther King Jr. epitomizes the best in Baptist peacemaking: "True peace is not merely the absence of tension; it is the presence of justice." In this way the initial Baptist struggle for the right of religious liberty grew into a struggle for human rights; the Baptist Richard Overton, in fact, seems to be the first in history to develop an explicit doctrine of human rights, drawing on his own struggle for religious liberty and justice for the poor.[12]

This development can be seen as a maturing of the synthesis of the Anabaptist themes of peacemaking and following Jesus with Calvinist themes of justice, the sovereignty of God, and practicality. At times, Calvinist realism has eclipsed attention to the way of Jesus and become authoritarianism, militarism, or racism. It is true that Calvinism was also the historical source of constitutional democracy and parliamentary forms of government, and of religious liberty — but not without help from the free-church movement influenced by the Anabaptists. On the other hand, the Baptist version of Anabaptist hope for peacemaking initiatives has at times been overly optimistic and idealistic,[13] and could have used a healthy dose of Calvinist realism about the pervasiveness of sin. Many people view themes of peacemaking and following Jesus as impractical idealism. They label Anabaptists as sectarians and accuse them of withdrawal from the world. Refusal to participate in killing enemies, however, does not mean withdrawal from practical service in the world, be it the production of musical and artistic culture or participation in economic activity or public service.[14] In addition, it must be noted that

10. Dekar, *For the Healing of the Nations,* pp. 66-67, 81, 84, 95, 97, 99, 238, 248-49, 252, 257-58, 263, 266, 273.

11. Dekar, *For the Healing of the Nations,* pp. 63-64, 75-76, 83, 106-7, 110ff., 114, 127, 151, 155ff., 222, 230, 233, 235, 227.

12. Glen H. Stassen, *Just Peacemaking: Transforming Initiatives for Justice and Peace* (Louisville: Westminster Press, 1992), chap. 6.

13. Dekar, *For the Healing of the Nations,* p. 202.

14. See John Howard Yoder in *Authentic Transformation: A New Vision of Christ and Culture,* by Glen H. Stassen, John Howard Yoder, and D. M. Yeager (Nashville: Abingdon Press, 1996).

the Anabaptists did not withdraw from dialogue with other denominations; the magisterial Reformers withdrew from dialogue with them, and then persecuted them so severely for a full century that they had to emigrate or withdraw for mere survival.[15]

In *Authentic Transformation: A New Vision of Christ and Culture,* I have argued that one good solution comes from synthesizing the Anabaptist emphasis on following Jesus with the Calvinist emphasis on the sovereignty of God over powers and authorities and all of life. I also argued for including in this new ethic the Pentecostal emphasis on the Holy Spirit as the living God dynamically present rather than the static possession of any set of doctrines or institutions. The result is a peacemaking strongly grounded in the way of Jesus Christ, concretely interpreted. It is clearly not a way of withdrawal but a way of creating practical peacemaking initiatives in the world. God's will revealed in Jesus Christ is the will of the sovereign God for the world.

Recovering concrete attention to the way of Jesus as obedience to the sovereign God in practical ways in this world seems to be the direction Baptist peacemaking is taking. A strong practical bent characterizes Baptist peacemakers, since Baptists always want to know how any proposal will work in reality. Perhaps this comes from their themes of visible discipleship, visible churches, and actual obedience demonstrated in deeds. "A faith without works is dead," say the Baptists, quoting James, the letter Luther loved to hate. Baptists follow Jesus' words in Matthew 7:24-27: the one who not only hears Jesus' words but does them is the one whose house is built on the rock. Baptist peacemakers thus want a kind of peacemaking that works in the real world. Whenever I speak in churches on peacemaking, basing my talk on careful and incisive biblical exegesis, I almost never get questions about my exegesis; I always get questions about how my ideas will work in specific situations. This may be a mixture of the Baptist emphasis on visible discipleship with an American pragmatism, but it is characteristically Baptist nonetheless.

Baptist interpretation of the Bible also tends toward concreteness. We do not look only for broad theological generalizations or vague attitudes, but seek specific teachings and concrete ethics. This may be one reason the first Baptists were concerned to be faithful to what baptism

---

15. John Howard Yoder, *The Legacy of Michael Sattler* (Scottdale, Pa.: Herald Press, 1973).

means concretely in the New Testament. In his *Ethics: Systematic Theology*, James Wm. McClendon Jr. sees the heart of Baptist identity as our sense that the teachings about the New Testament church are teachings about the present church; we are to be New Testament Christians.[16] In its legalistic form, this can produce a rigidity and a lack of theological depth. But the best sociologists of religion, such as Robert Wuthnow, conclude that many churches have lost members because of the vagueness and generality of their teaching and preaching about the difference Christian faith makes for daily life. Furthermore, while these most general and least concrete of the churches have lost members, churches that are more concrete about what it means to follow Jesus have gained members.

In summary, it fits Baptist tradition to focus on the way of Jesus in the New Testament, spread religious liberty under God, seek churches that are modeled on the New Testament and have regenerate church members who follow Jesus, and emphasize the sovereignty of God over the world, justice, and practical peacemaking initiatives.

There are many Baptist individuals and organizations that are currently working for peace. The Baptist Peace Fellowship, under the leadership of Ken Sehested, and its newspaper, *The Baptist Peacemaker*, emphasize justice for all sorts of oppressed people. The Fellowship has prepared study materials on Martin Luther King Jr., taken effective initiatives to oppose racism, made connection with the tradition of Menno Simons, and worked to foster peacemaking groups in churches and to foster churches that teach and practice peacemaking. It has sent representatives to Latin America, Asia, and Africa in the pursuit of practical peacemaking and seeks to heal the spirit of violence in the United States. It has done all this in a spirit of worship, repentance, and evangelistic revival and has been remarkably effective.

Michelle Tooley, a Baptist professor of Christian ethics at Belmont College in Tennessee, has written *Voices of the Voiceless: Women, Justice, and Human Rights in Guatemala*.[17] She describes realistically the strong barriers against justice and human rights as well as the actual actions of groups of women struggling for these rights. Hers is not a book of ideals

---

16. James Wm. McClendon Jr., *Ethics: Systematic Theology*, vol. I (Nashville: Abingdon Press, 1986), pp. 27ff.

17. Michelle Tooley, *Voices of the Voiceless: Women, Justice, and Human Rights in Guatemala* (Scottdale, Pa.: Herald Press, 1997).

and wishes, but a description of actual actions being taken to work for justice and human rights and of practices that have in fact made a major difference in Guatemala. Without being specifically Calvinist, it does contain Calvinist themes of justice and practical realism. One woman described by Tooley is Rigoberta Menchu, who received the Nobel Peace Prize for her work for human rights after Tooley had already selected her work as a focus for her own book. Tooley is Chair of the Board of Witness for Peace and serves on the Board of Bread for the World. She frequently travels to Latin America on peacemaking missions and sometimes leads groups of North Americans there. Hers is not simply theoretical peacemaking, but practical and effective engagement.

Daniel Buttry, a Baptist pastor in Michigan and former Director of Peace Ministries of the American Baptist Churches, has written *Christian Peacemaking: From Heritage to Hope*.[18] In it he shows how two effective practices of peacemaking, nonviolent direct action and conflict resolution, are spreading around the world, preventing wars in Latin America, Africa, Asia, and Europe. He too shows the Anabaptist discipleship themes and practical Calvinist themes. His biblical basis emphasizes the Anabaptist themes of following Jesus and the Sermon on the Mount, and he interprets the Sermon on the Mount as containing practical, transforming initiatives of peacemaking. The book is largely a narrative of empirical effectiveness, telling the stories of practices of nonviolent direct action and conflict resolution on all four major continents. Buttry himself has traveled to Chiapas, Burma, Africa, Nagaland, and elsewhere, teaching the two practices of peacemaking he writes about; in so doing, he has helped achieve truces in some of those places.

My earlier book, *Just Peacemaking: Transforming Initiatives for Justice and Peace*,[19] seeks to combine attention to Jesus' concrete teachings and example of peacemaking as transforming initiatives with empirical descriptions of practical and effective practices of peacemaking. This book has led to an ecumenical project with twenty-three interdisciplinary scholars developing a consensus on a just peacemaking theory in *Just Peacemaking: Ten Practices for Abolishing War*.[20] It, too, pays attention to

18. Daniel Buttry, *Christian Peacemaking: From Heritage to Hope* (Valley Forge: Judson Press, 1994).

19. See bibliographic information in note 11.

20. Glen H. Stassen, ed., *Just Peacemaking: Ten Practices for Abolishing War* (Cleveland: Pilgrim Press, 1998).

Jesus' way as well as to practices that are effective in the real world. It shows that the international system is in fact being changed by these new peacemaking practices, and that war is being abolished in many places and in many cases. Once people see this change, it energizes them and guides church peacemaking groups in ways that are effective in the new international environment that we are entering, and that many do not yet perceive and understand. The ten practices include those that Tooley and Buttry describe, plus seven others:

A. Peacemaking Initiatives
   1. Support nonviolent direct action
   2. Take independent initiatives to reduce hostility and threat
   3. Use cooperative conflict resolution
   4. Acknowledge responsibility for conflict and injustice; seek repentance and forgiveness
B. Justice
   5. Advance democracy, human rights, and religious liberty
   6. Foster just and sustainable economic development
C. Community
   7. Work with emerging cooperative forces in the international system
   8. Strengthen the United Nations' & international efforts for cooperation and human rights
   9. Reduce offensive weapons and weapons trade
   10. Encourage grassroots peacemaking groups and voluntary associations.

Baptist Peacemaking Merges with Truly Ecumenical Peacemaking

In this way Baptist peacemakers embrace the differing emphases of Christian discipleship, the importance of following the way of Jesus and his teachings, and the sovereignty of God over the powers and authorities of this world, all in their quest for practical ways of working for justice and peace in the real world. I believe this is a fulfillment of the Baptist heritage and may lead us to recover key dimensions of that heritage. Baptist peacemakers hope to persuade Baptists to be true Baptists. We also hope to invite non-Baptists to join with us and show us how to be better Christians, faithful to God in Christ. We want not merely to invite others, but to persuade them also — we are evangelists, after all. And we do not want merely to persuade others, but to ask them also to persuade us and call us to deeper repentance, for we are children of the Great Awakening, of the Christian life as continuous repentance and joy in the Spirit, of Christian faith as death to sin and resurrection to life in Christ.

The Peace Heritage of the Churches of Christ

THOMAS H. OLBRICHT

The Churches of Christ bring a different witness to peace than most other confessional groups. At the turn of the twentieth century, many Churches of Christ leaders and members were pacifists. Pacifist views, however, eroded sharply during World War I and even more so during World War II.[1] Adequate knowledge of our pacifist heritage lingers in our churches, so that it is commonly agreed that the issue of military service is open for discussion. In churches where the topic has been aired, strong feelings are attached to the various positions. Debate over the issues of pacifism and involvement in the armed forces always arises during times of war or conflict.[2]

In *Freedom from War: Nonsectarian Pacifism, 1814-1914*, Peter Brock has, I think, appropriately positioned Churches of Christ in a chapter on the Disciples of Christ.

1. See Michael W. Casey, "From Pacifism to Patriotism: The Emergence of Civil Religion in the Churches of Christ During World War I," *Mennonite Quarterly Review* 66 (1992): 376-90. See also Casey, "The Closing of Cordell Christian College: A Microcosm of American Intolerance during World War I," *Chronicles of Oklahoma* 76 (Spring 1998): 20-37; Michael W. Casey and Michael A. Jordan, "Free Speech in Time of War: Government Surveillance of the Churches of Christ in World War I," *Free Speech Yearbook 1996*, ed. John J. Makay (Carbondale: Southern Illinois Press, 1997), pp. 102-11; Casey, "New Information on Conscientious Objectors of World War I," *Restoration Quarterly* 34 (1992): 83-96; and Casey, "Warriors Against War: The Pacifists of the Churches of Christ in World War Two," *Restoration Quarterly* 35 (1993): 159-74.

2. See Michael W. Casey, "The Courage of Conscience: Conscientious Objectors in the Churches of Christ During World War II," unpublished paper presented to the Christian Scholar's Conference at David Lipscomb University, Nashville, July 1991.

Their peace witness displays an important feature that comes to the fore in pacifist history only after 1914: pacifism as a permissible option for a religious denomination's membership . . . it seems to me that the idea of pacifism as a denominational option — an idea that prevails widely today, even in some sections of the Roman Catholic church — had first emerged among the Disciples. Or, at any rate, it appeared first in that body in more concrete form than in any other American church.[3]

Historically Churches of Christ have highlighted and sometimes basked in the light of our "peculiarities," posturing ourselves much like the peace churches, but with a different raison d'être. We have emphasized the name of the church, baptism by immersion for the remission of sins, vocal music, weekly celebration of the Lord's Supper, congregational independence, a-millennialism, non-creedalism, and, at times, unity for Christendom.[4] Pacifism, I think, has never played a key role in our distinctiveness, though it has sometimes been close to the surface, along with other issues such as the priesthood of all believers. Since World War I, pacifism, rather than being a peculiarity of the Churches of Christ, has been a peculiarity of certain persons within the Churches of Christ. The intramural disturbances were noted by H. Leo Boles (1874-1946) a leading minister and president of David Lipscomb College, now University (1913-1920, 1923-1932). In 1923, reflecting back on 1917, Boles wrote,

We were so divided on this question during the war that we could have no influence with governmental authorities. Our division became sharp and acrimonious. Brethren were alienated from brethren. Some suffered persecution and imprisonment; while others, it seemed, rejoiced that they were suffering. Many acted in a very unchristian way toward their brethren who for conscience' sake denied the right of government to compel Christians to engage in war and to kill their fellow men.[5]

3. Peter Brock, *Freedom from War: Nonsectarian Pacifism, 1814-1914* (Toronto: University of Toronto Press, 1991), p. 136.

4. The similarities may be seen by reading Donald F. Durnbaugh and Charles W. Brockwell Jr., "The Historic Peace Churches: From Sectarian Origins to Ecumenical Witness," in the *Church's Peace Witness,* ed. Marlin E. Miller and Barbara Nelson Gingerich (Grand Rapids: Eerdmans, 1994), pp. 182-95.

5. H. Leo Boles, *The New Testament Teaching on War* (Nashville: Gospel Advocate, no date [c. 1923]), reprinted in C. G. Ross, *War: A Trilogy; Three Perspectives — One Biblical Position* (Fort Worth: Star Bible Publications, 1994), p. 3.

It is not clear even today that a questioning of Constantinianism and war are matters on which we can find commonality with other confessions; these issues still divide our own community.

Indications that pacifism still is a viable option among us, however, may be found. Michael Casey, who has researched the history of individual pacifists, has found a few individuals who because of a common commitment to pacifism have established rapport with persons from the peace churches and other conscientious objectors.[6] Four years ago a Stone-Campbell history list was created on a server at Abilene Christian University,[7] and, from several recent postings, it seems that many persons among us entertain increasing reservations in regard to war and church ties with governmental agencies. Some are rediscovering the views of David Lipscomb, which advocate both anti-Constantinianism and pacifism, and finding themselves more in agreement with him than they anticipated. These leanings seem to reflect the shifting currents in the mainstream churches as well as in our own.

The question therefore arises as to whether historically there has been a mutual interplay between evangelical unification and pacifism. Perhaps the two are endemically related. If one is dedicated to unifying sisters and brothers, does one also refrain from maiming or killing sisters and brothers or, for that matter, any person, known or unknown? Members of Churches of Christ have had our own platform upon which unity might be attained; we have argued that the way to unity is the demolishment of all the nonbiblical distinctives that foster fragmentation. If all our friends and neighbors would forego the specifics in which their beliefs and actions run counter to Scripture, and which they have formalized in creedal expressions, then all of us can be one in Christ.

What is therefore needed, we in Churches of Christ have contended, is a common commitment among all Christians to the authority of the Scripture and to doing and believing nothing without a "thus saith the Lord." Furthermore, a means of reading Scripture whereby we will all understand the Bible alike is demanded. If we in the Churches of Christ

6. Michael W. Casey, "Churches of Christ and World War II Civilian Public Service: A Pacifist Remnant," in *Proclaim Peace: Christian Pacifism From Unexpected Quarters*, ed. Theron Schlabach and Richard T. Hughes (Urbana: University of Illinois Press, 1997), pp. 97-114.

7. A Churches of Christ university founded in Abilene, Texas, in 1906. The university enrolls four thousand students in undergraduate and graduate programs annually.

followed our own agenda, we would seek to lead churches, and likewise citizens, into peace and unity, refusing to kill our enemies, and would lead the way in biblical analysis. When we have completed these exegetical and hermeneutical tasks we will be one in faith and brotherhood. We will be at peace. But, some have asked, will we be at peace even with ethnic aliens and foreign nations? At one time the answer among us was, yes, we will be at peace, because by the authority of Jesus Christ we are neither to be angry in our hearts nor kill. But we have lost confidence in our ability to deliver the goods on either front. We have been ambivalent on anti-Constantinianism and war since we ourselves are confused and embarrassed, and perceive, I think correctly, that we should follow the witness of the peace churches as they explicate Scripture. The leading preachers for the Churches of Christ in the decade before War World I were almost unanimous in embracing pacifism. Moves by government agencies, however, soon brought harassment to several of these leaders and not a few either abandoned pacifism or became silent. Reflecting back on the situation in 1917, Leo Boles wrote:

> Hundreds and thousands of good people, both men and women, were wholly at the mercy of the popular spirit. They had never been taught what attitude a Christian should take toward war. They had not studied the question for themselves, and were drafted and driven into war before they had time to consider what was the mind of Christ on the subject. Even the leaders of the church and preachers in general were unprepared to give instruction to those who in prayer sought earnestly for guidance. Preachers and elders were ignorant, it seemed, of the Bible teaching on this subject, and in making a hasty decision were guided more by the "God of War than by the Prince of Peace." The shepherds of the flocks were confused and could give no aid to the helpless young men who turned to them for instruction.[8]

The Churches of Christ

In order to appreciate the views on peace among members of the Churches of Christ it is important first of all to situate this brotherhood among other American churches. The Churches of Christ in America result from an in-

8. H. Leo Boles, *The New Testament Teaching on War*, p. 1.

digenous American movement seeking to restore the gospel and church of the New Testament. For this reason the term "Restoration Movement" has been employed as a self-designation, though this particular phrase is not widely employed by outsiders. Three sizable constituencies now exist from the late-eighteenth-century beginnings: (1) The Christian Church (Disciples of Christ), (2) The Independent Christian Churches, and (3) The Churches of Christ. The Churches of Christ are the conservative wing of the first major split in the movement and were identified as autonomous by the Federal Census Bureau in 1906. The Independent Christian Churches first moved toward a separate, more conservative conclave within the Christian Church (Disciples of Christ) in 1927, and withdrew officially in the late 1960s.

Churches of Christ have approximately two million members throughout the world, most of whom are in the United States.[9] The majority of those in the United States are located in the region running from Pittsburgh to El Paso with the northern border extending from Pittsburgh through Indianapolis, St. Louis, Wichita, and Albuquerque, and the southern through Atlanta, Montgomery, Baton Rouge, Houston, and San Antonio.[10]

The roots of the Restoration Movement extend backward to the period after the Revolutionary War, when some religious Americans grew restless over autocratic structures, European control and theology, and denominational boundaries. These pressures caused reform in the mainline churches but also resulted in independent constituencies springing up in various regions. Four such independent groups in partic-

9. For excellent demographic maps for Churches of Christ in the United States see Peter L. Halvorson and William M. Newman, *Atlas of Religious Change in America* (Atlanta: Glenmary Research Center, 1994), pp. 179-81.

10. The standard histories are the following: William E. Tucker and Lester G. McAllister, *Journey in Faith* (St. Louis: Bethany Press, 1975) [about the Disciples of Christ]; James B. North, *Union in Truth: An Interpretive History of the Restoration Movement* (Cincinnati: Standard Publishing, 1994) [about the Christian Churches, NACC]; Richard T. Hughes, *Reviving the Ancient Faith: The Story of Churches of Christ in America* (Grand Rapids: Eerdmans, 1996) [about the Churches of Christ]. See also the recent accurate and fair assessment written by a Roman Catholic: Richard M. Tristano, *The Origins of the Restoration Movement: An Intellectual History* (Atlanta: Glenmary Research Center, 1988). For a judicious, but perhaps conservative estimate of the demographics of membership of the Churches of Christ, see Mac Lynn, compiler, *Churches of Christ in the United States* (Nashville: 21st Century Christian, 1997).

ular should be mentioned: (1) Virginia's, led by James O'Kelly (1757-1826), a dissident Methodist minister; (2) New England's, led by persons of Baptist heritage, chiefly Abner Jones (1772-1841) and Elias Smith (1769-1846); (3) Kentucky's, the result of the efforts of Presbyterian Barton W. Stone (1772-1844); and (4) the group in Pennsylvania, West Virginia, and Ohio, led by Thomas (1763-1854) and Alexander (1788-1866) Campbell, born in North Ireland, and Walter Scott (1796-1861), born in Scotland.

Early in the 1830s the churches from the Stone and Campbell groups began merging in Kentucky. This amalgamation expanded to churches in Pennsylvania, Ohio, Virginia, Tennessee, Indiana, Illinois, and Missouri, and several churches from the New England Jones-Smith and Virginia O'Kelly movements also became a part of the Stone-Campbell merger. After the Civil War the Christian Connexion churches (those that did not merge with the Stone-Campbell movement) established headquarters in Dayton, Ohio. In 1931 they merged with the Congregational Church, then with the Evangelical and Reformed Church, to form in 1957 the United Church of Christ.

By 1850, Alexander Campbell, because of his journal editing, book publishing, debating, lecturing, and founding of Bethany College, became the best known leader of the movement. His outlook left a permanent stamp on all his descendants regardless of their location on the theological spectrum. His views certainly influenced the Churches of Christ, although the perspectives of David Lipscomb of Nashville, Tennessee, modified certain of Campbell's positions in the latter part of the nineteenth century. Thomas and Alexander Campbell were themselves highly influenced by the Scottish Enlightenment, which emphasized reason as opposed to enthusiasm and the importance of exterior constructs for the church as opposed to inner feeling. They modified their reform views — that is, the heritage of John Calvin — accordingly, though they remained far more Reformed than they themselves recognized.

The churches of the 1832 merger, usually going by the name Christian Churches, multiplied rapidly, becoming the fastest growing indigenous American church and reaching a million members before 1900. After the Civil War, however, differences going back to the beginning of the movement reappeared. The first of these had to do with state and national mission societies; such societies had widespread support, but regional differences and embitterments over the war and reconstruction led to estrangements. The liberal leaders gained the upper hand in the mission societies, prompting the conservatives in former Confederate states to withdraw and grow increasingly critical of the societies. In the early 1870s the leadership for the opposition, Tolbert Fanning and David Lipscomb, published *The Gospel Advocate* from their base in Nashville, Tennessee. (Fanning began it in 1855 and Lipscomb reissued it in 1866 when the war was over.) At a somewhat later date, Austin McGary (1846-1928) promoted the opposition in Texas, founding The Firm Foundation in 1884. A dispute over instrumental music was the cause of the differences in this case. By 1895 several of the conservative churches rallied around *The Gospel Advocate*.

I turn now to the views of three important leaders in our history who were pacifists. Accessing their views provides an insight into perspectives within the Churches of Christ.

Alexander Campbell

Alexander Campbell (1788-1866) has throughout the years been an important intellectual leader for all his descendants — even those who deny the connection, as have some in the Churches of Christ. Campbell came to America in 1809 at twenty-one years of age. It is likely that he came in contact with pacifist ideas in North Ireland or Scotland, possibly through reading the works of Soame Jenyns (1704-1787).[11] He commented several times on war and Christian involvement in it in *The Christian Baptist*, published from 1823-1830.[12] In a work on the political ethics of Alexander Campbell, Harold Lunger has located him on Roland Bainton's left-wing religious spectrum.[13]

11. Harold L. Lunger, *The Political Ethics of Alexander Campbell* (St. Louis: The Bethany Press, 1954), p. 262; Soame Jenyns, *The Works of Soame Jenyns* (London: T. Cadell, 1790), 4 vols.

12. Campbell was also an admirer of the Glasgow professor Thomas Chalmers (1780-1847), who was against war, but favored defense when a nation suffered attack. Campbell also corresponded with William Ellery Channing (1780-1842), a leader in the peace movement, and in 1836 on a visit to Boston Campbell preached in Channing's church. See Peter Brock, *Freedom from War: Nonsectarian Pacifism*, pp. 24 and 47.

13. Harold L. Lunger, *The Political Ethics*, pp. 17, 18. See Roland H. Bainton, "The Left Wing of the Reformation," *Journal of Religion* XXI (April 1941): 124-34.

Alexander Campbell can best be understood against the background of the "ideal type" of left-wing Protestantism classically exemplified by the Anabaptists and Spiritual Reformers of sixteenth-century Europe. Roland H. Bainton describes four characteristics of this radical sect wing of the Reformation: the ethical note, or the ideal of a pure church; Christian primitivism, or the attempt to restore primitive Christianity on the basis of a biblicism of either the Old or New Testament; a heightened sense of eschatology, which in some instances passed over into revolution but more often took the form of a passive and patient enduring of present evils while awaiting the early coming of the millennium; and the radical separation of church and state. All four of these notes were present in the thought of Campbell, and each helps us better to understand his political ethics. Some were modified during the 1830's and early 1840's as he made the transition from a radical sect position to a more denominational point of view.

Later Lunger remarked that Campbell "seems to have felt little affinity with the Anabaptists" since in his debate with N. L. Rice (1807-1877) he was careful to disassociate himself from them, and more particularly from the "Munster fanatics." "What have we to do with the Anabaptists?" he asked.[14] He clearly wanted to position himself with religious primitivists who nevertheless welcomed modern progress and enlightened government.

When Campbell immigrated to America he shared some of the euphoria about the prospects and freedom there. But as the years wore on he became increasingly pessimistic about the basic direction of government and came to believe that the solution to human amelioration was the rapidly accelerating movement of which he was a part and which he in turn identified with the kingdom of God. Campbell was a post-millennialist. He believed that human governments were in decay while divine government, the church, was ascending. He began to express these views in *The Christian Baptist* (1823-30) and later in the *Millennial Harbinger* (1830-1870). In 1833 he wrote:

---

14. Harold L. Lunger, *The Political Ethics*, pp. 18, 19, quoting a debate between the Rev. A. Campbell and the Rev. N. L. Rice in *On the Action, Subject, Design and Administrator of Christian Baptism*. See also, *On the Character of Spiritual Influence in Conversion and Sanctification* and *On the Expediency and Tendency of Ecclesiastical Creeds, as Terms of Union and Communion Held in Lexington, Ky., from the Fifteenth of November to the Second of December, 1843* . . . (Lexington: A. T. Skillman & Son, 1844), p. 873.

We begin to doubt the permanency of our own political institutions; and men are now proving that no parchments, constitutions, or forms of governments can throw efficient barriers in the way of the cupidity, ambition, and pride of man. . . . Politicians stand aghast; but the students of the Bible know that the atheism, infidelity, and mammonism, which inwardly work in all the governments of the Old World and the New, must consign them all to perdition.[15]

Campbell believed that while the holding of political office was not off-limits to the Christian, it was better that the believer abstain from political affairs and that the thoughtful Christian not seek office.[16] He did agree that voting was a responsibility, but did not do so with a great deal of enthusiasm. He implied that he voted more according to principles and policies than by party.[17] He felt strongly, however, about the need to support common school (what we would now call public school) legislation.[18] He discouraged involvement in the various improvement societies, arguing that Christians should instead put their energies into building up the kingdom of God.

Instead of putting it in the church's power to do that good, you weaken her power just so much as you give of your time, your means, or your favor to these institutions. Every shilling you give to a Temperance Society, as such, you, as a professed Christian, abstract from the church. . . . Also, every hour you spend . . . in said society . . . you . . . give . . . away forever from your Christian and church duties.[19]

Campbell held the somewhat unusual position of favoring capital punishment but opposing a Christian's involvement in war. He supported this apparently contradictory view by arguing that when a designated officer executes a murderer this is done under the auspices of God, but when a soldier slays another soldier it is he who makes the decision and does the killing.[20]

15. Alexander Campbell, *Millennial Harbinger* (1833), p. 12.
16. Harold L. Lunger, *The Political Ethics*, p. 59.
17. Harold L. Lunger, *The Political Ethics*, p. 61.
18. Thomas H. Olbricht, "Alexander Campbell as an Educator," in *Lectures in Honor of the Alexander Campbell Bicentennial, 1788-1988* (Nashville: The Disciples Historical Society, 1988), pp. 79-100.
19. Alexander Campbell, *Millennial Harbinger* (1845), p. 108.
20. Harold L. Lunger, *The Political Ethics*, p. 247.

Campbell set forth his most systematic pacifist views in his "Address on War," presented to the Wheeling Lyceum on May 11, 1848. The audience was no doubt religious in orientation but the event was not created as a religious gathering. For that reason, perhaps, Campbell commenced with utilitarian reasons for opposing war. He provided statistics in regard to the tremendous financial burden imposed through warring, mentioned the loss of life and deterioration of public morals that resulted from war, and identified wars as irrational. He asked whether a Christian nation had a right to wage war against another Christian nation, but then declared that there are no Christian nations, putting aside the possibility of a just war or a war of defense by arguing that a Christian could not be involved in a war of any sort.[21] The chief text he employed was John 18:36: "My kingdom is not from this world. If my kingdom were from this world, my followers would be fighting to keep me from being handed over to the Jews. But as it is, my kingdom is not from here." In regard to the wars of Israel, Campbell argued that killing was in those cases appropriate because God was king and commanded it. The government was not republican, aristocratic, or monarchial, he argued, but, rather, a "theocratic" government "of the most absolute character . . . God was, therefore, in person the King, Lawgiver and Judge of the Jewish nation."[22]

On the question of just wars, Campbell first observed that governments do not permit soldiers to determine whether or not a war is just. He then reported on a study furnished by the Peace Society of Massachusetts, which concluded that no wars were purely honorable or for reasons of self-defense alone. He therefore declared that,

> If the end alone justifies the means, what shall we think of the wisdom or the justice of war, or of the authors and prominent actors of these scenes? A conscientious mind will ask, Did these two hundred and eighty-six wars redress the wrongs, real or feigned, complained of? Did they in all cases, in a majority of the cases, or in a single case, necessarily determine the right side of the controversy? Did they punish the guilty, or the more guilty, in the ratio of their respective demerits? No one can,

21. Alexander Campbell, "Address on War, Wheeling, Virginia 1848," in Alexander Campbell, *Popular Lectures and Addresses* (Nashville: Harbinger Book Club, 1861), p. 344.

22. Campbell, "Address on War," pp. 348-49.

indeed, no one will, contend that the decision or termination of these wars naturally, necessarily, or even probably, decided the controversy so justly, so rationally, so satisfactorily as it could have been settled in any one case of the two hundred and eighty-six, by a third or neutral party.[23]

Campbell later offered a concrete proposal as to how wars may be arbitrated through an organization that, in conception, anticipated the United Nations.

> Why not have a by-law-established umpire? Could not a united international court be made as feasible and as practicable as a United States court? Why not, as often proposed, and as eloquently, ably and humanely argued, by the advocates of peace, have a congress of nations and a high court of nations for adjudicating and terminating all international misunderstandings and complaints, redressing and remedying all wrongs and grievances?[24]

As to his reasons why Christians ought to refrain from war, Campbell referred to biblical texts, citing for the most part passages from the gospels. He summed up with these arguments:

3. The prophecies clearly indicate that the Messiah himself would be "THE PRINCE OF PEACE," and that under his reign "wars should cease," and "nations study it no more."

4. The gospel, as first announced by the angels, is a message which results in producing "peace on earth and good will among men."

5. The precepts of Christianity positively inhibit war — by showing that "wars and fightings come from men's lusts" and evil passions, and by commanding Christians to "follow peace with all men."

6. The beatitudes of Christ are not pronounced on patriots, heroes and conquerors, but on "peace-makers," on whom is conferred the highest rank and title in the universe: — "Blessed are the PEACE-MAKERS, for they shall be called the SONS OF GOD."[25]

23. Campbell, "Address on War," p. 357.
24. Campbell, "Address on War," pp. 362-63.
25. Campbell, "Address on War," p. 363.

David Lipscomb

Alexander Campbell's views were embraced by many leaders in the movement, one of whom was Tolbert Fanning (1810-1874) of Tennessee, a teacher of David Lipscomb (1831-1917). Lipscomb went beyond Campbell in the Civil War years, even declaring that Christians should neither hold public office nor vote. As editor of *The Gospel Advocate* from 1866-1917, he was champion of the forces that resulted in the Churches of Christ being identified as a separate religious body in the Federal Census of 1906. He was also the most persistently heard voice among the churches that ended up comprising the Churches of Christ. It was, no doubt, the result of his influence more than any other that most of the leading preachers in the Churches of Christ favored a pacifist position as World War I approached.[26]

Under the teaching of Fanning, Lipscomb apparently came to favor a pacifist position early on. Nevertheless, he was inclined prior to the Civil War to look favorably upon the United States government because it was democratic; in 1855 he identified democracy as "the first fruits of Christianity" and spoke of the ballot box as holy.[27] Lipscomb voted only once, for John Bell of the Constitutional Union Party in 1860, and, with the coming of the war, he changed his mind about Christians' participation in government and made his declaration that a Christian should not vote. He began publishing his views on Christians and the government in *The Gospel Advocate* in 1866-1867. These were first collected and published as a book in 1889.[28]

26. David Lipscomb was born in Tennessee. His family lived for a time in Illinois (1834), but soon returned. He received his college degree after attending Franklin College, headed by Tolbert Fanning, from 1846-1849. He lived on a farm most of his life and made his living chiefly though that means, and he commenced preaching in 1854. He and Tolbert Fanning revived *The Gospel Advocate* after the Civil War in 1866. In 1891 he, along with James A. Harding and William Lipscomb, founded Nashville Bible School (which was named David Lipscomb College after his death). The best biography of Lipscomb is Robert E. Hooper, *Crying in the Wilderness: A Biography of David Lipscomb* (Nashville: David Lipscomb College, 1979). On the significance of Lipscomb see Robert Hooper, *A Distinct People: A History of the Churches of Christ in the 20th Century* (West Monroe: Howard Publishing Company, 1993).

27. Hooper, *Crying in the Wilderness*, p. 110.

28. David Lipscomb, *Civil Government* (Nashville: Gospel Advocate Company, 1889).

In 1862 Lipscomb was the leader among a group of Middle Tennessee preachers who petitioned the Confederate administrative head in that area to exempt members of the churches from military service and other hardships resulting from a pacifist position.[29] About the petition Lipscomb wrote:

> This document was signed by the elders and evangelists of ten or fifteen congregations, and was the means of saving all those members of the church who would take this position, set forth above, and stand firmly to it, from service in the war through which we have passed. A petition of similar nature varied only to suit the changed demands, was presented to the Federal authorities.[30]

These Churches of Christ preachers recognized that they were not accorded the same privileges as the Historic Peace Churches so they ended the petition by stating

> We respectfully petition of you that those members of our churches, who are now, and have been striving to maintain a position of Christian separation from the world, its strifes and conflicts, may be relieved, on terms equitable and just, from requirements repulsive to their religious faith, and that they may be, at least, placed upon a footing similar to that in which denominations holding a like faith are placed.[31]

In the document, the leaders argued that the Bible in its teachings is "more binding upon the subjects of the Kingdom of Jesus Christ, than the rules and regulations of any human government or power."[32] Further-

29. Lipscomb, *Civil Government*, pp. 128-30. See also David Edwin Harrell, "Disciples of Christ Pacifism in Nineteenth Century Tennessee," *Tennessee Historical Quarterly* XXI (September 1962): 267-69.

30. David Lipscomb, *Civil Government*, p. 130.

31. Lipscomb, *Civil Government*, p. 130. The failure of the United States government to recognize the pacifist strain in the Churches of Christ is one of the downsides of pacifism being an individual matter. The peace churches arranged for the Civilian Public Service camps in World War II, and at least two hundred persons from the Churches of Christ were enrolled in these camps. *Firm Foundation*, 27 April 1943, 12. While some money was raised to support these individuals, they were basically recipients of orchestration supported by the peace churches. See Donald F. Durnbaugh and Charles W. Brockwell Jr., "The Historic Peace Churches," pp. 190-92.

32. Lipscomb, *Civil Government*, p. 128.

more, they maintained, Christians are in general to obey the government, but they are not to do so if what the government requires conflicts with explicit teachings of the Scriptures. The preachers thus based their request to be released from military obligations on their belief that the instruction of Scripture not to kill took precedence over the governmental requirement to serve in the army of the Confederacy.

Lipscomb's main effort in the early part of *Civil Government* was to establish, primarily through citations from the Old Testament, the diabolical nature of human government. For Lipscomb, the progenitor of all human governments was Babylon, which from the beginning embodied the human propensity to pursue its own interests rather than those of God. Quoting Genesis 9:9-10, but also Josephus, Lipscomb charged that Nimrod launched the first government, which in turn stood in opposition to God.[33] Lipscomb pounced upon statements concerning Babel or Babylon as the result of the significance he attached to Babylon in Daniel. "The design and purpose of this beginning of human government on earth was to oppose, counteract, and displace the government of God on earth."[34] Human government in its origin and practice therefore stands diametrically against God.

> It is clear that human government had its origin in the rejection of the authority of God, and that it was intended to supersede the divine government, and itself constituted the organized rebellion of man against God. This beginning of human government God called Babel, confusion, strife. It introduced into the world the organized development and embodiment of the spirit of rebellion, strife and confusion among men. God christened it Babel. It soon grew into the blood-thirsty, hectoring Babylon, and subjugated the surrounding families, tribes and kingdoms to its dominion, and became the first universal empire of the earth, and maintained its sway until the days of Daniel.[35]

Even Israel was guilty according to 1 Samuel 8, since she demanded a king and thereby replaced the Lord God. Elsewhere, Lipscomb argued that Israel is the only approved nation. Clearly Lipscomb's description of the foundations for human government as a punishment for sin is special

33. Lipscomb, *Civil Government,* pp. 8-9.
34. Lipscomb, *Civil Government,* p. 9.
35. Lipscomb, *Civil Government,* pp. 9-10.

pleading. It is built upon selected texts which are stretched and misused in such a way that nationalism is seen as foreign to God. But if that is the case, why is God so concerned to bless the nations through Abraham and his seed?

The basis for this flaw in all human governments, according to Lipscomb, is their penchant for personal gratification, a flaw which is endemic, even in democracies.[36] "But it is not in man to form government in which the selfish element will not prevail, and which will not be used to tax and oppress the ruled for the glory and aggrandizement of rulers."[37] This flaw too often occurs even in traditional Christian groups; as Lipscomb writes, "[t]he introduction of human additions into the Divine institution has the same tendency."[38]

Because all governments are based on self-interest and therefore flawed, in Lipscomb's view, God permits them to exercise this self-interest in destroying one another. Moreover, God's people are called upon to assist in this destruction as in the destruction of the Canaanite groups.[39] Even though these nations do this out of self-interest and for their own purposes, God is able to use their destructive inclinations to rid himself of human governments that stand against his hegemony. It is interesting that Lipscomb seems to think these efforts began with Nimrod and have continued ever since. How is it then that he opposes God's people engaging in warfare? Christ and Christians help destroy human governments not through the shedding of blood, but through the destruction of sin. The desired result comes about through suffering on the cross and the servanthood of believers.[40] God has rules for his kingdom (for example, those found in chapters 5–7 of Matthew) but, according to Lipscomb, no human government can operate on these rules.[41] The difference between God's kingdom in Israel and his kingdom through Christ is one of extent, not kind. The kingdom of Israel was regional, the kingdom of Christ is universal and spiritual.[42] The church is the kingdom of God.[43]

---

36. Lipscomb, *Civil Government*, p. 23.
37. Lipscomb, *Civil Government*, p. 24.
38. Lipscomb, *Civil Government*, p. 40.
39. Lipscomb, *Civil Government*, p. 37.
40. Lipscomb, *Civil Government*, pp. 52-53.
41. Lipscomb, *Civil Government*, p. 57.
42. Lipscomb, *Civil Government*, p. 76.
43. Lipscomb, *Civil Government*, p. 83.

Although Lipscomb's investigations of the Scriptures focused primarily on the Old Testament, he also emphasized the importance of the Sermon on the Mount, though he did not discuss it at length. He wrote:

The sermon on the Mount, embraced in the fifth, sixth, and seventh chapters of Matthew, certainly contains the living and essential principles of the religion the Savior came to establish, those which must pervade and control the hearts and lives of men, without which no man can be a Christian.[44]

It is not clear in *Civil Government* whether or not Lipscomb believed that Christ would return to reign on earth. He does seem optimistic, however, that sin, and hence civil government, will be destroyed. He believes that Christ will accomplish this, apparently though church members on earth, and that it will be done without the sword, peacefully. For this reason, church members should commit themselves to the work of the church rather than to that of earthly kingdoms. The problem is that most governments are sustained by Christians. If Christians would get out of governments, the governments would collapse, and with no human governments in existence the reign of God would finally take over and God's kingdom would be all in all.[45] The collapse would not be sudden, as all versions of pre-millennialism hold, but would happen over time, as true Christians exit their roles in human government and accessions to the Kingdom increase, defeating sin by so doing. Lipscomb believed that the God-designated purpose of human governments was to punish the wicked, and that through wars even corrupt state churches are destroyed, Catholic as well as Protestant. God thus permits governments to destroy each other and to destroy denominations. Human governments are temporary, however, and in the new time, Lipscomb argued, there will be neither human governments nor human denominations.

Lipscomb carried his agenda to an extreme by attempting to prove that none of God's people had ever served in government. He argued that Joseph and Daniel were forced to serve in Egypt and Babylon against their will and that neither Cornelius nor the Philippian jailor continued in office. He further tried to make a case that Erastus of Corinth was not a

44. Lipscomb, *Civil Government,* p. 133.
45. Lipscomb, *Civil Government,* p. 88-91.

city treasurer, but a church treasurer — a case that others have attempted, but without great success.[46]

Another question has to do with anti-Constantinianism. The peace churches have traditionally argued, as they reconstruct church history, that the major departure from the true faith came with the hegemony of Constantine. Lipscomb cannot begin with Constantine because he sought to prove that human governments have always corrupted God's rule over men, even before Constantine. He did believe that Constantine perverted the kingdom of God, but saw this as an incremental change rather than, as the peace churches saw it, the critical fork in the road.[47] "But the so-called conversion of Constantine greatly accelerated and spread the custom" of Christians participating in government, he writes.[48] Surprisingly, Lipscomb seemed to approve the Montanists (those wild-eyed charismatics!), but did so because they all, like Tertullian, rejected human governments. On the other hand, he was very critical of other "forefathers" who might appear much more like bedfellows — for example, the Puritans — because they created a human government. (Though he did, it should be noted, find Roger Williams more praiseworthy.)[49]

Asked what would happen if, in fact, all humans became Christians of his stripe and human governments disappeared, Lipscomb responded that God was able to ensure that the mail would be delivered and other governmental services carried out.[50] He believed that President Garfield, a seminary graduate and member of the Christian Church, was corrupted by governmental participation, a fact Garfield himself recognized. At first incorrectly believing that Garfield no longer waited on the Lord's table, Lipscomb continued to be certain that Garfield no longer preached. He attributed that neglect to the corruption brought about by involvement in human government.[51]

46. Lipscomb, *Civil Government*, p. 110.

47. As to the sources for Lipscomb's ideas on civil government, he seems to have been in a stream of American apocalypticists, but he certainly nuanced his position so that distinctive features were apparent. The text of *Civil Government* suggests that he has not so much read the Anabaptists firsthand, but has primarily read about them through reading the historians Mosheim (1694-1755), Orchard (a nineteenth-century British Baptist historian), and Armitage (1819-1896).

48. Lipscomb, *Civil Government*, p. 120.

49. Lipscomb, *Civil Government*, p. 127.

50. Lipscomb, *Civil Government*, p. 136.

51. Lipscomb, *Civil Government*, pp. 138-39.

When it came to working for governments, Lipscomb rejected serving as postmaster or on juries. He believed, however, that Christians could be teachers since teaching has nothing to do with the administration of government.[52] Voting, on the other hand, was impermissible, since those who secure office through such votes are involved in the administration of human government. Lipscomb did not even approve of voting in favor of efforts to ban alcohol, betting, gambling, or prostitution, since to do so would be to fight evil with evil.[53] When Christians start voting for what seems a good cause, he argued, they are on the slippery slope heading toward full governmental participation.

The best and most positive summary of Lipscomb's position is perhaps found in a statement near the end of *Civil Government:*

> If the church ever attains to its primitive purity and efficiency it must be by a return to this clearly established principle of the separation of all its members from worldly governments, and the consecration of the affections, time, means and talents of all its members to the upbuilding of the church of God and the salvation of the world.[54]

H. Leo Boles

H. Leo Boles (1874-1946) was the last major leader in the Churches of Christ to write and speak openly about pacifism.[55] Certain key leaders, even now, consider themselves pacifists, but they have not written or spoken on the subject in the last several years, and members of the churches generally do not know that they are pacifists.[56] Boles was an important figure as sometime editor of the major religious periodical *The Gospel Advocate* and president of Nashville Bible School, later to become David Lipscomb College (now University).[57] In 1923, he commenced writing a

---

52. Lipscomb, *Civil Government,* pp. 141-42.

53. Lipscomb, *Civil Government,* p. 144.

54. Lipscomb, *Civil Government,* p. 128.

55. J. D. Bales published *The Christian Conscientious Objector* (Berkeley: Self-published, 1943), but he was not then a major leader; by 1950, when he might have been considered such, he had reversed his position and favored Christians participating in war.

56. One such example is the late M. Norvel Young (1915-1998), former president of Pepperdine University.

57. H. Leo Boles was born in Jackson County, Tennessee, and lived most of his life in Nashville. See Robert Hooper, *A Distinct People,* pp. 92-94.

series of articles in *The Gospel Advocate* which were later collected into a booklet and widely distributed.[58]

Now that World War I was over, Boles wrote, an examination of the war issue could proceed with less passion since war had now become generally unpopular;[59] it was therefore now appropriate to discuss the matter of Christians' involvement in war. Boles limited his remarks to involvement in war, rather than addressing the larger questions of God's part in war, war in the Old Testament, or the question of whether some wars are more just than others.

> Be it remembered that we are studying the Christian's attitude toward war. We are not discussing whether any other person or nation may engage in war. We have nothing to say at this time about one who is not a Christian engaging in war. The present study is, Does the New Testament teach that a child of God should engage in carnal warfare? The investigation is not that some wars may be more justifiable than others. War, any war, all wars are antichristian, and therefore a Christian should not engage in war. The nature of war is contrary to the nature of Christianity; the spirit of war is opposed to the spirit of Christianity; the "God of War" is antagonistic to Christ.[60]

Christianity, Boles argued, has a peaceful and loving spirit which stands in stark contrast to the vengeance and hatred created by wars. He then quoted numerous texts in the New Testament to validate this claim.[61] He cited a few Old Testament passages as well, but only to support the claim that "Christ was to come as the Prince of Peace. He is to reign over a kingdom of peace, and his subjects are to be peacemakers. His gospel is a gospel of peace, and his church is to pursue a peaceful mission."[62]

It was especially from the Sermon on the Mount that Boles developed the view that Christians should abhor war. From the Sermon, Boles emphasized that Christians are to turn the other cheek and love their ene-

---

58. H. Leo Boles, *The New Testament Teaching on War,* reprinted in C. G. Ross, *War: A Trilogy; Three Perspectives — One Biblical Position.* The page numbers in subsequent references refer to Boles' document alone.

59. Boles, *The New Testament Teaching on War,* p. 2.

60. Boles, *The New Testament Teaching on War,* p. 5.

61. Boles, *The New Testament Teaching on War,* p. 7. Among these are John 13:35, Ephesians 4:2-3, 2 Corinthians 13:11, and Romans 12:19-21.

62. Boles, *The New Testament Teaching on War,* p. 9.

mies, as well as purifying "the motives and affections of the heart." "When such unholy motives and intentions as hatred and revenge are prohibited, the spirit and nature of war are prohibited."[63] He particularly thought that the charge to love one's enemies negated any possibility that Christians should engage in war.

> The distinguishing duties of the Christian are sacrificed when that one goes into carnal warfare. The publican, the Gentile, the sinner, and the world love those who love them and hate those who hate them; they attempt to destroy those who would destroy them. Now, if the Christian loves only those who love the Christian, he is no better than the publican, the sinner, or the world.[64]

He also found in the Beatitudes a call for a special Christian demeanor.

> Does any one believe that the poor in spirit, meek, and merciful, subjects of Christ's kingdom, could ever slaughter their fellow men in war? When one engages in war, one must abandon the practice of all the characteristics mentioned in the Beatitudes. No teacher of war or officer, in training soldiers, ever teaches the Beatitudes as a part of the knowledge or qualifications required of the soldier of carnal warfare.[65]

Boles also highlighted John 18:36, "My kingdom is not from this world." Christians cannot go to war with other Christians; they cannot go to war with their neighbors; they cannot go to war with their enemies; they cannot go to war on behalf of the kingdom of God.

In response to the claim that Christians should engage in war and kill if their government orders them to do so, Boles argued that the responsibility of war cannot be transferred from the soldier to the government or army.

> As no Christian can make resignation of his moral agency, he must ever be responsible for his conduct. As long as his conduct is directed by his own will, or as long as he submits his will to another to be used by another, so long will his personal responsibility continue. I cannot

---

63. Boles, *The New Testament Teaching on War*, p. 14.
64. Boles, *The New Testament Teaching on War*, p. 14.
65. Boles, *The New Testament Teaching on War*, p. 15.

conceive of the Christian's responsibility ceasing when he becomes a soldier.[66]

Boles also argued that the right or wrong of wars cannot be determined by whether the war is defensive or offensive. "It matters not whether they be offensive or defensive wars, the practice of soldiery cannot be a duty of the Christian. To the Christian, a war between armies or nations is only a great big fight between two opposing forces."[67] He further rejected the claim that a Christian "has a right to resist with carnal weapons an intruder on the rights of life, honor, or property"[68] or to "resist the murderer of himself or family with physical arms," arguing against those who said that "he has the right — yea, it is his duty — to resist with deadly weapons the one who assails the honor of mother, wife, or daughter; that he may use deadly weapons in defending his right to property."[69] Boles ended his book by citing others in the restoration movement who supported pacifism and by quoting those who had participated in war and as a result viewed it as scandal.

Boles, therefore, is the last major leader in the Churches of Christ who issued a clarion call to engage in war no more.

The Outcomes

Does the pacifist position of these leaders in the restoration heritage continue today? More, it seems, among ministers than elders, and in varying degrees in the different wings of the movement. In 1984 Laurence C. Keene produced a study called "Heirs of Stone and Campbell on the Pacific Slope: a Sociological Approach."[70] On the question of whether Christians should bear arms Keene discovered the following results:

66. Boles, *The New Testament Teaching on War,* p. 18.
67. Boles, *The New Testament Teaching on War,* p. 35.
68. Boles, *The New Testament Teaching on War,* p. 39.
69. Boles, *The New Testament Teaching on War,* p. 39.
70. Laurence C. Keene, "Heirs of Stone and Campbell on the Pacific Slope: A Sociological Approach," *Impact Disciples of Christ on the Pacific Slope* 12 (1984): 5-91. The number of members of each group on the western slope is about the same with the Churches of Christ the largest, the Independent Christian Churches second, and the Disciples last, with about 100,000 for each group. The number of responses were about equal in the reverse order.

	Should	No
Church of Christ Elders	54.3	28.7
Church of Christ Ministers	27.3	47.0
Independent Elders	75.2	22.8
Independent Ministers	44.4	44.4
Disciples Elders	53.7	30.6
Disciples Ministers	17.9	45.2

The results show that elders were about twice as likely to favor participation in war as ministers. Furthermore, the Churches of Christ and the Disciples held about the same views while the Independents were much more likely to favor bearing arms. There were differences in respect to age groups as well; Keene found that "[a]mong the Church of Christ and Disciples elders, the younger groups were significantly against 'bearing arms.' The older elders were strongly in favor of it. Among the Independent elders, all three age groups were in favor of bearing arms."[71]

Another manner in which these groups differ is in terms of their support of government through symbols and sermons. The influence of Lipscomb is still strong in the Churches of Christ; I have been in above a thousand different Churches of Christ buildings throughout the world and have never seen a flag displayed in an area where worship took place, unless it was in a facility not owned by the church. Almost all Independent churches, on the other hand, display flags in the place of worship the week of the Fourth of July, and most have sermons on patriotism. Very few Churches of Christ ministers preach sermons on patriotism. The Disciples' practice is somewhere in between the Churches of Christ and the Independents.

Another interesting gauge of current opinion is the discussion of pacifism on the Stone-Campbell internet list. Of seventeen participants who entered into this discussion, ten identified themselves as pacifists while seven argued for fighting only in just wars. No one argued that Christians should fight in any war at the demand of a government. These seventeen individuals, however, are not representative. We know little about them other than that they had internet access and were interested

71. Laurence C. Keene, "Heirs of Stone and Campbell," pp. 67-68.

in discussing the subject. The seventeen are scattered across the United States and Canada, and few of them are located in the states in which the highest percentage of Churches of Christ members live. Those who favored pacifism based their opinion on the statements of Jesus and the difficulty or even impossibility of identifying a just war. Not much discussion of a biblical theology regarding life or peace occurred on the list. Those who wished to discuss just wars believed that this position was the predominant one among Churches of Christ members rather than pacifism. The desire for peace on the current scene is not a strong motivation in Churches of Christ, though the postmodern attack on power may turn the tide in that direction.[72]

The statement of one of the Stone-Campbell list participants, Jerry Gross, gives some flavor of sentiments among the churches in the days of Vietnam and after.

> At Vanderbilt in the late '60's I was a distinguished military graduate who accepted a commission as a career officer in the US Army Corps of Engineers from the ROTC program. During that time I also began to preach for some of the churches (sic) of Christ in the Nashville area. While in engineering graduate school at Vanderbilt I began to have concerns of conscience about what Lipscomb and H. Leo Boles called "carnal warfare." Although I had been in the churches of Christ all of my life, I had never heard one sermon or lesson on the topic. After finishing graduate school I entered the army as an engineer officer. After completing Ranger School . . . I was stationed at Ft. Stewart, GA where I also preached each Sunday for the local Church of Christ. I made trips back to Nashville and sought the advice of my spiritual mentors but they seemed ill prepared to help me in my struggle. When I received my orders to Viet[n]am, I filed an application to be classified as a "non-combatant conscientious objector." When I informed the congregation of my decision, I was strenuously opposed by several of the male members. While in Viet[n]am, working on a general's staff at an army construction agency, I received word that my application had been approved by the Department of the Army. I resigned my commission as a Captain, rejoined my family in Tennessee, secured a position as a preacher with a church in West Tennessee, and attended Harding Grad[uate School] to prepare myself for a life of ministry.

72. This discussion took place 16 February 1995 through 10 March 1995.

218

Since that time I have struggled with the issue of pacifism and warfare. I think it is important to point out that Just War theories are of little help to young men (and women) who are facing military service. Opting out of a particular war (Viet[n]am), or a particular mission (the bombing of Dresden) as a Just War advocate is not possible in the military service. As far as the military is concerned, you are either a pacifist or you are not. Hence, the easy dismissal of pacifism that I have witnessed does not serve very well our young men and women who may have to face their own decisions about participating in future wars.[73]

Conclusions

It is clear that when the occasions arise, members of the Churches of Christ are willing to discuss matters of war and peace. Because of widespread differences, however, these subjects are not frequently discussed in the churches, and some congregations even prohibit taking them up on the grounds that ill will or even splits in the church may result. Because of our historical position, we in the Churches of Christ do have a contribution to make to discussions relating to war and peace. The atmosphere now exists which makes it possible to enter into such discussions with persons of other confessional groups. A start, if high-level scholars can be recruited, is the publication of documents on war and peace from a biblical perspective. It is my expectation, however, that securing recruits will be difficult because our premier professors are not very interested in either anti-Constantinianism or pacifism.

73. An e-mail on the "Stone-Campbell@Bible.ACU.edu" list, 18 February 1995.

The Fragmentation of the Church and
Its Unity in Peacemaking: A Report

University of Notre Dame
June 13-17, 1995

Background

1. A consultation meeting June 13-17, 1995, at Notre Dame, Indiana, was a third meeting on the pilgrimage toward the unity of the church in a "Common Confession of the Apostolic Faith Today," focusing on the apostolic character of the church's peace witness. This consultation, sponsored by the Faith and Order Commission of the National Council of Churches of Christ in the United States and Joan B. Kroc Institute for International Peace Studies of the University of Notre Dame, builds on the work of the World and National Councils in exploring the common ground for a conciliar communion, and specifically on two previous consultations, at Bethany Theological Seminary, Oak Brook, Illinois, in 1990 and Douglaston, New York, 1991.

2. Previous work on the history of the church's confessional tradition, *Faith to Creed,* and the results of the previous consultations in this series, *The Church's Peace Witness,* provided historical and biblical foundations for the present discussion. This consultation provided a significant opportunity to explore the link between ecclesiology and peacemaking, in dialogue with the Historic Peace Churches. This report is prepared for the work of Faith and Order of the National Council of Churches of Christ in the United States of America. Members of Orthodox, Anglican, Ro-

man Catholic and Protestant churches presented a variety of the positions of the churches over the question of peace and the relationship of the church to society, the impulse of the churches' contribution to the quest for visible unity, and the present developments that might place the relationship among these churches in a new context. These studies in the United States take place against the background of the Gospel imperative to peacemaking and the unity of the church. Faith and Order's *Confessing the One Faith* provides an articulation of where some churches are on this pilgrimage at this time.

3. The previous consultation provided encouraging common ground in the churches' approach to the biblical witness. It also furthered discussion on the relevance such witness is given in the churches' contemporary approaches to the question of peace and its centrality in the church's confession:

> The statements [of the churches produced during the 1980s] generally agree that peace is a central theme in Scripture, that it is rooted in some way in the eschatological reign of God, and that Jesus did not resort to violence. They differ in their estimate of the relevance of biblical views of peace, war and violence for church in the contemporary context. . . . It may be that the statements' shared concern for peacemaking is beginning to inform the churches' appropriation of Scripture in ways that relativize the traditional interpretations that have undergirded confessional divisions along just war and pacifist lines. The fact that all these statements have recently been produced by these groups does seem to indicate that concern for peace witness, which had earlier been left largely to the historic peace churches, has now become important for virtually all Christian groups. (*The Church's Peace Witness,* p. 210)

The convergence in ecclesiology was less clear from the earlier consultation, therefore the present discussion invited papers from Lutheran, Reformed, Roman Catholic, Mennonite, Brethren, Churches of Christ, and Assemblies of God perspectives. Significant responses were incorporated into the discussion from Orthodox, Baptist, Methodist, Anglican, and Quaker perspectives.

4. The divisions in the Body of Christ in the world are a counter witness to the peace sought and proclaimed by the church as the follower of the Prince of Peace who prayed that his disciples might be one. The

221

movement toward unity among the churches is itself a sign and model of their peacemaking vocation. The consultation considered a wide range of theological, historical, and ethical perspectives on the relationship of the unity of the church, peace among the churches, and the churches' peacemaking vocation in the world.

5. In this consultation the churches have been encouraged to speak out of the specificity of their histories and traditions, seeking common ground in Jesus Christ and the common elements shared in the quest to be faithful to the church's call to be united in peacemaking. As the consultation has looked at the origins of the churches' alienation, their various resources for unity and witness in peacemaking, hopes have emerged for reconciliation in the apostolic faith, formation in Gospel discipleship, and common witness in the world.

6. We lament that Christians have used their faith to further hate and violence. Nevertheless, events of the last decade have also shown that the peacemaking efforts in the world and the responses of the churches have made a difference in human history. While areas of disagreement continue, the fact that peacemaking is an essential element of the apostolic faith is acknowledged by all. We continue to recognize divergences in the approach to this apostolic mandate in our pilgrimage toward full communion.

Learnings

7. We are agreed, on the basis of the Apostolic Tradition, that Christians, following our Lord and Savior Jesus Christ, are called to be peacemakers. We consider this a common confession of the faith once delivered to the apostles, basic to our Christian unity. In a world of violence, be it in the streets or in warfare, churches affirm that peace is the will of God, and that peace has been shown to us most clearly in the life, teachings, death, and resurrection of Jesus Christ. Peacemaking is most deeply rooted in Christ and the unity of the church, and such unity is a gift of the Holy Spirit linked to repentance and forgiveness. Through the power of the Holy Spirit, we are enabled to practice peacemaking as a way of participation in the life and death of Christ. A primary vocation of every believer is love, out of which peacemaking flows. Our peace with God impels us toward peace with neighbor and love of enemies.

8. In the face of the fragmentation of the church we are agreed on the importance of spiritual formation for unity in peacemaking. Both pacifist and non-pacifist churches find themselves in a world where evil has become multifaceted in ever more insidious ways, ranging from a hierarchy of violence to the arrogance of power politics, intertwined with economic greed and pervasive military power. In our church communities, we want to train our members for peacemaking, helping them to develop a wider repertoire of responses to evil and violence and to enemies. As Christians many of us would endorse, instead of "fight or flight," Jesus' way of creative nonviolence which confronts enemies, unmasking sin and injustice. Formation or training in peacemaking is important on an ongoing basis, not just in times of crisis or war. Some participants have recalled the missionary injunction of Jesus "to be wise as serpents and innocent as doves" (Matt. 10:16) as a call for healing and a symbol of sharp discernment and vigilance against the sin of playing God (Gen. 3:5). Others have recalled the many ways of spiritual formation in the past, be it monastic discipline, penitential discipline for those who have killed as soldiers or guardians of the peace, or critical involvement in the affairs of this world.

9. Among many represented at this meeting, criticism of the just war theory has deepened. Nuclear warfare stretched the capabilities of the just war theory. Moreover, nation-states seldom use just war criteria as a basis for deciding whether to enter a war, considering issues in the continuation of a war or assessing the consequences after a war has finished. For some, the just war tradition is an unused resource that can enhance peacemaking if seriously taken into account by Christians. Most wars since the close of the Cold War are civil wars.

10. At the Notre Dame meeting, we affirmed the importance of hearing each other's church histories as a means of understanding each other's positions on peacemaking. Repentance of past persecutions of peacemakers, disowning the anathemas of past confessions, and forgiveness will further our future dialogue. We can affirm our common history in the early centuries of the church, including a common history of martyrdom during those first centuries. We recognize that those church traditions that have claimed the first-century church as the primary model of the church have often claimed the first-century church's peace position.

11. We also recognize in the histories of the American churches the difficulties and changes with regard to the peace position that occurred

especially during World War I, in many of our traditions. In addition, the shaping impact of World War II, Vietnam, and the Cold War in general has left a greater legacy of testing and reviewing the churches' capacity for peacemaking, and has resulted in renewed attempts to articulate, and in greater understanding of our diverse attempts to articulate a theology of peacemaking.

12. We are agreed that some form of critical participation in civil government and in the surrounding society is appropriate. We are interested neither in complete withdrawal from society nor in uncritical absorption into the dominant culture.

13. We are agreed that, at some point, Christians may be called to obey God rather than human authorities. Our ultimate loyalty is to God, and to the church, the people of God. Our primary identity is Christian. At some point, the issue of peacemaking may be a question of allegiances, or of idolatry. We saw the relevance of eschatology for sustainable and hopeful peacemaking. Peacemaking is dependent on hope in God's deliverance of the righteous, God's judgment on the unjust and fulfillment of peace in God's reign.

Points of Contention

14. A) While we are in agreement that all Christians should be striving for peace, there continues to be significant disagreement over the best ways to pursue peace. Some individuals and traditions hold that to follow Jesus is to relinquish all contemplation and taking of violent action toward another human being, created in the image of God, for whom Christ died. Others wonder if the love of neighbor may at times call for effective intervention — even armed intervention — to save innocent parties from hostile aggression. Would this action be an honorable means of action or cause Christians to become what we hate?

15. B) While the various churches may come to embrace clear positions on peace and nonviolence as normative for Christians, churches also struggle with what to do with members who choose another path. What is the significance of this diversity within each church for the unity and healing of divisions among the churches? Should particular strategies and stances toward peacemaking become obligatory, or should churches simply give clear witness to the truth they have received? Then again, how mean-

224

ingful can a testimony be if it goes unheeded by the church's members? While churches do not want to become dictatorial, they clearly desire to provide accountability for maintaining their convictions, while at the same time providing pastoral care for those who dissent for reasons of conscience.

16. C) Marks of the church are of central concern, but as of yet, we have no full agreement as to what are the necessary marks. Some wonder if they should include gathering in the name of Jesus and Christ-like discipleship — even leading to suffering. This being the case, a clear connection between the death and resurrection with Christ experienced in the Eucharist and baptism may be understood to extend to ethical stances in the world. For the Christian, one must be willing that self should suffer for truth, and not that truth should suffer for self.

17. D) Understandings of church and state continue to be matters of concern. On one hand, the responsibility of states to protect and order a society is appreciated; on the other, Christians may feel pressured by the state to go against conscience. We recognize the tensions between the polarities of charisma and institution within the church, and affirm at each step solidarity with Jesus and his teachings.

Struggles faced by developing church traditions may include questions of survival and the sense of being disenfranchised. Conversely, the temptations of more established church traditions may include challenges of inertia and the inability to change directions.

As churches accumulate greater influence, governments and powers become more interested in influencing their directions. Within this situation, Christians must be wise as serpents so as not to be co-opted into unholy alliances which threaten our ability to be innocent as doves (Matt. 10:16), and loyal to our common Lord.

18. E) Peacemaking would be furthered considerably if at least Christians could agree not to kill each other. Should not our loyalty to our common Lord supersede our loyalties to family, home, and state? On the other hand, why should Christians be willing to kill or harm non-Christians for whom Jesus also shed his blood? They too are beloved by God and created in the divine image. How could Jesus' followers commit acts of violence against those he commands us to forgive? Then again, just war criteria have often been invoked with the specific intention of limiting violence, conflict, and casualties. It is the question of the use or nonuse of force in the common goal of peacemaking that remains unresolved within the churches.

Recommendations

In the face of the increasing complexities of Christian unity and peace-making the participants of this consultation make the following recommendations:

19. A) That definitions of unity, mission, and peacemaking be well-grounded in an understanding of the apostolic faith as a source of power to create regional and global ways of peacemaking, with a focus on un-masking the reality of evil and on the church as the community of the meantime between Christ's first and second coming. As the community of the interim (the people of "the way," Acts) the church has been empowered by the Lord to bear his witness in the world, to live as a sign and foretaste of the age to come, and to announce his coming lordship.

20. B) That unity and peacemaking require special programs of faith formation, in and among the churches, that assist in developing the skills of nonviolent Christian living and understandings of the churches and their quest for visible unity.

21. C) That the churches develop programs of prayer for peace, for the unity of the church, and for one another. These prayers nourish communion in Christ and move Christians to the conversion to God's will for the unity of the church and the peace of the world.

22. D) That the churches provide opportunities for a dialogue of conversion, whereby Christians can encounter one another in their common quest for understanding, deepening their commitment to peace and justice in the world, and growing in their zeal for the unity of the church.

23. E) That those churches who have condemned one another's positions on pacifism and engagement in the world reconsider whether these condemnations can be put aside through public acts of reconciliation. That those churches which in the past have persecuted the Peace Churches, or have contributed to the estrangement of other churches, can find occasions for public repentance and petitions of pardon in communal acts of reconciliation, forgiveness, prayer, and confession together.

24. F) That Faith and Order, in the National Council of Churches, explore the relationship of the apostolic character of the churches' faith and order as they develop from traditions of continuity and traditions of restoration.

25. G) That the conciliar work on justice, peace, and integrity of creation consider unity in common confession, sacramental life, and mu-

tual accountability for the process of common witness and action in the world.

26. H) That further study be done in the relationship of the church as the People of God in the context of national and ethnic identity.

Contributors

LOIS Y. BARRETT
Commission on Home Ministries,
General Conference Mennonite Church

ALEXANDER BRUNETT
Archbishop of Seattle
Chair of Ecumenical and Interreligious Affairs, National Conference of
  Catholic Bishops

MURRAY W. DEMPSTER
Vice President for Academic Affairs and Professor of Social Ethics,
Vanguard University of Southern California, formerly Southern
  California College

DONALD F. DURNBAUGH
Professor Emeritus of Church History, Bethany Theological Seminary
Archivist, Juniata College
Fellow of the Young Center for the Study of Anabaptist and Pietist
  Groups, Elizabethtown College

JOHN H. ERICKSON
Professor of Canon Law and Church History,
Associate Dean for Academic Affairs,
St. Vladimir's Orthodox Theological Seminary

Contributors

Eric W. Gritsch
Professor Emeritus of Church History,
Gettysburg Lutheran Seminary

Jeffrey Gros, FSC
Associate Director, Ecumenical and Interreligious Affairs,
  National Council of Catholic Bishops

Paul Meyendorff
The Fr. Alexander Schmemann Professor of Liturgical Theology,
  St. Vladimir's Orthodox Theological Seminary
Chair, Faith and Order Commission, National Council of Churches

Lauree Hersch Meyer
Retired Associate Professor of Theology,
Colgate Rochester Divinity School

Thomas H. Olbricht
Distinguished Professor of Religion Emeritus,
Pepperdine University

Thomas D. Paxson Jr.
Christian and Interfaith Relations Committee of Friends
  General Conference
Chair, Department of Philosophical Studies,
  Southern Illinois University at Edwardsville

James F. Puglisi, S.A.
Director, Centro Pro Unione, Italy

John D. Rempel
Mennonite Central Committee Liaison to the United Nations
Member, Inter-Church Relations Committee, Mennonite Church,
  USA

ALAN P. F. SELL
Chair of Christian Doctrine and Philosophy of Religion,
Director of the Centre for the Study of British Christian Thought,
The United Theological College, Aberystwyth, Wales, within the
    Aberystwyth and Lampeter School of Theology of the
    University of Wales

GLEN H. STASSEN
Lewis Smedes Professor of Christian Ethics,
Fuller Theological Seminary